Praise for *The Courage to Raise Good Men*

"A rare and brilliant achievement . . . and an invigorating celebration of human possibility."
—Harriet Lerner, Ph.D.

"*The Courage to Raise Good Men* inspires so much confidence in its author and raises so many interesting issues that I wished it had been twice as long . . . [Silverstein] has mastered her discipline and [has taken] it a step further . . . [for] it is the personal thread that drives the book and provides its most affecting moments."
—Helen Epstein, *The Boston Globe*

"It is fascinating to see how through therapy [Silverstein] helps families of adolescent boys handle problems."
—*The Seattle Times*

"An important and liberating contribution . . . Silverstein and Rashbaum convincingly skewer the childraising 'experts' who have insisted, paradoxically, that women should be full-time mothers and that mother-love is toxic to boys."
—Barbara Ehrenreich

"Literate, perceptive, and provocative—sure to heat up the fires of the gender debate."
—*Kirkus Reviews*

"[A] stunning work . . . [Silverstein] has woven an exquisite and complex tapestry, blending the personal, the cultural, and the psychological. *The Courage to Raise Good Men* is a unique and totally original book, which I recommend to any man who has ever had a mother, any mother who has ever had a son, and anyone who has ever had a family."
—Andre Gregory

PENGUIN BOOKS

THE COURAGE TO RAISE GOOD MEN

OLGA SILVERSTEIN is one of the founding members of the family therapy movement here and abroad. A faculty member and therapist at the Ackerman Institute for Family Therapy since 1972, she also has her own private practice and is coauthor of *The Invisible Web: Gender Patterns in Family Relationships*.

BETH RASHBAUM has been a freelance book editor and writer since 1983.

The Courage to Raise Good Men

Olga Silverstein

AND

Beth Rashbaum

PENGUIN BOOKS

PENGUIN BOOKS
Published by the Penguin Group
Penguin Books USA Inc., 375 Hudson Street, New York, New York 10014, U.S.A.
Penguin Books Ltd, 27 Wrights Lane, London W8 5TZ, England
Penguin Books Australia Ltd, Ringwood, Victoria, Australia
Penguin Books Canada Ltd, 10 Alcorn Avenue, Toronto, Ontario, Canada M4V 3B2
Penguin Books (N.Z.) Ltd, 182–190 Wairau Road, Auckland 10, New Zealand

Penguin Books Ltd, Registered Offices: Harmondsworth, Middlesex, England

First published in the United States of America by Viking Penguin,
a division of Penguin Books USA Inc., 1994
Published in Penguin Books 1995

7 9 10 8 6

The names and identifying details of the patients discussed in this book
have been changed to protect anonymity.

Grateful acknowledgment is made for permission to reprint the following copyrighted works:
Excerpts from *Rabbit at Rest* by John Updike. Copyright © 1990 by John Updike. Reprinted by
permission of Alfred A. Knopf, Inc., and Penguin Books Ltd. "Disobedience" from *When We Were
Very Young* by A. A. Milne. Copyright E. P. Dutton, 1926. Copyright renewed A. A. Milne, 1952.
Used by permission of Dutton Children's Books, a division of Penguin Books USA Inc. and
Methuen Children's Books. Excerpts from *The Story of Ferdinand* by Munro Leaf. Copyright
Munro Leaf and Robert Lawson, 1936. Copyright renewed Munro Leaf and John W. Boyd,1964.
Used by permission of Viking Penguin, a division of Penguin Books USA Inc. Excerpts from *Before
and After* by Rosellen Brown. Copyright © 1992 by Rosellen Brown. Reprinted by permission of Farrar,
Straus & Giroux, Inc. Advertisement by Tommy Hilfiger reprinted courtesy of Tommy Hilfiger Advertising.

THE LIBRARY OF CONGRESS HAS CATALOGUED THE HARDCOVER AS FOLLOWS:
Silverstein, Olga.
The courage to raise good men/Olga Silverstein and Beth Rashbaum.
p.   cm.
Includes bibliographical references.
ISBN 0-670-84836-0 (hc.)
ISBN 0 14 01.7567 9 (pbk.)
1. Masculinity (Psychology).   2. Men—Psychology.   3. Boys—Psychology.
4. Mothers and sons.   5. Child rearing.   I. Rashbaum, Beth   II. Title.
BF692.5.S55   1994
155.43′2—dc20   93–30253

Printed in the United States of America
Set in Galliard
Designed by Jessica Shatan

What do we fear? That our sons will accuse us of making them into misfits and outsiders? That they will suffer as we have suffered from patriarchal reprisals? Do we fear they will somehow lose their male status and privilege, even as we are seeking to abolish that inequality?

—ADRIENNE RICH
Of Woman Born

Acknowledgments

Our mutual thanks go to our editor, Nan Graham, who has never wavered for a moment in the intensity of her enthusiasm for this project, or the intelligence she brought to it; to the many feminist writers, men and women, to whom our intellectual indebtedness is obvious, even when their ideas have not always coincided with our own; to my daughter Judith La Mattina, who produced many hours of endless transcripts with dispatch and skill, and who read with a critical eye; and to my husband, Fred Silverstein, who was always ready to help with whatever was needed, and who was also one of our best readers.

In addition, for my part I wish most of all to thank my son, Michael, who read and responded with an openness and honesty that gladdened my heart; Marianne Walters, Betty Carter, and Peggy Papp, my colleagues in the Women's Project in Family Therapy, the place where many of these ideas were incubated and enabled to flourish; the staff at the Ackerman Institute for Family Therapy, who kindly read the proposal and took staff meeting time to discuss it; the vast numbers of students and patients who shared their stories and lives with me; Beth Vesel, my agent, who urged, cajoled, and finally convinced me to write this book, and has been consistently supportive and encouraging throughout; my daughter Laura Silverstein, who administered my weekly dose of relief and good cheer by bringing my small granddaughter Molly to visit; and last but not least Steven La Mattina, Mark Slifstein, and Barbara Silverstein, all of whom read and offered loving support as well as concrete critical help.

—OLGA SILVERSTEIN

Thanks to my agent, Kris Dahl, whose interest in our work may in part be due to the son who was gestating at the same time the book was; to Lynda Madaras, my first reader, whose excitement was particularly important to me because of my respect for her work as a sex educator; to Joan Peters, Penny Stallings, Barry Secunda, Frank Rose, and Ethel Person, each of whom has seen and commented on various portions of the manuscript, sometimes skeptically and critically, sometimes with applause, always with kindness and tact; to Pat Strachan, who has been unflagging in her enthusiasm, from the very beginning; to Ellen Rashbaum and John Wallace, my sister and brother-in-law, whose gift of an airline ticket put me on the first leg of the journey that led to this book; and to my cousins Pat and Steve Mizel, who gave me a place to stay when the plane landed.

—BETH RASHBAUM

A Note from the Authors

This book was a joint project, but because the professional and personal experiences related within are those of Olga Silverstein, we chose to write in the first person.

Contents

1   Cautionary Tales: For Mothers of Sons Ages One
    to Six   1

2   Hero Tales: For Boys Ages Six to Twelve   37

3   The Myth of the Male Role Model, and Other
    Tales for Changing Times   75

4   The Adolescent Years: Establishing—and
    Enforcing—Masculinity   107

5   Leaving Home: The Young Man's Rite of Passage   149

6   Men in Relationships   183

7   What Do Women Want? What Do Men Need?   229

    A Note from the Author's Son   243
    Notes   245
    Index   269

ONE

Cautionary Tales:
For Mothers of Sons
Ages One to Six

Even Thetis, dipping her mortal boy
In Styx, dreaming of armoring him
Against both worlds, gripping her joy
In fatal fingers, allowed the dim
Danger of her handhold on his heel.

How could she bear to lower him
Knowing the yearning of the Naiads down below;
Hearing the sibilant whispers urging him to
Swim; feeling the small arched body
Straining to let go?

If immortal mothers are to such folly prone,
How am I to guard against the thumbprints
On my own?

MESSAGE TO MOM: HANDS OFF

I wrote that poem many years ago, when my son, Michael, my first child, was born. In those days I was very young and very inexperienced in all things having to do with babies. But already I knew, for it was the conventional wisdom of the time, as it still is today, that I could be a danger to my boy. Like Thetis, I might fail to let him go, and the love I felt for him might in some way damage the armor of his manhood, rendering him as vulnerable as Achilles—who of course died of a wound to that very heel by which his mother had once clung to him. *Hands (and thumbs) off,* we mothers have been warned.

Certainly I did my best to heed that warning. Perhaps I tried even harder than I might otherwise have done because when Michael was born his father was away, in the army, as was every other young man of my acquaintance, including my two older brothers and my two brothers-in-law, and I knew it was a terrible thing for a boy to be raised by a woman alone. But to my shame, I did not always succeed at putting the proper distance between us. Hence I found myself duly admonished by a succession of male authority figures, and racked with uncertainty about how to care properly for my son.

One day when Michael was about a year old and I was feeling particularly nervous—we were all nervous all the time during the war years—I took him to a pediatrician and explained that I had come because my baby seemed "tense." I think now that I was simply looking for a man to tell me Michael was fine, as indeed he was. The doctor looked at me sternly and told me I was hovering too much. "Get off the boy's back," he said. Which was the beginning of what I now see as the long process of my pulling back and monitoring myself.

A few months later, not long after Michael started to walk, I again went in search of male reassurance. This time I took him to a fancy specialist, because he was so pigeon-toed he was tripping over his own feet and I thought maybe he needed some kind of corrective shoes. This man was even sterner. "What this boy needs," he said, while shaking his finger at me, "is a little judicious neglect." Shame is an excellent technique to use on a mother, and I was very much ashamed. My baby was a boy and I was doing him wrong.

Two years after that I was still failing to be sufficiently neglectful in the eyes of the experts. Again in response to my concern about Michael's appearing "tense," our pediatrician suggested that he needed his independence. "Send him outside by himself," he advised. "By himself?" I repeated, in some surprise. He was only three and a half, and we were at that time living in the Bronx, in a pleasant enough but busy, populous, urban neighborhood. "Yes, you have to let him go. Stop protecting him all the time." So of course I did try to allow him to be more independent. In retrospect I would describe Michael as intense, rather than tense. His being a very intelligent child, acutely aware of and responsive to his environment, led naturally to his taking everything to heart. He didn't need to be off on his own; he needed someone to talk to about his many concerns—one of which, surely, was that he had just met his father, newly returned from World War II, for the first time.

Why was I so convinced that these men had hold of some inalienable truth about mothers and sons, I have to wonder now. Was it simply that I was so young and inexperienced I would have believed anything a man in a white coat said to me? Perhaps. But the idea that my little boy might be contaminated by mother love was with me from the beginning, as it is with most mothers. This fear was and is so embedded in our culture that even now, when 25 percent of our children under the age of eighteen are living in households headed by a single parent—usually a woman—we continue to believe it. Even most feminists believe that boys can't be raised by a woman alone, and the most sophisticated and liberated of women go chasing off in desperate search of a "male role model" for their fatherless sons. Psychiatrist Frank Pittman expressed the prevailing philosophy (perhaps better than he knew) in a magazine piece called "Men and Their Mothers": A woman "cannot raise a boy into a man," he said. And if there is no father figure on the premises, Dr. Pittman believes, as do most people, lay and professionals, that the boy will suffer unless his mother can find him one.

"A Boy for You, a Girl for Me"

In that old song "Tea for Two," a woman paints a rosy picture of domestic bliss for her beloved, evoking the family they will someday raise, the boy who will be his, the girl hers. This is a woman who has gotten the message about how things are supposed to work. The boy is always the man's. (And eventually, at least if you believe in the Freudian scenario, the girl is his too. To be a "Daddy's girl" is a charming and desirable goal, but a "Mama's boy" is a terrible thing.)

One way women learn how things are meant to be is that men make sure they hear it. From the moment they arrive at the hospital bearing a toy football for the newborn boy, the fathers are staking their claim. Obviously, the football is more a message for Mom than a gift for Junior.

Many of the symbols we use to denote gender are so much a part of our culture that we don't even think about how rigidly we adhere to them, but there are stories that occasionally open our eyes to their imprint on our collective psyche. A couple I knew were expecting twins. Amniocentesis had shown that both twins were girls, and the nursery was decorated accordingly. When one of the twins turned out to be a boy, the father insisted on a major overhaul of the decorating scheme, despite his wife's protests about the time and expense involved. "No boy of mine is going to sleep in a pink room!" he stormed, coming to the rescue of his helpless infant son, who might otherwise have been contaminated by his mother's— and infant sister's—feminizing influences. It seems unlikely that either the father or the mother could have worked up to a similar degree of hysteria about a girl baby sleeping in a blue room.

These same twins were treated very differently, beginning when they were less than a year old. Patrick was cuddled less, kissed only after a bump or injury, and allowed to cry much longer without being comforted. He was also tossed in the air more vigorously and held and played with more roughly, usually by his father, but occasionally by his mother as well—this despite the fact that Patty was a sturdier baby, with a birth weight almost a full pound higher than her twin's, and that Patrick was the fussier of the two. As their mother explained, her husband was very concerned that they not "spoil" Patrick. "I leave him to Charlie a lot," she said, "because I know I'm a softy and he needs a little toughening up so he can catch up with Patty."

It's not unusual for mothers to be collusive in this enterprise of "toughening up" their boys, as they try to get their sons to live up to their husbands' expectations (and their own). I heard recently about a five-year-old boy who spent the afternoon with a little girl the same age and, when his mother came to pick him up, emerged from the playroom wearing a barrette in his hair. The mother was horrified: "Well, thank heavens his father didn't see this," she confided to the little girl's mother, "or he'd be in big trouble." And so, by implication, would she, for no proper mother would have raised a son who would put a barrette in his own hair (or allow his playmate to do so either, it not being clear which of the two five-year-olds was responsible for this grave breach of manly decorum). Some months after I heard the original story, I was told that the little boy was no longer allowed to play with the girl, as she was deemed too feminizing an influence on him. Actually, she's a very outgoing, self-confident, adventurous, and even assertive child—all qualities we traditionally associate with males—while the boy is rather shy and uncertain.

In D. H. Lawrence's *Sons and Lovers* we watch a man lay claim to his son. As his wife dozes upstairs one Sunday morning, Walter Morel cuts one-year-old William's hair. When Mrs. Morel comes down, she finds him sitting with the child clasped between his knees, "cropped like a sheep, with such an odd round poll; and on a newspaper spread out upon the hearthrug, a myriad of crescent-shaped curls, like the petals of a marigold scattered in the reddening firelight. . . . 'Yer non want ter make a wench on 'im,' Morel said."

"Don't make a girl of him" is always the man's message, and most women go along with it. I don't mean to suggest that their husbands force it on them: the culture does. The fear of what would befall an insufficiently "masculinized" boy in this society is enormous, and women feel that fear as profoundly as men do. I have seen this fear time and again in my family therapy practice, when couples come in to deal with problems that have arisen with their sons because of what the mental health establishment conventionally diagnoses as "too much mother" (or "too little father"). But one of the most poignant of these cases, in which the father had claimed the boy as his own and the mother had ceded her stake in her son, concerned a child who was not even born.

Anticipatory Grieving: "A Son's a Son till He Gets Him a Wife"

The Gordons arrived in my office for their first session, having said they needed help because of Jean's depression. Indeed, she did look quite miserable, and very pregnant. My first question was, How long had she been feeling so bad? In response she began the following story: They were both in their mid-forties and had gotten married five years before, specifically because they wanted to have a child together. Alex already had a child from his first marriage, a ten-year-old daughter whom he saw quite regularly. As she reached this part of her recounting, Jean began to cry so hard she had difficulty continuing. "Is his relationship with his daughter a problem for you?" I asked.

"No, no, of course not. It's just that . . ." And out came the part of the story that concerned their efforts to conceive. Four years' worth of temperature charts, fertility drugs, intercourse on a schedule, and so forth, which naturally caused me to believe that what she was leading up to was a tale of a marriage that had failed just as the medical technology that had put such endurable stress on it succeeded. But that wasn't it at all. They had gotten through the rigors of the fertility battle with their relationship relatively intact, and had been overjoyed when Jean got pregnant. Both agreed that their problems began only when Jean went for her amniocentesis and they found out the sex of their child. She then went into a severe depression, which had still not lifted. At which point in her narrative Jean broke down again. "I'm seven months pregnant," she said, sobbing, "and it's a boy!"

For the first time Alex spoke, rather angrily: "I just don't get it. She was desperate about having a child. It was as though her life depended on it. I wanted one, sure, but I didn't have to have one. She did. Now we find out that not only is she pregnant, against all odds, but we are going to have a healthy little boy. And she's beside herself. I don't understand her."

"Of course you don't," Jean replied. "You already have a daughter. Now you'll have a son. You'll have two children, I'll have nothing."

When I questioned Jean about what she meant by that, she explained, "Well, you know, as soon as this child turns eighteen, he'll be gone. I go through the agony of getting pregnant and giving birth, and Alex gets a son. All I get is goodbye."

"Goodbye? You're going a little bit too fast for me. I don't understand."

"You know . . . everyone knows. 'A son is a son till he gets him a wife, a daughter's a daughter the rest of her life.'" Thus she expressed the conventional view that the boy is hostage to a future that will exclude his parents, in a way that a girl's future does not. But the distress she felt at that prospect went far beyond the conventional.

For the four years of their fertility ordeal, Jean explained, she had been picturing the baby they would finally have, and always it was a daughter—a companion, a friend "for life." Now only two months away from delivering, she was dreading the birth of their child, who seemed to her to be halfway out the door already, and Alex was as furious with her for her reaction as he was hurt, puzzled, and unhappy.

"So you're mourning the loss of a son who hasn't been born yet?" I asked, as I began to see the situation through her eyes. "You're getting ready to give him away."

"I'm not giving him away. That's the way it is. Everyone knows that. After the first few years a boy goes over to his father. And then he leaves home and that's it."

As if to make sure that I understood the boundaries properly, Alex broke in to explain: "I know what she means. I love my daughter, but she's very attached to her mother, and I don't begrudge that. It's how things should be. But I have some dreams too. I can take this boy to baseball games with me. I have a chain of sporting goods stores that I can turn over to him in time—not a bad thing to be able to pass on to a son."

Later sessions revealed that, having come from a family of three girls, and grown up listening to her father complain, half jokingly and half in earnest, that he had "no one to play with," Jean was all too ready to buy into the notion that girls are for mothers and boys for fathers. This was an idea that had only been reinforced when her mother said to her, after the birth of the last child, "Oh, I'm so disappointed. I wanted one for your father this time." So now Jean was trying to steel herself to make this gift to Alex, which she felt she owed it to her son as well as her husband to do. Why? Because, as Jean explained to me in that first session, "Boys need a man—the role-model thing, for sports and stuff."

"Sports? What else?"

"Well, I wouldn't want to turn him into a mama's boy, tied to my apron strings. He needs to learn about work, responsibility."

"Oh, I see. You don't work?"

At which both Jean and Alex began to laugh, and Alex explained that Jean worked very hard and was, if anything, overresponsible in her job as a social worker, feeling that she had to shoulder the burdens of the world. "It's one of the things we argue about. I'd like to play a little more, but Jean finds it difficult to enjoy taking time off."

Here was a woman giving up her child before he was even born because she was convinced that she had little to offer a boy. Her idea of doing what was best for him was to start preparing herself emotionally for the separation she would have to effect from him in order to enable him to be a proper man. So it was in fact she who was halfway out the door of her son's life!

The therapy consisted of getting both Jean and Alex to talk about what it means to be a man in this world, and the good qualities that each of them had that they thought they might like to pass on to their child. They also began to explore their family histories, at which point it became apparent why they were wedded to such an extreme version of the usual scenario involving a male child. But the Gordons were in fact typical, if not in their rigidity, then certainly in their basic view of "the way it is," in the father's insistence on laying claim to his son for the man's world ("She'd turn him into Little Lord Fauntleroy," Alex told me, by way of explaining why it was necessary for him to be the "role model"), and in the mother's collusion, however heartbroken. Most women, like most men, fear that a mother's influence will ultimately be harmful to a male child, that it will weaken him, and that only the example of a man can lead a son into manhood. Single mothers in particular are haunted by the dread of producing a sissy.

Mother Denial: In Myths and Movies, Rites and Rituals

There's nothing new about these beliefs, although at times of real change—now, and in the years during and immediately after World War II, as well as in the early years of this century—they get invoked with special urgency. The fact is, however, they are there to be invoked, for they have been with us for thousands of years, as we can readily see when we turn to the myths and fairy tales on which we were brought up.

Unlike men's movement leader Robert Bly, who uses these old mythologies as though they were proofs of certain immutable truths about the human psyche, I see them as accurate but time-bound descriptions of certain cultural realities that pertain during a given era. As Joseph Campbell, whom Bly claims as one of his mentors, puts it: "Mythologies are all conditioned by local geography and social necessity." Thus they both reflect and advance the beliefs of the culture from which they spring. Once the culture has changed, as I believe ours is in the process of doing, they will change. Until then, we will continue to hark back to the familiar, and to proclaim it eternal.

The typical Greek hero is a man who from his earliest days has been removed from the sphere of the mother—and often of the father as well (which would meet approval from Bly, who believes that a man must escape "parental expectations")—to be raised by an older man or god (Bly's "male mother" or "mentor" figure). In the story Freud used to such powerful effect, the infant Oedipus was sent away to die because an oracle told his father that his son would grow up to kill him. Years later the adult Oedipus, having against all odds survived, returns, unknowingly, to the city of his birth, where he kills the king, his father, and breaks the ultimate taboo by marrying his mother. He thereby destroys his family, and he comes close to destroying the kingdom of Thebes as well, for the gods strike it with a plague until the "unclean thing" (Oedipus himself) that has polluted its moral order is discovered and driven away.

Then there is the story of Jason, whose father fostered him out at birth to the centaur Chiron, who had earlier raised Hercules and would subsequently train Achilles. For Achilles this training in heroism came too late, for he had already been irrevocably marked by his mother's grasp and was thus doomed to an untimely death on the battlefield. But Jason would go on to win the Golden Fleece, and Hercules, one of those who accompanied him on that bold mission, would later perform the twelve great labors and achieve immortality.

If—unlike Oedipus, Jason, Achilles, and Hercules—a Greek hero is not conveniently removed from his mother sometime in infancy, he may have to get rid of her himself in adulthood. This was the case with Orestes, who killed his mother and then went one step further, denying the very meaning of the blood relationship between them. Arguing for Orestes' acquittal from the charges of matricide, Apollo explains during the trial: "The mother is no parent of that which is called her child," merely "nurse of the new planted seed that grows. The parent is he who mounts." To reject not just the individual mother but the principle of motherhood itself is, symbolically, a way of ridding oneself of all feminine influences, of killing off all remnants of the feminine within one's own psyche. The feminine,

Apollo is telling us, is no natural part of a man. That, I believe, is the real meaning of mother denial.

Such myths have been deconstructed in wonderfully intelligent ways, as well they should be. Alternative interpretations make it clear that those tellings that focus on the son's need to renounce the connection to the mother are ignoring the murderous role of the father. In the story of Oedipus, for example, it can be argued that it was neither he nor his mother who set the train of tragic events in motion, but his father, by choosing to sacrifice his son's life to preserve his own.

For now, however, I'm interested only in the usual interpretations of the myths, which construe them as a vehicle for the idea that a male child must be removed from his mother's influence in order to escape the contamination of a close relationship with her. The love of a mother—both the son's love for her, and hers for him—is believed to "feminize" a boy, to make him soft, weak, dependent, homebound. "Mama's boys" are sissies. Or in Freudian terms, mother love may be eroticized into something dangerous to the very identity of the child as male if it impedes a confrontation with and successful resolution of the Oedipal dilemma; for only through renunciation of the loving mother, and identification with the aggressor father, does the Freudian boy become a man.

This is the prevailing wisdom of our culture. Indeed, it may be said to have served our culture tolerably well for some thousands of years, during which we lived in an expanding universe, and men were required to sail off across the seas in search of one version or another of the Golden Fleece, to cross new frontiers, to fight in fierce hand-to-hand combat—hence to deny the "feminine" qualities in themselves, to be willing to endure long separations from their mothers (and other loved ones).

But our universe is no longer expanding in the same way. The frontiers we must cross are internal, not external. Warfare can lead to the extermination not just of our enemies but of all humankind.

Those feminine qualities that Bly and his cohorts are seeking to drum away on their weekend retreats may turn out to be precisely the ones men will need to survive in this drastically changed world of ours. Instead of rethinking the traditional verities, however, the mythopoetic male movement that Bly has forged sanctifies them, looking to the old myths for inspiration, seeing them as life-enhancing, believing devoutly in the necessity of removing the "soft" boy from his mother's sphere and turning him over to the male world. We remain trapped in our male mythology of masculinity and heroism. And we continue in our everyday lives to be profoundly affected by these myths—or, if we don't know them, by their descendants in our own time, the fairy tales we read our children, the movies we see, the television shows we watch.

The typical fairy tale, for example, involves a damsel in distress, who must be saved by a young hero. Snow White, Cinderella, Sleeping Beauty, Rapunzel—all are passive female figures awaiting salvation by a man. Here we have another way of killing mother off—making the central female figure in our popular dramas a young, helpless girl instead of an older, powerful woman. The young boy reader can then cast himself in the role of savior and protector of someone weaker than himself, which enables him to escape, in his imagination, from his real-life situation as a child very much in need of the protection of his mother. (I don't doubt the value of this imaginative exercise for the male child, though certainly I could wish there were something comparable to offer his sister.) In other fairy tales, like Beauty and the Beast, and the Frog Prince, there is a handsome prince, a cruel old witch, and a beautiful young maiden. The cruel witch is a version of the possessive mother who does not want her son to marry, and thus uses her magical spells and potions to make the hero repellent to the maiden. The witch's spell is overcome by the young maiden, who again becomes the central female figure in the drama, overthrowing the older woman.

Other stand-ins for mother appear in fairy tales like Hansel and

Gretel, in which a cruel stepmother persuades a loving father to abandon his children in the woods so there will be more for the two of them to eat. Moral one: Bad women control good men. The hungry children find a gingerbread house made of sweets and other goodies, and are enticed inside by a witch. Moral two: Bad women can seduce helpless children. The witch locks Hansel in a cage to fatten him up, the better to eat him. Moral three: Women feed on young boys. Beware of engulfing, hungry females. Gretel pushes the witch into the oven, thus saving Hansel. Moral four: The triumph of the young girl over the old witch. The children are then happily reunited with their loving father, the stepmother having been routed. Moral five: We would all be so happy together, father and children, if only we could get rid of the woman (mother) in our lives. This I see as the story of our times, the emblem of the new men's movement.

And then there's the American tall tale—of Paul Bunyan, John Henry, Davy Crockett, and so forth—from which women have been banished altogether. These are stories of men with enormous strength and courage, celebrations of the work ethic, appropriate to a frontier people for whom physical power was all-important.

Today we still think that mothers get in the way of masculinity, of all those qualities that lead to success, and the stories we tell reflect that belief as surely as the myths and fairy tales of earlier times. In most of the current genre of hugely successful blood-and-guts movies—the *Rambo, Die Hard,* and *Under Siege* type of saga that dominates Hollywood today—the heroes don't have mothers. In those movies where mothers do have some presence, they tend to be problematic, even if they are likable characters. *The Karate Kid,* for example, a typical movie in the ever-popular "achievement-of-masculinity" genre, shows us a single mother and her preadolescent son enjoying a warm, close relationship, which we are obviously meant to view as an obstacle to the boy's route to manhood, for the kids at school pick on the boy all the time and think he's a sissy. We understand that he needs a "male role model."

Fortunately, an old Chinese man who works in the building they live in befriends him, teaches him karate, and along the way imparts the necessary wisdom about what it means to be a man. So the young boy and his mother become increasingly distant, while he spends more and more time with his mentor, eventually achieving so much skill in karate that he enters a competition and is able to beat all the other, bigger kids. In the last scene, we see him lying on a stretcher, bloody, battered, but triumphant, with his mother standing proudly beside him. "My little man," she crows. Once again the culture has affirmed the assumption that a woman emasculates a male child, and only a man can lead a boy into manhood. And once again, the woman is ultimately collusive in this enterprise, as she celebrates the achievement of her bloody but unbowed manchild.

Boyz N the Hood tells another version of the inadequate-mother story, depicting a divorced black woman who comes to the conclusion that she lacks the authority to discipline her son, to shape him into someone with the inner toughness and self-control to survive in their ghetto neighborhood—this despite the fact that she is shown to be a very strong, competent person, able to stand up unflinchingly to everyone *except* her son. But since our culture believes that no woman is tough enough to handle an adolescent boy, in a very sad leavetaking she turns him over to her ex-husband. The rest of the story is about the son's journey to manhood, under the tough but loving guidance of his wise father.

In the context of African-American family life, in which nearly two-thirds of the households in 1991 were headed by single parents, most of them women, it is valuable to be reminded of the existence of fathers like the one depicted in this movie—a fine man who does a fine job of raising his son under very difficult circumstances. But does that reminder have to come at the expense of mothers, with the suggestion that they are not tough enough to do the job of raising sons? Do we have to put women down in order to affirm men?

Even those movies ostensibly trying to subvert patriarchal, male-dominant values end up affirming our conventional ideas about what is needed to produce a successful man in this culture. In the "happy ending" to *Little Man Tate*, for example, the child prodigy, unwilling to sacrifice his relationship with his mother, who has given him over into the care of a woman who can cultivate his genius, chooses the feeling world of his mother over the achievement-oriented world of his mentor. (Though both are women, only his mother is womanly; the other woman can't even cook!) Alas, even *Little Man Tate*, so acute about the cost boys pay for their exile from the relational world, still posits the same choice (which I would argue is a false one): the child must either love and be loved, or achieve. By choosing Mom, he thereby loses his chance at success.

In many cultures there are rites and rituals that symbolically remove an infant or small child from the world of his mother and turn him over to his father, to the community of men in general, or to the larger community—presumably in order to prevent the kind of outcome we see in *Little Man Tate*. Some of these rituals involve both girls and boys, some only boys, but the purpose is always the same. Although the United States is not a very ceremonial culture, even here there are a few ethnic and religious groups that enact rituals to effect that mother-child separation. The Mormons, for example, have a ceremony in which the father of the newborn (girl or boy) and several of his close male friends form a circle, each with one arm around his neighbor, the other beneath the baby, and then recite in unison: "We take you in our arms, and by the power of the priesthood, we give you a name and the Father's Blessing." Orthodox Jews also have several early-life ceremonies for boy children. Besides the ritual circumcision, which is celebrated very elaborately, there is a precircumcision custom in which young boys gather around the bed of a newborn baby boy and recite various prayers designed to protect him against having his soul snatched by Lilith—who, as Adam's first wife, might be seen as the very essence of the feminine principle. The boys are thus rescuing the newborn from the female (by implication his mother) and claiming him as one of their own. Later, when the boy turns three, there is a ritual haircut, during which the boy's father invites various male family members and friends to snip off small locks of the child's hair, signifying his passage from baby to boy, presided over by other males.

Few of us have managed to quell the uneasiness instilled by these cultural myths (and the attendant ceremonies). Mothers remain convinced that they are bad for their sons, and fathers—any fathers—are good. Again I turn to my practice for an example.

Fear for the Fatherless, Overmothered Son

Kate called to make an appointment to see me because she was worried about her five-year-old son, Stephen. There were three younger siblings in the family, she told me, by her second husband, Yeno, but Stephen was the son of her first husband, who had died when the child was still an infant.

I suggested that the entire family come in for the first session, but when Kate and Yeno arrived they were alone. Kate explained that Stephen had made such a fuss about coming that they had decided not to push him, and had therefore decided to leave the other children home too. A little further into the session it became clear that this had been Yeno's decision—he thought I was foolish to think they could talk with the children present—but I did not belabor the point, since it was clear that it would be counterproductive to get into a power struggle with him. He had an agenda of his own, and as far as he was concerned that was what they were in my office to accomplish. In his eyes, the problem with Stephen was that Kate spoiled the boy. Though he tried to discipline Stephen, Kate often usurped his authority, with the result that Stephen was a sissy—cried if his feelings were hurt, didn't stand up to his brother, Jacob, who was two years younger, preferred playing with his two baby sisters, and so forth—but there was nothing wrong with the boy that a few good beatings wouldn't cure. The only reason Yeno had agreed to see a "shrink," he said, was that he hoped I would convince Kate to let him be the "real father" that Stephen obviously needed.

What was Kate's version of the problem, I asked. "He just always seems so unhappy and depressed," she said, "sometimes for no reason. If he cries and I ask him what the trouble is, he won't answer me, and Yeno always says, 'I'll give you something to cry about if you don't shut up!' Which makes him cry even harder. And when Jacob takes his toys away, Stephen never fights back, even though he's much bigger. I tell him he has to learn to fight, but he just gets this sad look on his face and goes away from me."

"And then half the time you run after him," Yeno accused her, "and that makes him an even worse sissy."

"Yeno's way of encouraging him to toughen up is by roughhousing with him and Jacob," Kate explained, "but Stephen doesn't like it. So it always ends with Stephen crying and Jacob and his father making fun of him. I know Yeno means well and that Stephen has to learn, but . . ."

"Learn what?" I interrupted. In reply, Kate and Yeno described what it meant to be a man in their culture—which was working-class conservative Hungarian. The conventionally macho qualities they listed were one thing they seemed to agree on.

As the family history emerged during the first two sessions, both of which were with Kate and Yeno alone, Kate explained that one of her main motivations for remarrying had been to provide Stephen with a proper male role model. After her husband died, Kate moved in with her mother, who cared for Stephen while Kate went to work. Grandma had her own notions of how to keep Stephen from becoming too soft, which included strict toilet training, sending him outside in the cold with only a light jacket for warmth, never allowing him to sit on her lap, and so forth, but she was nonetheless a loving, caring presence. Once the first terrible shock of widowhood had passed, Kate began to enjoy the independent life she had built for herself—the job, the new circle of friends, the feeling that she could manage on her own. But urged on by her mother, who was very concerned about what would happen to Stephen if he continued to be raised by two women, she began attending a Hungarian social club to look for a husband. There she met Yeno, a recent Hungarian immigrant who was much older than she as well as very Old World in his views. While for herself she might have preferred someone younger and more Americanized, Yeno was a decent man, made a good living in construction, and, as a "man's man," seemed tailor-made for the task of leading her fatherless son into manhood.

Instead, the little boy who had been a happy, outgoing, and lovable, if somewhat high-strung, child, cared for by two women who between them had provided both the nurturing and the discipline he needed, was now whiny, miserable, and sullen. Caught in his mother and grandmother's mythology of masculinity, the victim of mistaken notions about how to whip a boy into manhood, he was in the process of being turned over to Yeno, who had nothing but contempt for him. He had lost his mother and grandmother and gained an image of male behavior that was predominantly aggressive, demanding, and angry.

Over the course of the six or so sessions we had together, half of which involved the whole family and half Kate and Stephen alone, I tried to reinforce Kate's own instincts about what her unhappy little boy needed. Though in her mind she believed the conventional wisdom that every boy needs a father, she knew in her heart that something had gone awry with this plan. The very fact that she had brought the family into therapy, over Yeno's objections, meant that she had grave doubts about the course she was on with her oldest child.

In other families facing these issues it is often possible to help the father learn to value qualities like those Stephen had in such abundance—emotional availability, the kindness and tenderness I saw him display toward his little sisters when they were all in my office, the imaginative and creative temperament that was evident in the drawing and reading he chose to do while the other three children played with toys. Ideally, the father comes to love and accept the child for who he is. But for a variety of reasons having to do with his own family history, the culture that had shaped him, his age, and the limited time and energy he was willing to give to the therapeutic enterprise, that was too hard a task for Yeno. What we were able to accomplish was an understanding that Stephen was a "different" kind of child, who could not be expected to follow in Yeno's steps but would instead benefit more from his mother's attentions. Thus I helped to validate Kate's feelings for her son, to free her to do what her instincts told her to do, and to neutralize Yeno's impact on Stephen's world. Stephen was greatly relieved, and his depression soon lifted.

While Yeno could not be said to have learned any real affection for his stepson, he did at least acknowledge that there are different ways of being a man in this world. Thus, he backed off from his own strenuous efforts to "whip Stephen into shape," and he ceased blaming Kate for "spoiling the boy."

Mother blaming, however, is one of our culture's favorite indoor sports. For reasons they do not really understand, it is particularly popular with sons (who are aided and abetted by virtually the entire mental health field).

MOTHER BLAMING: ENTER DR. FREUD AND HIS DISCIPLES

Three old women sit around a pool in Miami Beach, arguing over the merits of their respective sons. "My David is so wonderful to me," the first one says. "On my seventieth birthday he gave me a beautiful catered dinner, and invited all our friends." "That's very nice," said the second lady, "but my Aaron is really something. When we celebrated our fiftieth wedding anniversary he threw a huge party for us, and bought airline tickets to Miami for all our friends in New York." "Well," said the third, "Benjamin is also very good about special occasions. But that's not the only time he remembers. Do you know he pays a psychiatrist a hundred and fifty dollars, three times a week, just so he has someone to talk to about me?"

Despite his understanding that the mother is usually the source of the child's first intimate relationship and will thus always remain the first love, Sigmund Freud himself attributed much less importance to the boy's relationship with his mother—once he's past infancy—than to his relationship with his father. It was in the Oedipus complex, the working out of the boy's desire to kill his father so that he might sleep with his mother, that Freud located the nexus of all psychological meaning and complexity—and of much else besides. "The beginnings of religion, morals, society and art converge in the Oedipus complex. . . . The same complex constitutes the nucleus of all neuroses. . . . It seems to me a most surprising discovery that the problems of social psychology, too, should prove soluble on the basis of one single concrete point—man's relation to his father," he proclaims.

Perhaps the emphasis on fathers was Freud's way of overcoming the mother-centered home, which was a relatively recent phenomenon in his time, the result of the Industrial Revolution, when the world was divided into a male-dominated work sphere and a female-dominated home sphere. Seen this way, the Oedipus complex was a sexualized theoretical model of the potential destructiveness of a woman to her sons, an elaborate rationale for the need to distance the mother from her sons so that they would develop properly. Or as psychologist Paul Olsen described the Oedipus complex, it is "the cornerstone of a philosophy invented by a male who needed to play down the dependence on Mother (Freud never dealt with true infantile dependence) and paint it sexual, as if the boy had active genital wishes to copulate with his mother."

In any case, the mother was not the prime actor in most of the domestic dramas that Freud described; she was simply a desirable object, which the father owned and the son wished to own. From this you might expect that in the eyes of those who followed and popularized Freud, Mom would be off the hook, absolved of any responsibility for the psychological well-being of her son in the post-infancy years, provided she simply allowed him to withdraw from her, as he would naturally do in the process of learning to identify with his father. But this is not how things turned out.

By creating an image of the child (male and female alike) as the generally unfortunate product of his parents' own neuroses, Freud—or more to the point, his popularizers—created in parents everywhere hope for the opposite outcome: that if they could only usher him through his successive oral, anal, genital, and Oedipal stages, in a spirit of good mental hygiene and without imposing their own neuroses on him, they would produce a well-adjusted, happy child. Previously the goal had been to produce a physically healthy and God-fearing, moral, or at least well-socialized child, which could be achieved (depending on what school of advice you listened to) either by trusting to nature or by curbing it. The goal was obvious, the means relatively straightforward. But a psychologically healthy child? Never in the history of all the advice books on child-rearing had parents been given such total responsibility (read "blame") for such a broadly and amorphously defined outcome. And given Freud's conceptualization of the unconscious—how it operates in destructive ways in the unpsychoanalyzed, hence unaware adult, how it can be seriously if not irrevocably damaged by an unaware parent's mishandling of the child—never had such weighty responsibility rested on more precarious grounds.

Freud could also be said to have given new intellectual ballast to the idea that boys and girls were to be raised differently, for the working out of the Oedipus complex, on which a proper sexual identify depends, was different for the two genders. Girls identify with their primary love object (but must give up their active genital strivings toward her in exchange for a passive, receptive stance toward Father), while boys have to make a switch in identification from Mother to Father. In the eyes of the man who saw the root of all cultural and psychological meaning in the father-son relationship, the mother played a negligible role in all this. She was basically just to stay out of the way as her son forged his route to manhood via his identification with his father and his renunciation of her.

Those who followed Freud, however—and this included both the Freudians (among them Ernest Jones, Melanie Klein, Karen Horney) and their seeming opposites, the behaviorists, under the leadership of John B. Watson—shifted the awesome responsibility squarely into Mother's lap. For both groups, whatever their other differences, shared Freud's belief in the crucial formative influence of early life experience, and both differed from Freud himself in their realistic acknowledgment that such experience generally occurs in the presence and under the influence of Mother.

The serious attack on mothers began in the years during and immediately after World War II, with popular social commentaries like Philip Wylie's *Generation of Vipers,* first published in 1942, and successful enough to have gone through twenty printings by the time of its reissue as a "classic" in an author-annotated version in 1955; and *Their Mothers' Sons,* by no less an authority than Edward Strecker, psychiatrist, consultant to the Surgeons General of the army and navy, and adviser to the Secretary of War, which was first published in 1943, then reissued in 1966. These books suggested that "Mom" had emasculated her sons (not to mention her husband, according to Wylie) and was thereby threatening the very fabric of this country (most particularly the strength of the armed forces, according to Strecker). Similar ideas had found their way into a 1943 book called *Maternal Overprotection,* by psychiatrist David Levy, which described twenty cases of the terrible syndrome named in the title—nineteen of them involving boys! Boys were clearly the children most at risk from Mom's own unconscious, unresolved neuroses (mainly those concerning her "femininity").

After the war, Mom's anxiety about the effects she was having on her children (if not the country) could only have been exacerbated by Benjamin Spock, whose main contribution to her worries was his popularizing of the notion of the perfectibility of the child, a goal for which she of course bore almost complete responsibility. The original *Dr. Spock's Baby and Child Care,* published in 1945, simply assumed that Mother would stay home to take care of her children, and almost all the advice was directed to her. She was to be affectionate but not too affectionate, warm but not too warm, to foster independence but to set boundaries, and so on. And with respect to her son, specifically, she was responsible (and still is, in the latest, fortieth anniversary edition) for facilitating his orderly progress through the stages of the Oedipus complex by not being too "permissive and affectionate" (at least, not by comparison with how the father treats him).

Mothers have continued right up to the present to be the main culprits not just in the popular advice books but in the professional literature as well. Researchers who in 1985 published a review of the relevant journals found that "the authors of the 125 articles read for this study attributed to mothers a total of 72 different kinds of psychopathology."

The result of this barrage of mother blaming has been to intimidate mothers, to make them doubt what are often their own best impulses. What mother guided by the childrearing experts of today, or those of any time in the last five or six decades, has not feared for the damage she might inflict on her sons by being either too loving (overprotective, overclose, smothering, seductive, devouring) or the reverse (unresponsive, rejecting, castrating, cold, hostile, angry)?

We're all familiar with the consequences of error on Mom's part, especially if she errs on the side of being too involved with her son. Then he may be impotent, unable to love another woman in adulthood, homosexual, even murderous.

For impotence (not to mention self-hating, woman hating, and of course disinclination to marry and reproduce), we can turn to Sophie Portnoy's son Alex and his famous *Complaint*. "What radar on that woman!" he expostulates to his psychiatrist. "The thoroughness! For mistakes she checked my sums; for holes, my socks;

for dirt, my nails, my neck, every seam and crease of my body." Not to mention "the further recesses of my ears" and his bowel movements (as women were in fact urged to do in that era's books on childrearing). As a consequence of Sophie's maternal ardor, Alex appears to despise her, himself, and women in general.

Though one commentator has attempted a reframe of the usual reading of this book, seeing both mother and son in a positive light ("Alex Portnoy, assistant commissioner of human rights . . . might not have been drawn to his vocation without a mother who had shown him, albeit in exaggerated form, the power of commitment and conscience"), there is in fact very little in Philip Roth's story about Alex's noble profession, and a great deal about his ignoble sexual depradations on women, especially those of a different ethnicity and class (from himself and his mother), they being the only women with whom he can "perform." Roth is clearly a dedicated Freudian, who meant Sophie to be a monster of obsessive love, and Alex to be a mother-created mess. Indeed, the whole hysterical tale is told in the office of an analyst—analysts being of course the last hope for men trying to overcome the legacy of castrating, seductive, overclose mothers. Thus Alex's analyst is given the closing line in the book: "Now vee may perhaps to begin. Yes?"

One could wish for Alex a better analyst than Dr. Spielvogel, who quite predictably believes that the symptoms of Portnoy's complaint "can be traced to the bonds obtaining in the mother-child relationship." If Alex were my patient, I would like to explore his feelings not just about his mother but about his father as well. "The potent man in the family," Alex tells Dr. Spielvogel, was his father's oldest brother. The father himself he portrays as a pathetic, failed man. Apparently, Dr. Spielvogel doesn't pick up on this. Might Alex's compulsive need to prove his masculinity (via his "plentiful" acts of "exhibitionism, voyeurism, fetishism, auto-eroticism and oral coitus") possibly have something to do with his father? Might this brainy Jewish boy, who lacked such conventionally valued male attributes as athletic skill and physical strength, have resorted to a kind of compulsive sexuality in adulthood, as he searched in himself for the "potency" he felt his father did not have? This we will never know, for Spielvogel, Roth, and Portnoy himself all seem persuaded that his problems are caused by his mother.

Turning now from impotence to inability to love a woman other than the mother in adulthood, we may look again to D. H. Lawrence's *Sons and Lovers*—but Lawrence's portrayal of the "bonds obtaining" in family life is considerably richer and more complex than Roth's. The son whose shearing was described in the passage quoted earlier would eventually die, but another son, Paul, who is the Lawrence figure in this autobiographical novel, becomes his mother's great favorite. And what happens to him? He is unable to love another woman, Lawrence tells us, because his needy, possessive mother always gets in the way. " 'I can't bear it,' " Mrs. Morel tells Paul, trying to talk him out of his growing infatuation with his first love, Miriam. " 'She'd leave me no room, not a bit of room—' And immediately he hated Miriam bitterly." He is later unable to leave his mother for his second love, Clara, either. Telling Clara he is going to go abroad for a while, he confesses that it " 'shall hardly be for long, while there's my mother.' 'You couldn't leave her?' 'Not for long.' 'And if you made a nice lot of money, what would you do?' she asked. 'Go somewhere in a pretty house near London with my mother.' 'I see.' "

Paul Morel and his mother are often cited by Freudians as an example of the damage an unhealthily close mother-son relationship can cause, and there are many passages in the book that suggest Lawrence may have agreed with this assessment. But it might be interesting to speculate on the possibility that Paul's father was at least as destructive to his son's love life as Paul's mother, if not more, for it was Walter Morel's relationship with his wife—characterized by occasional drunken batterings, witnessed by the children—that had caused Paul to picture adult love between men and women as a violent, brutal thing. Certainly it was Walter who was responsible for Paul's squeamishness about the physical act of love, and Lawrence is quite clear on this point:

> A good many of the nicest men [Paul] knew were like him, bound in by their own virginity, which they could not break out of. . . . Being the sons of mothers whose husbands had blundered rather brutally through their feminine sanctities, they were themselves too diffident and shy. They could easier deny themselves than incur any reproach from a woman; for a woman was like their mother, and they were full of the sense of their mother. They preferred themselves to suffer the misery of celibacy, rather than risk the other person.

As with the Morels, the violent father often produces a son who cannot connect with women, physically or emotionally, for fear of hurting them and thus repeating the family patterns. Mrs. Morel is not the only obstacle to Paul's relationships with Clara and Miriam.

Of course the most extreme and most dreaded version of the inability to form a sustained romantic relationship with a woman in adulthood is homosexuality, and there the experts have had a field day with mothers. Novelist Edmund White, in *A Boy's Own Story,* captures the general drift of the message from said experts, and how familiar it sounds! When the adolescent protagonist of the novel seeks help from a psychiatrist in hopes of being "cured" of his homosexuality, the good doctor sees him for several sessions and then announces that he has discovered the root of the boy's problem:

> Difficult as my father might be and obsessed with him as I might have been, Dr. O'Reilly had decided my dad was merely a son of a bitch but not the true villain, not like Mom. It was she who had broken past the immunological barriers of my frail psyche and infected every last inch of my soul. It was she who'd ensnared me in silk fetters, she who'd shorn my strength and blinded me to the

gross imposition of her will. Indeed, she'd so thoroughly invaded me that scarcely anything of my own remained to me.

This diagnosis was reached despite the fact (which presumably had been conveyed to the psychiatrist) that "As a little boy I'd scarcely known my mother; she'd seldom been home and I'd been left to my nurse." White tells the story humorously, so that we are meant to see through it, but his vignette of Freudianized mother blaming is hardly even exaggerated, capturing only too accurately the spirit and imagery of a certain kind of psychiatric discourse about mothers.

Alfred Hitchcock's *Psycho* did the same for a mass audience, in a story about a man whose mother had been so destructive in her closeness to her son that he went beyond even homosexuality to . . . murder! Thus at the end of the film, by which time Janet Leigh has been slashed to death by the knife-wielding Tony Perkins and the mummified corpse of the demented innkeeper's mother has been discovered propped up on a chair in the cellar, a psychiatrist is brought in to explain the workings of his tormented psyche. It was Norman Bates's mom who made him a killer of women, we are solemnly informed.

Given the litany of damages a mother can inflict on her son by too much love (or, in some versions, too little), it should come as no surprise that women try to be obedient to the injunctions of their culture. This means acknowledging their sons' masculinity—hence their difference, and by implication superiority—from the earliest days.

MAMA'S LITTLE MAN

> James James
> Morrison Morrison
> Weatherby George Dupree
> Took great
> Care of his Mother
> Though he was only three.

James James
Said to his Mother
"Mother," he said, said he:
"You must never go down to the end of the town,
If you don't go down with me."

—A. A. Milne
When We Were Very Young

Bossy little thing, wasn't he, this James Morrison Weatherby George Dupree? No such words would ever be attributed to a little girl, for that kind of assertive, active role is thought to belong properly only to the male gender, in whom it takes shape at a very early age. In *You Just Don't Understand* Deborah Tannen describes the different languages men and women speak, and demonstrates quite convincingly that these differences are observable in even very young boys and girls. However, since children of both sexes are raised mainly by women, certainly until they learn to talk, we have to wonder how it happens that boys acquire a language that is different from that of their mothers.

We don't have to look far for the answer. From a boy's earliest days he is taught a perception of himself as male—as a member of the more powerful, privileged, aggressive gender group. That's what was being inculcated at a family dinner table I was present at one night, where a one-year-old boy was burbling away happily to himself, while his six-year-old sister, who was recounting an incident that had occurred at school that day, was told by their father to be quiet because her brother was talking. Out of the differing perceptions of self that boys and girls are given come the different "languages"—behavioral as well as linguistic—that men and women "speak."

I know from personal experience, as well as from my practice and from numerous studies, that the forging of the "little man" is a social process that begins virtually at birth. Indeed, thanks to amniocentesis, which can reveal the gender of a baby some five months before birth, mothers can now get an *in utero* head start on the process of socializing their boys. Thus mothers (as well as fathers and other family members and close friends) who know the gender of the child while it is still in the womb have been observed to talk to it more, use more nicknames and baby talk, and touch and stroke the mother's belly more often if the child is a girl. "Hey, how ya doin' in there, big guy?" is about all the typical *in utero* boy can expect. While such actions are not likely to have much effect on the unborn child, they are revealing of the parents' own socialization, and predictive of the kind of socialization they will soon be passing on.

Since parents behave differently toward their children on the basis of the gender of the child, it is not surprising that they also perceive the child differently on that basis. In one study, the parents of fifteen newborn sons and fifteen newborn daughters were interviewed within twenty-four hours of the children's birth, and despite the fact that the infants did not differ in birth length, weight, or Apgar scores (doctor-assigned ratings of color, muscle tone, reflexes, and heart and respiratory rates), the parents viewed their sons as "firmer, larger featured, better co-ordinated, more alert, stronger, and hardier—and daughters as softer, finer featured, more awkward, more inattentive, weaker, and more delicate." Responses like these on the part of adults toward children must surely result in what a similar study called a "reality-defining quality." In other words, the children will end up fulfilling their parents' gender-stereotyped expectations.

Certainly I am no stranger to those expectations, on either my own or other people's part. I remember that when the nurse in the hospital brought me my newborn son for a feeding, she handed me the squalling little bundle with his red face and his hands knotted up in fists and said to me, "Oh, boy, is this guy strong-willed! He knows what he wants and he wants it *now.* You better feed him immediately, because he's got a temper." Believing absolutely in the existence of that will and that temper, I did feed him right away. But when my next baby, a little girl, started screaming from hunger, the nurses would bring her to me with the explanation that she was upset and needed soothing. So I would croon to her, "Oh, sweetie pie, you're unhappy. What's the matter? Tell Mommy all about it," and I would continue to talk quiet nonsense to her and stroke her and sing to her until she quieted down. Only then did she get the nipple. So from day one I was active in establishing and adhering to the male/female, instrumental/expressive divide, which is a product of the belief that boys and men are primarily oriented toward activity, achievement, and power, girls and women toward nurturance and relationship. (It was Talcott Parsons, the most pre-eminent American sociologist of the 1950s and 1960s, who formulated the theory of the instrumental father and the expressive mother, a sex-roles theory that was valuable insofar as it was descriptive, but harmful when prescriptive, as he certainly intended it to be.)

The ways in which parents enact the gender division are relatively subtle during the early years, especially in infancy. Up until sometime around kindergarten age, when a boy is first expected to "measure up" against a peer group, most parents these days will kiss and cuddle children of both genders, read them bedtime stories, give them nightlights if they are frightened, minister to their tears, and allow considerable leeway in the degree to which their male children conform to conventional expectations of masculinity (my earlier barrette story notwithstanding). Today's parents' magazines, for example, are filled with commonsense exhortations to allow small boys to play with dolls (or at least stuffed animals) if they choose. Even Dr. Spock, who in earlier editions of his book was very concerned about reinforcing sex roles, now feels that he shouldn't have been so "horrified" when one of his own sons asked for a doll at the age of three.

Nonetheless, subtle differences in the way boy and girl children are treated do persist, and mothers still worry, sometimes even at the breastfeeding stage, about the dangers of being "overclose" to their sons. "Overcloseness" is a concept perpetuated largely by the mental health field, and one that I myself no longer believe in. Certainly there are mother-son relationships that are close, very close, not so close, not close enough. But how can two people be "overclose," any more (regardless of what the pop psychology bestsellers tell us) than they can love each other too much?

Mothers can, of course, be invasive, controlling, abusive, dependent, anxious, manipulative, demanding, and so forth, just as men can be. But those aren't synonyms for "overclose" (and are not used as such except to describe women). Nonetheless, if a mother is contentedly nursing her six-month-old infant son and his little hands are playing with her breast, his eyes are looking deep into hers, and she feels a profound sense of connection to him, she is also likely to be feeling a quiet undercurrent of worry: Is this all right? Am I being overclose? As this thought crosses her mind, she may stiffen imperceptibly, break the gaze, maybe even pull away. Over the course of time similar anxieties, and a similar response to them, induce a subtle yet pronounced distancing. Enough of this kind of behavior and the baby begins to give up on her, to absorb at an unconscious level that his mother is somehow uncomfortable with him, that she is pulling back from him, that their closeness is problematic. Soon he responds in kind, so that his mother, who wasn't aware that she herself was the original actor in this scenario of withdrawal, eventually assumes that the withdrawal was his, not hers.

This explanation—that the son gradually moved away from his mother, as boys are meant to do, while the mother sat passively by, longing for her child but recognizing that he must deny her—pleases everyone and eventually comes to be believed by everyone, including the child. Its underlying assumption, that the boy chooses to withdraw, that such a choice is within his power, ratifies the very gender roles that it helps to instill. Moreover, it reassures us that the Oedipus complex has been satisfactorily resolved. "If it had been up to me, I would never have let him out of my lap," the mother says of her manly young adolescent with barely concealed pride, "but he started to pull away by the time he was six. From then on all he ever did was follow around in his daddy's footsteps." The fact that it may have been she (perhaps inspired by Spock) who engineered that switch, by stepping back and urging her reluctant husband and son to spend more time together, will long since have escaped her mind, if she was ever conscious of it in the first place. Often in the course of therapy the boy will remember it—not with any apparent sadness, for it is not permissible for a boy to long for his mother. Instead he will generally say something to the effect that he remembers how hard on him his father was when he was just a little boy, but he understands now that it was for his own good because he was a mama's boy and he needed toughening up. Mother, father, and son are all united in their belief that from a very early age the boy began moving away from his mother. In mother-headed households, he may even have begun bossing her around, or at least resisting her authority.

In some families, even when these "little men" cause big problems they are a source of pride. They may be monsters, but since their parents perceive them as admirably masculine, the satisfaction of having produced such a child generally compensates for the trouble they cause (as far as the parents are concerned anyway). So when one of these children is brought in for therapy, it's generally not the parents' idea.

Mama's Little Tyrant

When Ginny spoke to me on the phone, she sounded more angry than worried. "I'm calling you because the nursery school [she mentioned a very well known and prestigious school] said that my son, Bret, is out of control and that I should seek help for both of us."

"And what do you think?" I asked her.

"I think *they* need help if they can't manage a three-year-old. But I'd like to come in and talk to you. Maybe I need to look for another school and you could help me go about finding the right one." After ascertaining that she and her son lived alone, her husband of eight years having left her shortly after Bret was born, I made an appointment for the two of them to come in.

Ginny was an attractive young woman in her early thirties who showed up still dressed in her nurse's uniform. "I came straight from work," she apologized. As we talked about Bret's problems at school, where the teachers were upset with him because of his habit of hitting and biting and throwing things at the other children, Bret gradually moved from his mother's lap, to a chair, and then to the floor, where I had placed a box of toys.

Didn't Ginny share the school's concern about his behavior being out of control, I wanted to know? "He's a boy, for heaven's sake! He's just a normal, active, energetic kid, strong-willed like his father," she began to explain, only to break off as she caught sight of Bret lobbing a block in her direction. She deflected it in mid-flight and, with an embarrassed little laugh, told me, "He doesn't like me to talk to other people. The problem is he doesn't see me that much." When I asked, "How much is not much?," however, it turned out that Ginny worked from 8 to 3 every day but picked Bret up at school and then spent almost all of her evenings with him, as well as all of her weekends.

"So you're together a good deal," I commented, just as Bret hurled another block, which hit the window behind his mother.

I waited for Ginny to act, but she seemed to be waiting for me. "I guess you want me to see what the school means," I commented. Still she did nothing, so I stood up, removed the blocks, and left only the soft toys on the floor. Bret started to wail. Ginny went to him, throwing me a reproachful look, but when she tried to pick him up he bit her arm and slid screaming and kicking to the floor.

"What an unhappy little boy," I commented, whereupon Ginny's eyes instantly filled with tears. "Why don't you take him out to the waiting room so we can continue? The receptionist will keep an eye on him." No, that would be too distressing for Bret, according to Ginny, so we agreed to cut the session short and have her return for another appointment on her own.

Telling Ginny that Bret was an unhappy little boy was a low blow, I knew, but I also knew it was the only way to get through to her. The aggression and hostility that had aroused the concern of his teachers were, for reasons I did not yet understand, points of pride with her, proof of his "strong will," so we were not going to get anywhere if I aligned myself with his teachers and pronounced him "out of control." But "unhappy"—that was something she would have to think about.

Indeed, at our next session, after a few opening remarks of a rather belligerent nature ("You think I spoil him, don't you?"), Ginny subsided into a long silence and then suddenly blurted out, "Why did you say that Bret is unhappy?"

"That's what I saw. Tell me what you see."

"I see a boy who's a charmer like his father, and has his father's temper. He's a handful but I don't mind. I like strong men—" at which she broke off and laughed nervously.

In the sessions that followed I heard about Ginny's failed marriage to a much older man she thought of as a brilliant artist, a charismatic, romantic figure whose stalled career she had supported with her nursing job. Bernard was very upset and angry when, after two abortions, she refused to end a third pregnancy and gave birth to Bret. Eight months later he walked out on her and she never heard from him again. Thus her first assertion of her own desires led directly to the end of her marriage. I heard about her parents, who seemed to live at a chronic low level of depression, born of disappointment in themselves and each other. And I heard her vision of herself: dull, dreary, reliable, finding meaning only in service to others, first her parents, then her imperious, demanding husband, and now her equally imperious son. Her main concern about Bret, she explained, was that "he could end up like me."

Ginny's therapy involved a reassessment of both herself and the husband whom she had so romanticized. Her own journey was a slow one, for it was hard for her to acknowledge the existence of her strengths and charms, which were many. But the reassessment of her husband, when finally she attempted it, was almost instant. She decided to track him down in Paris, where, she had heard from friends, he was living, still trying to make a go of it as an artist. "He's just an unhappy, disappointed, middle-aged man, not too unlike my father," she said in wonderment upon her return. Once she could see Bernard's "strong will" as selfishness, his defiance as petulance, his temper as born of a low threshold for frustration, his demands on her during all the years she had catered to him as babyish rather than manly, she ceased to glamorize those same qualities in her son and began in earnest to exert the necessary control over him. Very quickly Bret was transformed from the miserable little tyrant I had first seen into a lively, rambunctious, but happy child.

The elevating of a young boy over his mother, and over any other females in his life (especially teachers, as happened in Bret's case), is a very common phenomenon in single-parent homes headed up by women. And while the psychological circumstances that give rise to it are different in every family, what all these families share is a need to be reassured that the boy is suitably male.

In my own family the elevation of the boy was a multigenerational tradition. My father was absent during his sons' childhood, first as a soldier in the Hungarian army during World War I, followed by three years as a Russian prisoner of war; then, shortly after repatriation, as an emigrant to America, where he lived for seven years before being able to send for his wife and children. My mother, capable and intelligent as she was, guarded the male prerogatives of her young sons by making them the men of the family during those years, and they were indeed "good fathers" to their younger siblings—my sister and me. Thus, by the time I myself was a young mother with an infant son and a husband who was also in the service, the situation had a certain familiarity. I was then living in a one-bedroom apartment that my sister and I shared. With all the men we knew away in the war, the two of us used to joke that baby Michael was the only man around.

At some level I actually believed that. Thus I wrote letters to my husband extolling Michael's manly virtues—when he was three months old. He lifts his head: he's so strong! He screams at the top of his lungs when he's hungry: he's so bossy! He wriggles around a lot when I hold him: he's so independent! As the months and years passed, I worried ever more about the effects of his not having a father and tried, not always successfully, to obey all the male authorities who warned me against giving in to my desire to protect him. He fell: I tried not to notice. He cried: I'd tell him he was a big boy and everything was okay. But still I would often hold him and kiss him when he seemed unhappy. Maybe if you were here, I wrote my husband guiltily, I wouldn't be such a hovering mother.

Meanwhile, I was always aware of trying to make Michael into someone his soldier father would be proud of when he returned. That this meant toughening him up, keeping him somehow free of all those "womanly" feelings of empathy and attachment that would prevent him from being a good soldier in his own turn one day, was a source of enormous sadness to me. I would look at my adored baby boy and weep to think of the war his future might hold. And yet I would also look with horror at those few pale, unfortunate 4-F males who had been left behind, unable to serve their country. Who would want to have mothered one of them?

When the war ended, all the men in my family had miraculously survived, and they returned as conquering heroes. I stepped aside to allow my husband and my son to get to know each other. Frankly, I was relieved. At last Michael had a father, who would know how to lead him into manhood. And yet I was also bereft. There was my little boy, being tossed about in the air and handled vigorously, if lovingly, by a big, rough-bearded stranger, and looking quite uneasy about the dramatic change in his life.

Soon, however, Michael had become Mike, he and Fred seemed to have established a good solid father-son relationship, and I had a new baby—this time a daughter, on whom it was permissible to lavish all my dammed-up feelings of love and tenderness. And now that Michael had attained the age of three, the myth of his independence was well under way. It would be several decades before I began to understand that it was only a myth, and that it had not necessarily served him (or me) well.

TWO

Hero Tales:
For Boys
Ages Six to Twelve

> She loved me for the dangers I had passed,
> And I loved her that she did pity them.
>
> —WILLIAM SHAKESPEARE
> *Othello,* act 1, scene 3

In the prepubescent set, two of the most popular movies of recent times—indeed of any time—are *Home Alone* and its nearly identical spinoff, *Home Alone 2.* The plot of the original is about what happens to eight-year-old Kevin when his family flies off to Paris over Christmas vacation and accidentally leaves him behind. It, like its successor, shows us a little boy who is incredibly brave, resourceful, smart, clever, active, and aggressive, not to mention wise in the ways of the heart, and kind.

Waking up to an empty house the morning of the flight and gradually realizing that he's on his own, Kevin breaks into a wild dance of celebration as he exclaims, "I made my family disappear. I'm free!" Give or take an episode or two of harmless mischief making, he then proceeds to behave with rather remarkable sobriety (by the standards of his age group), clipping discount coupons from the newspaper, going grocery shopping ("I got milk, eggs, and fabric softener," he will later tell his mother), inquiring of a sales clerk whether the toothbrush he has chosen is approved by the American Dental Association, taking himself to Christmas Eve services at a nearby church, and so forth. Admittedly, he is frightened of the next-door neighbor, rumored to be the "Shovel Murderer," and he does have a brief moment of terror when he hears some incipient burglars snooping around. But he overcomes his fears, declaring as he emerges from his hiding place, "This is ridiculous. Only a wimp would hide under the bed. I can't be a wimp. I'm the man of the house!"

The rest of the movie involves his ultimately successful efforts to foil the burglars, with a subplot in which he counsels the neighbor, an embittered old man who is estranged from his own family, and thereby demonstrates that he is as sweet as he is fearless. What a guy! And how perfectly he speaks to the fantasies young boys have about themselves.

Not to weigh this creampuff of a movie down with an overly heavy-handed analysis, I would still venture a few observations about what those fantasies are: first and most important of all, that a resourceful eight-year-old man-in-training doesn't *need* a family (though he may nonetheless be glad to see them when they return); that he can take care of himself (at least as long as the credit cards hold out and the pizza delivery man continues to come); that through a combination of quick-wittedness, courage, mechanical cleverness, and physical agility he can triumph over all adversity; that given the chance, he will become a hero. Parents, too, love the hero they think they discern in their little boys.

Though girls as well as boys have flocked to see the two *Home Alone* movies, making the first the highest-grossing comedy in history, I've heard several stories about girls (and at least one forty-five-year-old woman) who found the basic premise—a child abandoned by his family—quite upsetting. One little girl had to be taken home in the middle of the movie, another had nightmares for some weeks after, and my woman friend told me it called up fears of loss and desertion she thought she had long since put to rest. If there are any boys (or men) having similar reactions, nobody's talking about them. In fact, those who can afford to are probably rushing such boys off to the nearest therapist, since we think there's something terribly wrong with a male child who doesn't aspire to Kevin's brand of heroism.

To me the movie is alarming. Reading between the lines, in a way writer-producer John Hughes no doubt never intended, I see a sort of retribution tale, in which our young hero responds to the pressure put on males in our culture by declaring his total independence. *Who needs 'em?* is his attitude toward his family, which I think is a perfectly appropriate reaction from any child who has been trained for such independence from his earliest days. Not that there's any suggestion of family pathology in the movie. Far from it. Kevin's family may be a bit chaotic, but they love him very much, as he does them, and they appear to be the idealized all-American family in every way, which would mean that they place a very high value on male autonomy. By doing all they can to encourage it, they ensure that their son becomes suitably "masculine" in his behavior, as Kevin certainly is. The various kinds of myth making we engage in—the cautionary tales for mothers, the hero tales for boys—are for the purpose of ensuring that manly end product.

MEN-IN-TRAINING

Give or take certain variables pertaining to race, ethnicity, and class, the man we would like our boys to grow up to be would look something like this: aggressive, independent, brave, rational rather than subjective, active, ambitious, competitive, logical, adventurous, strong in body and mind, capable of separating feelings from ideas, unemotional or at least able to hide his emotions, decisive, and gallant toward the weak (mainly women and children, though in Kevin's case the weak were represented by the old man from next door). He is the male ethos incarnate, a veritable Superboy. And, thanks to the distance that his mother has dutifully put between them, he's not at all like her. Or, as we commonly say, he's not a wimp (the very word Kevin used), not a wuss.

Like Superman, he can maintain his nonsissy or non–Clark Kent status only by remaining aloof from the Lois Lanes (and mothers) in his life. He can rescue them, but unless he is willing to give up his "supermanly" powers, he can't become emotionally involved with them. And like Christopher Reeve in *Superman II,* he may discover that if he does choose to give up his mask of invincibility for the sake of a relationship that allows him to express all the parts of his personality, his Lois is disappointed. When she gets the new, sensitive, "relational" man she thinks she wanted, she finds out she still longs for the impassive man of steel, the superhero, for she, too, has grown up on the myths about masculinity. Thus both men and women believe there are really only two choices: a man can be Superman, or he can be the stumbling, bumbling, falling-all-over-his-own-feet Clark Kent.

Though we may think it ageless and immutable, our conception of what constitutes the ideal man is culture-bound, fluid, and, in its latest incarnation, relatively new, having emerged in the wake of the Industrial Revolution. That was when the factory replaced the farm as the main unit of production, and home and work spheres became two distinct entities, with women remaining in the one, while the men went off to the other—the factory, the office, the construction site (and, as ever, the battlefield). When new transportation technology made suburban living possible in the late nineteenth century, the division became more explicit than ever. As cultural historian John Demos put it, "Suburbs . . . soon became the epitome, in spatial terms, of the work-home dichotomy."

With the genders occupying such distinct spheres and performing such different tasks, it was natural that each be allotted those personality attributes suitable to its particular functions. Not that this represented a total break with the past. Dividing the world into two spheres merely resulted in an exaggeration of the division that already existed between the sexes. The workplace valued "instrumental" qualities, those attributes long associated with men, since thousands of years of patriarchy had seen to it that men developed the qualities needed to exercise authority. Home life required "expressive" qualities, which of course have always been women's special province, since it has always been women who bore and reared the children. But until the Industrial Revolution there was more of a crossover, since men's and women's lives were so much more intertwined. Women often worked side by side with their men, and men were intimately involved in the lives of their children. Afterward the two spheres diverged, and so, too, did our notions of masculinity and femininity—so much so that we may be uncomfortable when one person displays characteristics of both.

Thus, it has become the developmental task of latency-age boys (post-Oedipal and prepubertal) to acquire those attributes we consider manly and, not incidentally, to jettison the rest. It is acknowledged, however, that boys of that age are in transition between two stages of development, boyhood and early manhood, and also that they live in two worlds—a private, generally female-dominated one, where it's sometimes still okay to be a little boy, not very different from a little girl, and a public one, where it's usually not. Again, this has been so since at least the time of the Industrial Revolution, when not only did the male and female spheres come to be seen as separate, but childhood (at least among the middle classes) was granted a special, discrete status, as a prolonged interlude between infancy and adulthood when the rules governing adult life are sometimes suspended. Males over the age of five or six were to be put in school and treated as children, rather than sent out to fields, factory, or apprenticeship as miniature adults. How long this hiatus lasted depended on the station in life the boy was expected to assume, family finances, and other variables.

Although boys in our culture are allowed a certain amount of movement to and fro in the latency years, they do get the message about where they're headed, and they get it early on. Unlike the mothers of Sparta, of course we do not lead our six-year-old boys to the edge of the forest and send them forth, expecting them to emerge some time later as men. The distancing I've been describing between mother and son is relatively subtle during the first five or six years of life, and the behavior expected of boys at this stage is not much different from what we expect of girls. Nonetheless, there is one rite of passage that we could call our own version of the Spartan initiation ritual: the first day of kindergarten.

With more and more children in day care, that particular initiation may no longer be the dramatic event it once was. By this time, many boys will have had plenty of experience at being separated from their mothers. But kindergarten is still the testing ground on which a young boy takes his place among his peers. At day care he'll typically have been with children ranging in age from a year or so to four or five, and the expectations are relatively relaxed: children, boys and girls alike, go to day care to be taken care of. A kindergarten boy's classmates are all his own age, however, and he's entering the institution where he is to be schooled for success and achievement. From the first day on he's expected to "measure up" to his peers, to demonstrate to them that he's a regular guy. Only if he does so can he and his mother prove that they have both done their jobs well—she by making it possible for her son to disengage easily from her, he by having learned the all-important lesson: big boys don't cry.

Boys and girls alike are prone to tears at their kindergarten debut, of course, but it's only the boy's tears that are cause for concern or outright alarm (not to mention mother blaming). As described in the previous chapter, in a variety of subtle ways the mother has been preparing her little boy for this public ceremony of leavetaking virtually from birth. If he fails the test, and clings to her at the threshold of the kindergarten class, she's likely to get a lot of dirty looks from the other mothers (and occasional father), especially if she doesn't ignore his tears and dislodge his little fingers from her skirt. Then we know she's a bad mother, who is turning her son into a sissy. The teacher generally says, "Just leave him alone, he'll be fine," at which point, if she has any hope of redeeming herself and her son in the public eye, Mom is expected to stride firmly away, abandoning him to his new life.

No such expectations apply to girls and their mothers. It's not a mark against either if a woman's daughter cries during the first days of school; and if the mother chooses to stay and comfort her daughter, even to make excuses for her, such as "She's very attached to me," there's no stigma. This is the double standard in action, cutting both ways—consigning boys to a prison of denied, repressed emotions, girls to a domain of feeling and vulnerability, which, a few feminists to the contrary notwithstanding, our culture views as inferior.

It's not as neat as all that, of course. The particulars of class, ethnicity, and individual psychology differ from family to family, and so, too, do the measures of masculinity. Some families will value stoicism and stiff upper lips from a very early age, others will allow tears right up to adolescence; some applaud physical strength and athletic skills in their boys, others prefer more bookish accomplishments; some expect at least the ability to defend oneself, others applaud outright aggression—and so forth.

And no matter what the value system of any given family or ethnic group, some mothers will resist outside pressures, becoming silent saboteurs of the culture that is trying to shape their sons to a mold they don't much care for. Often this will result in a counterreaction from the fathers, with neither parent fully conscious of the content of the mixed messages directed at the child. For example: If a mother is lying in bed with her arm around her eight-year-old son, reading a story to him, the two of them lost in their own world, and the father happens to walk in at that moment, he may feel uncomfortable with their closeness. Typically, he'll say something like "Let me do that," take the book out of the woman's hands, and seat himself at the edge of the bed to continue the reading—all without necessarily being aware of what he is doing or why.

A couple of years later that same little boy may come home and, in an atmosphere of cozy intimacy, over milk and cookies, tell his mother everything that happened that day at school; but if his father happens to come into the room while this scene is taking place, he's likely to issue an order ("Time to wash up for dinner") or make some practical inquiry ("Did you do your homework yet?" "How did the game go?"), thus switching the tone from the expressive to the instrumental. Both mother and son will then tacitly cooperate in changing the dynamic, again without the conscious awareness of any of the protagonists in this quiet domestic drama. The talk will die down, and soon they'll move apart, the boy to his room, the mother to her dinner preparations or whatever, and Dad is left none the wiser. It's their little secret from him that they still have these talks. And it's certainly a secret from the outside world.

Beginning at around nine, ten, or eleven, depending on the specifics of the culture in which he lives, a boy's feelings for his mother, which are usually still very strong and loving, must go underground. Neither his peers nor his father will feel comfortable with them. Until then, however, many young boys do remain close to their mothers, and may therefore be encouraged, or at least allowed, to show more evidence of what we think of as the "feminine" aspects of their personalities, which are many.

Boys between the ages of six and twelve, especially during the first half of that time span, before the manhood training has intensified, will sometimes give way to tears, occasioned as often by hurt feelings as by skinned knees. They also have all the caretaking impulses girls do, bringing stray puppies home, picking up little birds that fall out of trees to nurse them back to health, vying to bring the class hamster home over Christmas vacation. Moreover, they can be wonderfully sweet and open, talkative and close, loving and affectionate, just as girls can be. Generally, they learn to disguise these qualities well, however, just as they learn not to acknowledge the feelings they have for their mothers, and their adult observers see only what the boys wish them to see (which fits in readily with what the observers expect to see).

In *You Just Don't Understand,* for example, author Deborah Tannen remarks that one of the most extraordinary things about the differences between the two sexes is how far back they go chronologically—a point she illustrates with an experiment involving same-sex pairs of second-grade boys and girls, who were observed behind a one-way glass. Told by the researcher to discuss "something serious," the girls look each other in the eye and tell each other stories about illnesses and accidents that have befallen those they know—that being their idea of what constitutes "serious"; the boys, however, avoid "serious" altogether in favor of telling each other jokes, some of which are scatological ("tu tu" in the underpants is popular with this age group), making fun of the researcher, and running around a lot. To Tannen this is a demonstration of girls and their need for relatedness, boys and their need for status and independence, which is how many feminist psychologists and thinkers now describe the differences between male and female. I don't see it quite that way.

What I know about boys in the second grade is that they are often in an agony of uncertainty about what kinds of feelings they are allowed to have. The nervous energy, the fidgetiness and fooling around that Tannen conveys so well in her description, have much less to do with what she sees as the desire to "flout authority" than with the fact that a boy this age is often flooded with feelings for which he has no outlet. Having gotten the message that "big boys don't cry," he's learned its corollary: "big boys aren't supposed to have certain feelings (of fear, uncertainty, sadness) at all"—a very problematic message, since he's well aware that he himself does. Having gotten the message that he's not to be a "mama's boy," he knows he mustn't allow anyone, not his father and certainly not his friends, to see how strong his attachment is to his mother. What he therefore does with his many "unacceptable" feelings is to disguise them with shows of bravado.

Feeling vulnerable and wanting to cry, he may instead make funny faces, spew forth a stream of scatological epithets, bounce off the walls from sheer nervous agitation, or smack the kid next to him. Wanting to run to his mother, he may mock his friend's connection to *his* mother. Psychiatrist Stephen J. Bergman tells us, "When I was a boy, one of the worst nicknames you could use on your boyhood friends was to call them by their mother's name. 'Hi Roz! Hey Myrna!' " Even more poignant, family therapist Eric McCollum recalls that when he was in grade school and one boy beat another in a fight, "he would tell his victim to 'Run home to Mommy.' Of course, that comfort was exactly what most of us needed when we were beaten but the taunt made our need shameful, a sign of defeat. The lesson was clear: Don't want your mother too much. Don't need her."

Not until later does the repression of feeling become automatic and therefore easy. For now, the forbidden feelings are still fairly close to the surface, where they often cause confusion and discomfort, to the boy himself as well as to his family and friends. Boys who seem to stray from the socially sanctioned path toward manhood make us uneasy.

BAD BOYS

We were the boys.
The ones who got into things first,
And thought about it later.
Who smiled with smiles that charmed,
and apologized sincerely.
The boys they rooted for and wanted to succeed
Even though we broke the rules.
The ones smart enough to give back something

Even as we were taking.
And somehow Mom knew that it would
All turn out OK.

So runs the copy for a recent advertisement for a line of men's clothing. How perfectly it describes not just the qualities we admire in our boys but also the active participation of women in fostering those qualities in their sons. From Huck Finn to Dennis the Menace, James Dean to Bruce Willis, we love our bad boys!

Conversely, we are uncomfortable about the "good boys" among us. When I read that ad, I couldn't help remembering Eugene, a boy from the neighborhood in the middle-class New York suburb we lived in when our children were young. Eugene was a timid youngster of about ten, not athletic, not particularly social, given to puttering around in the garden with his father or just swaying aimlessly to and fro on his porch swing. He seemed a sweet child, kind to the little girls on the block, polite to adults. As a consequence he was ostracized by his more adventurous and overtly "masculine" peers, who considered him whatever the equivalent of a "nerd" was at that time. Meanwhile, we grown-ups wondered if Eugene was one of those "good boys" we read about in newspapers who wake up one morning and out of the blue murder their parents (or, God forbid, the child next door). Was our neighborhood harboring an incipient Norman Bates, we asked ourselves. For in a world where there was perfect consensus on what was meant when we said "boys will be boys," any child who did not fit the norm was not just suspect, but possibly dangerous. We made Eugene the repository of all our fears and confusions about masculinity, which had been heightened by raising sons in the years following the return of their hero fathers from World War II.

Unlike Eugene's mother, I had the good fortune to have a son the same age who was "all boy," even if he did fall a bit short of the "bad boy" ideal. In fact, a year or two earlier I had worried about Michael for what seemed to me his excessive tenderheartedness. Though he was a strong, sturdy, athletic child, he hated to fight, indeed refused to fight no matter what the provocation. Unfortunately, because he was also a studious, serious kid who got good grades, he was picked on a lot. I used to say things like "I don't know what's to become of you, you're too soft. How are you going to make it in the world? Everybody takes advantage of you." But then one day he came home and told me he had beaten up one of his tormentors: "Rex finally got to me and I knocked him down," he said, through tears.

"So why are you crying?" I asked, secretly thrilled that he had finally stood up for himself.

"Because I'm afraid I really hurt him."

"Oh, Michael," was all I got out, before he announced with sudden decisiveness, "I'm going to go back and make sure he's okay. You come with me. We have to go pick Rex up."

"No way, Michael. You knocked him down and it's about time. He's a bully who's been bothering you for months. Good for you that you finally got back at him."

"You don't understand," he said, still very agitated. "I have to go see if he's all right."

That's who Michael was, and I worried about him accordingly. Gradually, however, he seemed to toughen up a bit. He played baseball, competed hard against the other boys, and didn't bother much with girls—or with me.

When Michael was ten years old, however, things changed for a while. My third and last child, Judy, was born during a year that was probably the most difficult in the life of our family. I came home from the hospital suffering from various complications of childbirth, which caused me to be confined to bed, while almost everyone else in the family and the neighborhood had been laid low by an epidemic of the flu. With my husband, my seven-year-old daughter, Laura, and both grandmothers ill, Mike had to run the house single-handedly—and he did. He carried water, food, and tea to each of us, went to the store, picked up medications, entertained Laura, and with the greatest tenderness carried the new baby to me for her feedings. During that brief terrible period, he was absolutely central to the life of the family, and in touch with the most wonderful, caring, nurturing parts of himself.

Although the responsibility of doing so much must certainly have been a burden on a child so young, in retrospect I see it as a positive thing to have happened to Michael. He rose to the challenge in the most natural of ways, for it obviously tapped something within him that craved expression. At the time, however, I was concerned that it would reawaken in him too many of those tenderhearted feelings I thought had gotten in his way before. So as soon as I was back on my feet, I accelerated my admiration for his achievements in the outside world, while covertly discouraging his participation in the inner life of the family. He, like his father, surely had "more important things to do." Laura I yelled at for not cleaning her room, but Michael was exempt from mundane housecleaning duties because he was studying for a big exam or playing Little League baseball or running for class president.

The observe side of that proposition was that as the boy in the family Michael was held to different, more rigorous standards. When he and Laura got into a fight one day, because Laura had been pestering him, as younger sisters will do to their older brothers, he finally hauled off and hit her. I was furious. "You must never, ever hit a girl!" I thundered, the implication being "You're too good for this—why would a fine young man like you hit a helpless, stupid little girl?" This despite the fact that Laura was more than able to take care of herself. He stiffened up and didn't say anything, as was his way when reprimanded. He never did hit her again, but he didn't talk to me much either.

That summer when I sent him off to camp and leaned down to kiss him goodbye, he pulled back and stuck out his hand to shake mine. "Do that to my sister, not me," he admonished, reminding me of the rules I'd obviously forgotten—rules about gender-appropriate behavior that I myself was partly responsible for establishing.

Michael's growing up, I thought with both sadness and pride. *He doesn't need his mother anymore.* Even if he did, he couldn't possibly let that be seen in front of his peers. Thus I accounted to myself for the distance he put between us, and I sanctioned it—with no sense that I was at least as invested in that distancing as were Michael and his peers.

Though I was hurt by Michael's refusal to kiss me, I accepted it as not just inevitable but desirable, for I was trapped, like most of the women of my generation, in the postwar ethos of a husband-and-child-centered way of life. If we were lucky enough to have sons, particularly sons as multitalented and bright as mine, we saw their access to the outside world as a glorious gift we were meant to encourage, with no recognition of what it might cost them in emotional connectedness. The price they paid would not become evident until years later (though we were well aware of the price we paid). Michael was my hero, my great accomplisher. Or maybe my accomplishment.

If I could do it over again, I think I might have found a way to tell him how I felt about that handshake. Not in public of course, since respecting a child's feelings requires that one not embarrass him in front of others, but perhaps in a letter in which I could tell him how sad I was that he didn't want to kiss me anymore, even though I understood and would honor his need to act like the other boys.

Michael's own recollection, only recently shared, is that it was around this time that he became conscious of turning away from the family, toward an intense involvement with the competitive world outside, where the rewards were many and tangible. The little boy got lost in the process of becoming a "real boy." What I realize now is that that couldn't have happened without my collusion. In my eagerness to give him access to the wonderful world of opportunity that awaited him beyond the threshold of our home (a world I simply assumed to be closed to me), I left the door wide open, never understanding that it didn't swing both ways. The sweetness and eagerness to connect were the necessary trade-offs for his accomplishments, of which we were all inordinately proud. And if I missed him—his emotional presence in the family—well, good mothering was all about sacrifice.

The "Ancient Maternal Betrayal"

In the name of being a good mother, and training a boy for the role we expect him to assume in life, a woman may of course go much further. But the underlying motivation remains recognizable, even in extreme circumstances. A colleague of mine has told me the story of his own childhood, which was marked by the severe beatings that his father gave him from the time he was about eight. For the smallest of infractions, like leaving his muddy boots in the front hall, Lawrence's father would beat his son bloody with either a stick or a belt. Meanwhile his mother would cry in the next room, never daring to interfere—though on the one occasion when his father had threatened Lawrence's sister with a beating, their mother had stood between the two and prevented it. In later years Lawrence asked his mother why she had allowed him but not his sister to be beaten, and she had explained that she thought it would have been wrong to intervene "between two men." She said, "Your father was a good man. He knew he had to toughen you up, because you were a soft, sensitive little boy. I couldn't do it. I didn't have the heart to do it. But I had to be strong enough to let him do it."

In the name of being a good mother, sometimes we sacrifice our very beliefs about right and wrong, abandoning our sons to the prevailing culture. As Adrienne Rich has put it, "The fear of alienating a male child from 'his' culture seems to go deep, even among women who reject that culture for themselves every day of their lives." She is writing about those women who, despite being feminists and pacifists, are nonetheless uneasy about forbidding their sons to play with toy guns because they do not wish to "emasculate" them, to make them "misfits and outsiders" in their world.

No sooner do I read those words than I think of two feminists whose writings about their family life describe exactly that kind of ambivalence. Though they, like Rich, are speaking specifically of guns, their more far-reaching agenda is to question the kind of heroism our culture values, and the violence and aggression implicit in it. Describing her son's upbringing, Judith Arcana tells us, "Originally, I tried to outlaw all guns—but found that he became obsessed with them, and fashioned make-believe guns out of everything. So I bought a Day-glo pink plastic squirt gun, and restricted its use to bathroom and porch. I know how to compromise."

Jane Lazarre recounts the complexity of the feelings she has toward her second son, who seems somehow more fragile and vulnerable than her first:

> I am acutely conscious of my desire to feminize him, to protect him from masculinity, to keep him from moving out of my world. Only rarely do I give in to this subversive urge—I have a fear of his losing his bearing altogether; that without *masculinity* in its most conventional sense . . . he will falter, stay so close to me that he will not be able to walk away at all.
>
> Determined that he be strong enough to negotiate the world (that ancient maternal betrayal), I may encourage his growing involvement in baseball which he clearly appropriates from his brother and friends without any authentic interest of his own, appropriates because he yearns to be a boy, too, to be a man. I may even buy him a toy gun if he begs me enough. Still, I am aware of the urge, the desire, to keep him tied to my world, and I wonder what sort of human being would result from the shameless determination on the part of a mother to feminize her son.

I, too, wonder what would happen if we didn't cooperate in pulling back from our sons, even pushing them out. What would be the results not of "feminizing" our sons, for that is not how I see it, but of allowing them to be themselves, with whatever unique mix of the "feminine" and "masculine" is natural to each of them? Of standing up to the culture when it seems to us to exact too great a moral or emotional cost? Of helping our sons to stand up to it as well, to see themselves as strong, indeed as "manly," insofar as they have the courage to make their own choices?

Perhaps the bravest mother I know of in this respect (and it's surely no accident that we encounter such a mother only in fable form) was the mother of Ferdinand the bull, in the children's story by Munro Leaf. Ferdinand didn't want to butt heads with all the other little bulls, preferring instead to sit quietly and "smell the flowers." Though his mother worried that he'd be lonely without the company of his peers, "she was an understanding mother" and she "let him just sit there and be happy." A mother of uncommon strength of character, she allowed her son to be himself, and he was indeed very happy with the life choice he made. When by an unlikely concatenation of circumstances he got the chance to be the star of the bullfights in Madrid, something every other bull in Spain dreamed of, he opted not to fight but to sniff the fragrance wafting down at him from the flowers worn in the hair of all the ladies in the audience. This got him shipped home in great disgrace, where for all anyone knows, the author tells us, he may still be sitting under a tree, happily smelling the flowers he loves. A salutary tale—for both mothers and children.

As far as Michael's using his fists was concerned, I did not do as well as Ferdinand's mother. Yes, when his father was away during the war I had looked at him in his cradle and wept to think of the violent world into which he had been born, which might one day claim him too, but I didn't make the connection between the war I feared and the playground battles I sanctioned. I bought into the culture, and despite having thought myself something of a bohemian for a brief time in the days before I married, I was basically an insider in that culture.

For those who are outsiders there may be an even greater temptation to embrace the culture and thereby try to gain admittance to it; or, alternatively, there may be something in their experience that gives them the strength to say no. Writer Audre Lorde, as a black woman and a lesbian, seems to fall into this latter category. Her son, like mine, did not want to fight, but when he was eight they moved to a new school and he became the neighborhood target. One day when he returned home in tears she grew furious with him and "started to hiss at the weeping child. 'The next time you come in here crying . . .' "—only to stop herself in horror. She realized that she was seeing in him a child too much like the fat, scared little girl she had been during her school days, and that her fury at her own past impotence, her grief for his suffering, were clouding her judgment, leading her into victim blaming.

> This is the way we allow the destruction of our sons to begin, in the name of protection, and to ease our own pain. *My* son get beaten up? I was about to demand that he buy that first lesson in the corruption of power, that might makes right. I could hear myself beginning to perpetuate the age-old distortions about what strength and bravery really are.

Lorde then decided "Jonathan didn't have to fight if he didn't want to, but somehow he did have to feel better about not fighting." Urged by a friend to tell Jonathan that she, too, had once been afraid, had once run away, she took him into her lap the next time "he came in crying and sweaty from having run away again" and did just that. "I will never forget the look on that little boy's face as I told him of my . . . after-school fights. It was a look of relief and total disbelief, all rolled into one." For him, this was an important first step in understanding that "power [is] something other than might, age, privilege, or the lack of fear," in unlearning the idea "that he can only be strong if he doesn't feel, or if he wins." For her it was a reminder of the necessity to stand up to society's "either/or . . . kill or be killed, dominate or be dominated" mode of thought.

The mother of sons stands in the position of having to create her complementary opposite, someone destined to behave in a way that works to keep both mothers and sons locked into the existing social structure, and perhaps ultimately locked in opposition to each other. A mother does not necessarily act to her personal advantage when she acts as the agent and nurturer of male personality traits. Quite the contrary. She promotes an attitude of condescension or even contempt toward those traits deemed feminine—in other words, her own. And having distanced herself from him at the proper time, she may raise a son who makes her very proud—a surgeon, soldier, scholar, stockbroker—but she's also likely to have lost her connection to him, and thus should not be surprised if their contacts are limited to Mother's Day, birthdays, and other ceremonial occasions. Moreover, the emotional cutoff she effects may not be to the advantage of her son, either, if it results in a man who is cut off from his tenderest feelings, at best unable to connect warmly, intimately, to women (and others), at worst given to acting out his feelings of alienation and anger in aggressive behaviors.

When a mother rears her son in the culturally mandated way, what destiny does she have in mind for him that is so different from what she wishes for her daughter? I'm reminded of a forty-year-old man who told me that his mother used to say to his younger sister, when she was still in grade school, "Be nice to all the other girls in your class, because you never know who they'll marry." Even though most women now work outside the home, making them at least theoretically capable of achieving success, rather than marrying it, and even though there are endless amounts of talk about the "new man" and "the new father," who will value the kind of emotional connectedness that women enjoy, we still seem intent on raising our sons and daughters as though they were marked for two distinct worlds, both of them several decades behind the times.

And despite all the data provided by sociobiologists intent on showing the biological roots of gender difference ("nature" is winning the public relations battle over "nurture" these days), we still seem to operate on the peculiar assumption that our boys enter this world gender-free and will remain so unless we teach them what masculinity is. Thus, we are as intent on this sex-role socialization process as any tribal society that uses brutal initiation rites to train its male young for a world in which physical threat and material scarcity are the dominant realities. That the training we give our boys may be increasingly irrelevant to either gender in an information- and service-driven post–cold war global village—this, alas, is an idea still in the nascent stages.

THE ELEVATION OF THE SON

The teaching of the boy starts early and accelerates fast. Much of it takes the form of educating him about the rights and responsibilities accruing to his superior male status (as in "You must never, ever hit a girl!" or "Ladies first"). This elevation pertains especially to the most important woman in his life—his mother. He is to be not just distant from but superior to her; otherwise he may run the risk of being "unmanned" by her, which puts him on the road to being "henpecked" or "pussy-whipped" by women in later life. So the thinking goes. And again, women collude in it, for it isn't easy—indeed it takes considerable courage—to stand up to the culture in which we live. If there's any doubt about the ambivalence with which our culture looks on men who have abandoned the pose of superiority for more egalitarian relationships, we have only to look at the press coverage of Hillary Rodham and Bill Clinton in the early days of the campaign.

Even those of us who cling to the world view that saw women as helpless creatures, fit only for the domestic sphere and in need of the protection of their menfolk outside of it, are generally willing to concede that the world that gave birth to that attitude is gone. How odd, then, that we find it perfectly natural (and often rather endearing) to hear a father say to his eight-year-old boy as he walks out the door on his way to a sales meeting in another city, "Take care of your mother."

The father doesn't say to the mother, "Take care of my kid," although it is certainly she who will do the caretaking, not vice versa. No, "Take care of your mother" is the phrase that comes automatically to people's lips in response to the absence of a boy's father (whether due to routine causes like business trips or to death, divorce, or desertion). Since the boy is not literally expected to do anything, the phrase may seem to be just a hollow, harmless pleasantry. But in fact it is charged with meaning, for it carries the message to the boy that he is strong and competent compared with his presumably weak and incompetent mother. By raising our boys to a level so high that they see themselves as caretakers of women, we are preparing them, psychologically, to take their place in a world where men are still the dominant sex.

Thus, "take care of your mother,' a phrase as reflexive as "gesundheit" to a sneeze, as evocative of our anachronistic but still enduring fantasies about appropriate gender roles as any 1950s sitcom, is no empty saying but a powerful cultural signifier. And the idea underlying it, like any idea that is central to a culture's idyllic vision of itself, gets played out in myriad forms.

Jack and the Beanstalk is the fairy-tale version of our insistence on making "Mama's little man" not just a figure of speech, as it is when applied to children under five or six, but an actual description of the expectations our culture has for its males. Jack's mother, you may recall, was a poor, miserable widow who gave her young son, Jack, the job of selling their cow for the money they would need to live on. But Jack gets swindled on his way to the market and returns with something of much less value, which his mother again sends him off to sell, and which he again exchanges for something of even lesser value, and so on and so forth to the infinite despair of his mother, until finally he comes home with a mere handful of beans, which she pitches out the window in a fit of rage. In the morning they discover that a great beanstalk reaching to the sky has risen from their backyard. After Jack climbs the beanstalk, he defeats the giant at the top, lays claim to the golden harp and the hen that lays the golden eggs, and brings them back to earth so that his mother will have both everlasting joy and everlasting prosperity. In a story worthy of Freud, Jack the giant killer has proved himself his mother's hero.

The most recent attempt to capitalize on this age-old theme was the movie *Radio Flyer*. Despite the vast sums of money lavished upon it—for example, $1.1 million for the script and a shot at directing, an extraordinary deal for its virtually unknown writer—it proved a monumental bomb, both critically and commercially. Told as a flashback through the eyes of a man who is trying to impress upon his children the importance of promises (" 'I promise' are the two most important words you can ever say . . . the commitment can last your entire life," he solemnly intones), the story revolves around two little boys, Bobby and Mike, who look to be about seven and nine. Their father has walked off, and after waiting in vain for him to return, their teary-eyed mother packs the two boys and her few earthly possessions into her car and drives off in search of a new life out West.

At a roadside souvenir stand along the way, Mike and Bobby encounter the wise old man who elicits the promise that puts the plot into motion: "You boys take care of your mom, you hear?"

"We promised we would," the narrator (who is Mike grown up) tells his own little boys, "and we never broke that promise."

The stage is now set for a terrible tale of child abuse. The mother meets and marries a man with a drinking problem, who, unbeknownst to her, beats Bobby, the younger of the two, whenever he's had a few too many. Because they know their mother has at last found happiness with "The King" (as their stepfather likes to be called), the boys become partners in silence, hiding the marks left by the beatings, refusing to go back on their promise to take care of their mother. In a highly ambiguous ending, misted over by lots of fancy philosophizing about the uses of the imagination for transforming the grim facts of life, it appears that Bobby, with the collusion of his brother, commits suicide.

Despite engaging performances by the two young actors who play Bobby and Mike, and what the makers of the movie must have thought of as a surefire central conceit (How could "Take care of your mother" not be a winner?), *Radio Flyer* never found its intended audience. My theory is that the writer went too far. No matter how much a culture reveres its males, or in the case of our culture, no matter how desperately it is scrambling to restore to them the stature they have lost, a son is not expected to give up his life for his mother's happiness. Invoking the sanctity of promises in a story of two little boys who promise to take care of their mother results in the death (or at least the permanent disappearance) of one of them. It is hardly surprising that this theme turns out not to be a crowd pleaser.

The elevation of a young boy to some sort of hero status in relation to his mother need not result in death or severe injury for us to deplore it, however. In my opinion such elevation is always a kind of abandonment, with psychological rather than physical suffering the more usual outcome. I realize that it isn't intended as abandonment or understood as such—we think we are honoring our males, acknowledging their superior status, building their egos to prepare them for their future role—but that is in fact the result. Children, whether they are boys or girls, need parents who can take care of them, and of themselves. If instead the children are set up as the caretakers, they end up being cheated of their basic needs. Boys are especially vulnerable in this respect: dazzled by the Superman (and *Home Alone*) mythologies of his culture, every young boy is an incipient hero.

The Son as Caretaker

"We're having a problem with our youngest son, Billy," the woman's voice on the telephone explained. "He's nine years old and has never given us any trouble before, even seemed mature for his age, but now he's suddenly acting like a two-year-old. His father is very angry and I'm very upset." After ascertaining that Billy had two older half brothers who were away, one in college, one at boarding school, I made an appointment to see him and his parents together.

When they arrived I was struck by the contrast between the mother on the one hand and the father and son on the other. Julie was an extremely pretty, petite woman, maybe five feet tall, very delicate, with a piquant, almost childlike appearance. Her long straight blond hair was held back by a headband, her clothing consisted of a big shirt over tights worn with flat-heeled T-strap shoes, and she had big doe eyes that had been made to look even larger by the skillful use of makeup. In sharp contrast to her hulking, sober-faced son, she seemed youthful and carefree. Billy and his father, Bill, were both big strapping males, and both quite formally dressed (especially by the standards of a nine-year-old these days). Billy wore gray flannel pants and a white shirt and, following his father's example, shook hands with me in a serious fashion.

After a few minutes of hemming and hawing, in response to my attempts to elicit a description of the problem that had brought them to me, the somewhat flustered father winked at his son and came out with it: "I think it's one of these Oedipal things, you know. . . ."

"No, I'm afraid I don't."

Julie stepped in at this point. "Billy has become very dependent on me. Suddenly he wants to go everywhere with me. He refuses to go to school, doesn't want to go anywhere alone, and recently has even taken to sleeping outside our bedroom door, where we find him in the morning."

Given the almost universal tendency to explain a boy's behavior toward his mother in Freudian terms, it would have been easy to see Julie as a seductive mother and to accept Bill's notion that this was "one of those Oedipal things." With that formulation it would make sense to devise a strategy to put some distance between mother and son, which almost always involves bringing the father in more actively. But Billy at nine was in the middle of what are called the latency years; by definition, sexuality would not be prominent in his personality. Nor did his bearing toward his mother strike me as that of an incipient lover. Something else, I felt sure, was going on.

"When did all this start?"

"Right after the summer," Julie said. "We had a very good summer. Everyone was home: Jim, Bill's twenty-one-year-old son from his first marriage, came back for summer vacation from Yale; Luke, my son from my first marriage, who's fifteen, hadn't yet left for his first year at Choate; and even Bill was home all August, after spending much of the year away on business. So it was wonderful. I love it when all four of my men are home."

This is the kind of remark from a mother, particularly when said flirtatiously in the presence of a stranger, that would normally send a boy Billy's age running in disgust from the room. But Billy remained impassive.

As Julie continued her story, she explained that the time they had together had been particularly precious to her because they were the last days she would have with Luke before he went off to Choate. She was sad about his impending departure but had accepted it as a necessity because Bill had told her he was turning into a sissy under her influence.

"Luke didn't want to go," Billy broke in.

"Sure he didn't want to go," Bill explained with the beleaguered look of a man who's been over this ground many times before. "But Luke was too close to Mom, he needed toughening up. Julie agreed with that," he said, turning to me.

"Did you agree, Julie?"

"Yes, I guess I did. I told Luke, 'I still have Billy here, don't worry about me.' But he always worried after I married Bill. Bill is so big. He always thought Bill might hurt me."

"*Has* Bill ever hurt you?"

"The question should be," Bill broke in, "Has Julie ever hurt *me?*"

They both laughed, but I noticed Billy did not. His face remained expressionless, although flushed. Further questioning along these lines during subsequent sessions elicited the information that Bill and Julie played a lot of games with each other that focused on the disparity between their physical sizes. Bill would threaten to crush Julie if she didn't do what he said, and she would squeal, "Help, help, where's my hero?" so that Luke would come to her "rescue." These mock battles were a family joke to everyone but Julie's sons, who took them seriously. In fact, Julie described them as the means she had used to build Luke's self-esteem. Since Luke was small and slight, she worried that he wouldn't pass muster with the other boys. By making herself even smaller than she was and playing the victim, she thought she could make him "feel bigger."

Billy was the unhappy witness to the Luke-Julie dynamic, always feeling left out of the magic circle Julie had so carefully drawn around herself and the son whose stature she was trying to bolster. Six years younger than Luke, but almost as big, Billy did not seem to Julie to be in need of any similar bolstering. His physical size got in the way of her being able to see him as someone with any needs at all. Thus, in different ways, both Luke and Billy had been deprived of their rightful place as children in this family—Luke by Julie's efforts to cast him as hero to her damsel in distress, which was too burdensome a role for a child to have to take on, and then by her allowing Bill to send him away to boarding school so he wouldn't get too "soft," Billy by Julie's belief that he was big and strong and tough like his father and therefore didn't need a mother. Without understanding what she was doing, Julie had functionally abandoned both her sons.

After a number of further sessions Billy was finally comfortable enough to talk about his relationship with Luke, revealing the extreme jealousy he had felt over the special attention Luke got. "My mother was always talking to him. They had secrets. She always wanted him around to protect her. But when he left, he said to me, 'Take care of Mom.' So I did." Seeing the role of bodyguard as his only route to enjoying a real relationship with his mother, Billy had thrown himself into the cause. Hence his following Julie around, sleeping outside his parents' door, refusing to go to school, and so on. While Bill and Julie had seen him as a child regressing to inexplicably babyish behavior, in Billy's own imagination he was a giant on constant guard.

Julie was amazed by what she heard. She had had no idea that Billy had been jealous of Luke or lonely for her. Moreover, "I never realized he thought he was taking care of me"—a discovery that seemed to me to bode well. Often a woman's realization that her elevation of her son has unintentionally left him feeling stranded will cause her to mother him more appropriately. But she immediately followed up with: "I think that's real cute."

"Cute!" What greater putdown could there be for a boy Billy's age? It was going to take some doing to help Julie see the child in Billy without infantilizing him, which would be as hard on him as the elevation had been. For Julie, there seemed to be no middle ground between little boy and man. Both Julie and Billy needed to understand that it was legitimate for a nine-year-old to love and need his mother.

In short, the task of therapy was to take Billy off guard duty without disrupting his newfound closeness to his mother or pathologizing his need for her. Unfortunately, that proved very difficult with this family, because for reasons having to do with their own family histories, Julie and Bill were wedded to their game. An emotionally deprived childhood had left Julie feeling in need of a protector, while Bill's childhood with a chronically depressed, detached mother had resulted in a longing for a powerful connection with a woman. His children were at best an interruption to that connection.

Following the session in which Billy revealed his bodyguard fantasy, he apparently got enough validation for his efforts and enough assurance that his mother would be all right without him for him to be willing to return to school. With the problem behavior resolved, Bill and Julie canceled their next appointment, and never returned—perhaps because they felt their intricate dance of roles threatened by some of the questions that had been posed to them in therapy.

I suspect that in his attempt to win his mother's love, Billy may find other problematic ways of enacting his hero fantasies in the future, perhaps by engaging in overt battles with his father when he is an adolescent. At that time he will probably be sent off to boarding school, just as his brother Luke was when the relationship between him and Julie got too intense for Bill's comfort. Or if Julie objects too much, they may find another therapist, someone who will define Billy's struggle as Oedipal and therefore prescribe less mother, more father. If Bill proves reluctant to play his part in this scenario, however, which may well happen, since his relationship to his children always takes a back seat to his intense connection with his wife, boarding school may indeed be the "treatment" of last resort for this lonely boy, who only wants a mother.

The Son as Husband Substitute

There are many ways of elevating a boy to an inappropriate status, and many reasons for doing so. Often, if a woman feels frustrated by her husband's lack of ambition or drive, or by what she perceives as her own ineligibility for worldly success, she may make her son into the repository of all her aspirations for the future. Expected to achieve what his father could not, he becomes the pawn in a battle between his parents and, torn apart by conflicting loyalties to both, is left feeling confused, stranded, and alone. What he feels, however, may not be at all apparent from how he acts.

Ten-year-old Ben, for example, presented as a hostile youngster with an overload of pseudo-bravado. A tall, handsome boy brimming with tense energy, he swaggered into my office for our first meeting, having shoved his seven-year-old sister before him. Asked to take a seat, he slowly and ostentatiously fingered several items on my desk, all but daring me to reprimand him, before finally deigning to take the chair I had indicated to him. Ben and Lucy were in my office at my request, because after a couple of sessions with their parents, who had come to me for marriage counseling, I had inferred that the children, Ben in particular, were bearing the brunt of much of their mutual hostility. I wanted to see all four members of the family in action.

The problem, as Sara had described it in our initial session, was her husband, Maury. "He's a sweet man, a good man," she said. "Too good. He lives in another world. His boss takes advantage of him, he never stands up for himself. For him everything is always fine. Maybe for him—not for me." Maury worked as a pattern maker and cutter in a clothing factory, the same job he'd had when Sara had first met him twelve years before. "I've been trying to light a fire under him, get him to change jobs or make his boss give him a raise," she continued. "What kind of role model can a schlemiel like this be for his son?"

"Nothing is good enough for her," Maury retorted. "She'd like to wake up one morning and find herself married to a brain surgeon."

"For myself I don't care. It's Benny I'm worried about. I've given up on Maury, but Ben is young, he has such potential. If only Maury would take him in hand . . ." In this and the following session the main topic of conversation was Sara's insistence that Maury step in and discipline Ben, supervise his homework, intervene for him at school, where he was having trouble with his teachers—all things that Sara had previously done for Ben herself. But now that he was growing up, becoming fodder for Sara's ambitions for her family, she wanted the man of the house to take charge. It wouldn't be right for her to do it, she felt, because that would emasculate Ben—as she was sure any therapist would agree.

About that she was right: standard therapeutic practice would be to work with the father to get him to assume the role of disciplinarian. But like many men who feel undermined by their wives, Maury had taken recourse in what is commonly called passive-resistant behavior. He simply dug his heels in. I could see that trying to badger him into a role that came so unnaturally to him was going to be a dead end for this family.

"The boy is fine," he told me at our next meeting. "I don't know what Sara wants from him."

"He's not fine," Sara insisted. "He's only ten but already he's a cutup in school, he's in plenty of trouble with his teachers, and he's got a mouth on him. How is he ever going to get into medical school at this rate?"

"So what do you want me to do about it? It's *your* mouth he's got!"

It was clear how the argument would proceed, and obvious that I was going to have to meet Ben if we were to make any headway.

When I did meet Ben I quickly saw that *someone* would have to take charge of him, for he was rapidly careening out of control. Sara's pride in him was enormous. He was a very bright, verbal child who used wit as a shield, which had earned him the nickname "The Wiseguy"—a term whose multiple meanings were not lost on him, since he was an avid watcher of the TV program about the Mafia that went by the same name. When he was younger these qualities had perhaps been more appealing. Sara had seen his swagger and his temper as "spunk," his "fresh mouth" a promise that he would not be a "mealymouth" like his father. But now even she could see that the qualities she had previously enjoyed—indeed had held up to Maury, in Ben's hearing, as exemplary, as everything that he himself lacked—had turned ugly. He did not look much like a doctor-in-the-making.

Ben was clearly a miserable child, furious with both of his parents for making him their battleground, and torn between his love for his father and his hunger for his mother's approval and admiration. "All he ever does is watch TV!" Ben told me, echoing his mother's contempt for her husband. "All she ever does is yell at everybody. Nothing we do is ever good enough for her," he said, in an uncanny imitation of his father. His acting out of what had clearly become unbearable tension had made him rude, hostile, and provocative.

Once the family dynamic became clear, after a couple of sessions with everybody present, it was time to see Maury and Sara alone again. I began this fifth session by asking Sara where she got the idea that a "sweet" man (as she herself had described Maury) was somehow lacking strength.

"When I got married my mother warned me that life with Maury wouldn't be easy. She knew from difficult because she herself had such a hard life with my father"—another sweet, good man, who, in Sara's words, "never made anything of himself."

"Did your mother?" I asked.

"What?"

"Make something of herself?"

"Well, what could she do? In those days all a woman could be was a housewife."

"That's true. It was much harder when your mother was a young woman. I guess we all accepted the notion that a woman's success was achieved through her husband—or else through her son, as you're trying to do with Ben. But do you still think that's true?"

"No." Long silence. "Well, yes."

Both Maury and Sara laughed, thus paving the way for me to spend the next several sessions exploring with both of them their ideas about appropriate gender roles, so as to arrive at new, more workable definitions of what it means to be a man or a woman in these times and in their particular family. Sara worked part-time as a receptionist in a doctor's office, a low-paying job that was all she could aspire to given her high school education. It turned out that she had always wanted to be a teacher but had feared that Maury would feel put down if she were to pursue such a white-collar profession. Maury's response when this finally came out in one of our sessions: "Let me worry about that!"

For all his lack of drive and his passive ways, Maury had a sure sense of himself. On the one hand, this had allowed him to stand up to Sara in her ceaseless attempts to make him pursue job opportunities that he didn't want; on the other, it meant that he really was not threatened by the idea that his wife might have a higher-status or higher-paying job than his.

Since Sara was clearly the high-energy, ambitious, assertive partner, I urged her to make better use of those aspects of her personality. Before she had abdicated out of fear of "emasculating" Ben, she had been an excellent disciplinarian, as she continued to be for Lucy, and she was encouraged to return to that task. I worked at overcoming her reservations and convincing her that any parent, male or female, had a right—indeed a duty—to set limits for a ten-year-old boy. Similarly, she was encouraged to maintain her high aspirations, not just for Ben but for her daughter and herself as well. As the more approachable and emotionally available of the two parents, Maury was to help Ben deal more directly with his feelings by talking to him and eliciting the questions he needed to ask about his growing sexuality. That way both Sara and Maury would be doing what they were good at and what they felt comfortable with. Meanwhile, Ben could get back to the business of learning who he was, rather than feeling that he was meant to make up to his mother for what his father was not.

When I heard from them four years later, it was to get an invitation to Sara's graduation from college. She now has a teaching degree. At fourteen, Ben was quite the athlete, and not doing badly in school either. "He's an adolescent," Sara told me, "but he's kind of sweet." Maury was Maury, but the passive-aggressive routine was no longer necessary. "We still fight a lot," Sara said, "but it's about real stuff and I don't mind." Next to Sara, Lucy appeared to be the most ambitious one in the family. "We may still have a doctor in the family," as Sara summed things up, "but it probably won't be Ben."

The Son as Buddy

In single-parent families, it's common to see boys who have become their mother's "little man." Often these boys are very bossy children who patronize their mothers, who in fact do uncanny imitations of a certain kind of husband, being alternately possessive, protective, and seductive. This is one of the standard ways of elevating a son.

Another, less common variation on the theme is played out between single fathers and their sons. Having few cultural patterns for how to be the primary caretaker of a child, a man may turn to the buddy prototype as a guide to relating to a son if he has custody. Two guys "baching it" together is the jovial term he'll use to explain this living arrangement to himself and the boy. He's acting out of love, and with the best of intentions. However, expecting a boy to be a buddy to his father, like asking him to be a caretaker or a husband substitute to his mother, can make for a very lonely child.

"I'm concerned about my eight-year-old son, Peter," Spencer said when he called, after identifying himself as the custodial parent. "The school psychologist says he's depressed. Can a child that age be depressed?"

"Yes," I replied. "It's not too common, but it's certainly possible."

"Well, then, we'd better come in to see you."

Spencer began the first session by suggesting that Peter tell the "lady" what was bothering him. Peter shook his head silently.

"What has your Dad told you about coming here?" I asked him.

"That you were going to make me feel better."

"Oh, is that the problem? You feel bad?"

"Uh-huh."

"Do you want to tell me about it, Peter?"

"No."

Peter was very direct. Children in this age group tend to be cooperative and even eager to please adults. Not Peter. Though he was a polite child, he seemed cut off emotionally from the outside world, his voice barely audible, his answers all monosyllabic, his affect blunted.

"Would it be okay if I ask your Dad a few questions about you?"

Peter nodded, whereupon Spencer and I began discussing the recent changes he had observed in Peter's behavior.

"Peter has been living with me since his mother and I split up, when he was three. I work at home, so it's no problem for me. In fact, I love having him, and I thought he enjoyed being there. But recently he's started to stay in more than he used to, he's gotten very quiet, and he has trouble going to sleep. He goes to bed when I tell him to, but when I go in to check on him when I'm turning in for the night, at around eleven, he'll be lying there still awake. Then he has trouble getting up and getting started in the morning. Right, Sport?"

"Yeah."

"Any other problems at home?" I asked.

"No, Peter has always been a very good boy, and that hasn't changed. He's my buddy."

"What's happening at school?"

"They say Peter doesn't pay attention. He daydreams. Doesn't do his homework, doesn't prepare for tests, seems totally uninterested in everything."

Peter really was depressed, just as the school psychologist said. But why? Why would a child lie quietly in bed for two or three hours, never asking for a drink of water or a bedtime story or another fifteen minutes of television? I felt I needed to know more about the breakup of his parents' marriage, his relationship with his mother, and the circumstances that had led to his living with his father, which we explored in the next couple of sessions.

When Spencer and Doris had divorced five years before, Spencer told me, they agreed on joint custody for their two children, three-year-old Peter and his six-year-old sister, Kathy. Spencer moved to an apartment a couple of blocks from his ex-wife's, fixed up a room for the children, and had them three days a week to her four. The arrangement was amicable, and for a while everyone seemed comfortable with it. Last year, however, Kathy had objected to the disruptiveness of switching back and forth. Determined not to become a weekend father, Spencer had negotiated an agreement whereby Kathy stayed with Doris and Peter moved in with him.

My first thought on hearing these details was that Peter must be missing his mother. But that turned out not to be a plausible explanation, since the children had been told they were free to visit the noncustodial parent at will, and I was convinced from Spencer's account that he and Doris were scrupulous about not guilt-tripping or pressuring them. The familial atmosphere was "democratic," Spencer explained to me, with both children having been consulted in the negotiations that led to the current arrangement, and both aware that there was always the option to renegotiate.

Perhaps that was the problem: too many choices for an eight-year-old. Spencer's friendly, egalitarian "us boys together" attitude didn't seem conducive to allowing a little boy to be a little boy. Neither did his terms of endearment—"Sport," "Buddy," "Old Man." I wanted to find out more about the kind of day-to-day relationship they shared. Having found myself returning again and again to the image of that silent child lying in bed awake for hours at a time, I particularly wanted to know a little more about the bedtime ritual.

"What happens when you decide it's time for Peter to go to bed?"

"Well, he goes to bed at eight-thirty every night, and fifteen minutes beforehand I give him a warning, which is his signal to go wash up and brush his teeth."

"Do you read to him or have any kind of good-night chat?"

"No, I figured he wouldn't want to be babied that way."

"So what happens after he brushes his teeth?"

"I go in and kiss him good night, and then I expect he eventually goes to sleep."

"But lately he hasn't done that, has he?"

Guiltily: "No. But what can I do? It's not like I don't spend enough time with him. We do a lot of things together, don't we, Old Sport?"

This time I could see Peter visibly wince at the name. But he responded obediently: "Yeah."

"That's very important," I said. "What kinds of things do you do?"

"We play chess. He's getting pretty good too. Soon he'll beat me, right, Champ? And we play other games too. But we also *work* as a team. We cook together, we clean, we do laundry. We run a first-class bachelor pad. After dinner we sit in the living room together and I write while Peter reads or does his homework."

It was clear that Spencer was a concerned, competent, and loving parent. Having defined himself as one of the "new men," he had been involved with child care from the very beginning. But because Spencer was raised in a traditional home, where male and female roles were clearly defined—the mother taking on the expressive, nurturing role, the father the instrumental, teaching role—his idea of how to be the new man was, like many men's, limited. He could only translate it into the taking on of more instrumental tasks—more of the usual male teaching tasks, so that Peter was now a good chess player and a budding athlete—and also more of the practical tasks usually assigned to the female: cooking, cleaning, laundry. And he took them on with genuine enthusiasm, having learned the male value of doing things and doing them well. It hadn't occurred to Spencer, though, to take on any of the expressive tasks, and thus Peter wasn't getting what he needed emotionally.

"Let me tell you what I see, Spencer," I began. "You're a great instrumental father. You're good at playing and working with your son. Good male, father-type things. Task-oriented, enjoyable. These things will serve Peter well later, but right now he seems to need something else."

Anticipating what he thought I was sure to be getting at, Spencer broke in: "His mother?"

"Not necessarily," I replied. "I do think he needs mothering. And we could send him to his mother for that. But"—and now I issued a direct challenge to the "new man" in Spencer—"I don't see why you can't be the one to do it."

It was true that my initial instinct had been to send Peter back to his mother. The conventional wisdom of most therapists is that young boys need their mothers, older boys need their fathers (in part so that they can distance themselves from their mothers). But just as Ben's mother, Sara, in the family just discussed, seemed to me to be eminently qualified to play the "father" role of disciplinarian to her son, so Spencer seemed to me to be capable of "mothering" his.

We used our remaining sessions to discuss how to "do" mothering. I suggested, for example, that he could use the bedtime hour to talk things over with Peter. "If you shared some of your feelings with him, perhaps he might open up and share with you."

Spencer rose to the nurturing challenge. At first he felt awkward, but gradually he began to enjoy their talks. One night, he recounted a while afterward, he was telling Peter about how he felt after the divorce and he surprised both of them by starting to cry. "Then Peter started to cry, too, and there we were, crying and patting each other."

Now that's my definition of "the new man."

Not surprisingly, Peter perked up fast when his father gave him permission to be a child, not a buddy, and to experience a child's full range of emotions. His schoolwork improved, he started bringing friends home, and his whole demeanor changed. He loves spending time with his mother and sister, showing off his cooking skills.

Another new man in the making! Perhaps when there are enough of them, we can retire our hero fantasies and ease up on the boys who are expected to live them out for us.

But that day will never come if we continue to perpetuate the gender split. Our belief in that division is inaccurate and outmoded as well as harmful—as men like Spencer and Maury and women like Sara are proving all the time. At least one television show, the hugely successful (and much maligned) *Murphy Brown*, seems dedicated to making a similar point. Take the nanny arrangement worked out by anchorwoman Murphy and her housepainter/pal Eldin, which is one of sitcom TV's rare concessions to the psychological (if not the practical) realities of present-day life. After agreeing to Eldin's suggestion that he become the daytime caretaker of her infant son, Murphy asks him whether he really thinks such an unconventional arrangement can work: "The only problem I can see," Eldin tells Murphy, "is I have a slightly more developed feminine side than you do and that might confuse him." My prognosis is that Avery will do fine.

THREE

The Myth of the Male Role Model, and Other Tales for Changing Times

> If I could have one wish for my own sons, it is that they should have the courage of women.
>
> —ADRIENNE RICH
> *Of Woman Born*

THE NEW MAN: MASCULINITY PLUS ADD-ONS

Encouraging young boys to distance and differentiate themselves from women, and thus from the caretaking, nurturing aspects of their own personalities—the "feminine" parts—has been an effective means of creating a certain kind of man, it is true. And that man was well suited for his role as breadwinner in the free-market, capitalist world of work and public life created by the Industrial Revolution. But as the world has changed, with women participating more actively in the marketplace (man's world) and at least some men longing for the gratifications of intimacy (woman's world), the old idea of two distinct spheres is losing credibility. Perhaps this will be the beginning of the end of the gender split, for both men and women are now questioning the inventory of gender-appropriate qualities that each sex was bequeathed at that earlier time, recognizing that the split has become detrimental to all. Men like Spencer, the so-called "new man" (whose problems with his son were described at the end of the preceding chapter), are beginning to reclaim what has been lost to them. Our ideas about gender roles are in flux once again—which is all to the good in the long run but confusing at first.

Given the complexity of the demands currently being made on men, it's no surprise that they're feeling confused. In response to the deep-seated cultural and economic changes of the last several decades, men are now expected to be all that they once were and more—sometimes in ways that contradict one another, that are downright mutually exclusive. The "new men" are to continue to be strong, silent types while also being emotionally available. They are to be aggressive *and* empathetic, tough *and* gentle, hardheaded *and* sensitive, John Wayne *and* Alan Alda.

These emotional add-ons have put males in a terrible double bind. Hence the explosion of books, movies, weekend workshops, and therapies to help men cope with the increasing uncertainty about what a real man is. Does he take after real-life football player David Williams, who missed a game in order to attend the birth of his first child, and faced a $125,000 fine and possible suspension as a result? Or is he lying down in the middle of a highway to prove his toughness in imitation of football players in the movie *The Program*, as several boys were reported doing the day before the David Williams story broke? Should he be pounding his drums in the wilderness with some manhood guru, or attending fatherhood classes led by a psychotherapist?

Like their older brothers and their fathers, young boys are the victims of mixed messages about changing gender roles. Naturally, many of these messages come from their ambivalent fathers, who aspire to change but are uneasy about its consequences—and rightly so, for change will, as feared, mandate a loss of male privileges. (I would argue that what they stand to gain will more than make up for the loss, but that's an argument for another chapter.) One father I met recently told me with pride that as a "new man," he tried to be tolerant of the closeness between his wife and their nine-year-old son. This has resulted in the child's spending a lot of time in that female sphere the kitchen. Consequently, he now loves to cook. "Not that the boy isn't all boy," Bruce carefully explained to me, lest I underestimate his son's masculinity. "Brad is in Little League and plays a mean second base, but he also enjoys doing things with his mother." So while Bruce sits in the den watching a game on TV, feeling a bit lonely and kind of wishing his son would join him, he'll often hear Brad and his mother happily chattering away in the kitchen as they bake cookies. "It does get to me sometimes," he confessed, "and I'll walk by the kitchen and look in on them humming and baking and cleaning up and I'll wonder: Should I be doing something about this? But I always say to myself, 'No, let them be,' and I walk away without bothering them."

Brad is getting away with his cookie baking only because it's what I call an "add-on." If he weren't playing Little League, he probably wouldn't be allowed to bake cookies with his mom. Even so, he's just barely getting away with it, for what Bruce doesn't consciously understand is that his silent walking back and forth at the doorway is a clear sign of his disapproval. How much longer will it be before Brad accepts his father's tacit invitation to leave his mother in the kitchen and come watch a baseball game in the den? Or if he holds out, how long before the mother shoos him away and tells him to go keep his father company? Bruce's "new man" behavior, while more subtle than that of many other fathers, is just as likely to make his son feel caught in the tug-of-war that so often occurs between parents in these transitional years—the years when mothers may still be refusing, for just a while longer, consciously or unconsciously, to pull back from their sons.

Perhaps it's in response to their parents' ambivalence toward them, specifically toward their more "feminine" qualities, that young boys have made *Home Alone* such a staggering success. In a time of confusion about sex roles, when there is a longing to simplify the complex realities of the present, hero tales become extremely important for these boys, just as Robert Bly's mythopoetic men's movement has been for their fathers.

REWRITES OF "TAKE CARE OF YOUR MOM" AND OTHER RESCUE SCRIPTS

How the new man, and his son, are to relate to the new woman is perhaps the most difficult of all the gender-role conundrums, as is readily seen in any look at contemporary depictions of male-female relationships. Generally speaking, the pop culture products directed to males simply ignore the existence of women (except as sex objects or victims in need of rescue), because the issues they raise are too unsettling, and they therefore get in the way of male fantasies. But in the first of the wildly successful *Die Hard* movies, Bruce Willis tackles the problem head-on, with results that will be gratifying to wishful thinkers of both sexes. Willis plays a New York City cop visiting L.A. in an attempt to win back his estranged wife, who has left him to pursue a career when offered a high-level administrative job with a Japanese company. When he asks for his wife at the reception desk in the lobby of the building where she works and the clerk is at first unable to find her in the listings, he is stunned to discover that she has shed his last name (his brand, as it were) and taken back her own. What clearer sign could there be that she no longer needs him and he no longer owns her?

Fortunately for his dawning feelings of obsolescence, his wife's company is about to be taken captive by a violent gang of European terrorists, giving him an opportunity to single-handedly defeat the entire gang and thereby demonstrate the values of old-fashioned male heroism. Postmodern enough to be ironic in its embrace of these values—Bruce Willis declines the terrorist leader's nicknames of John Wayne and Rambo by saying, "I prefer Roy Rogers, I like his sequin shirts"—the movie is nonetheless an affirmation of them. But as a product of its time, it also pays lip service to the obligatory add-ons of emotional availability, empathy, respect for his wife as an equal, and so forth. Willis realizes during the course of the movie how much he loves his wife and child, and promises himself that if he gets out of this alive everything will be different, including his attitude toward his wife's career. His reward for embracing these new-man values? His wife takes back her married name at the end. Subtext: All these "liberated" career-women types really want is a little respect and a big hero. If ever there was a fantasy about rolling back the changes of the last thirty years!

That it's a popular fantasy is obvious from a look at the box office receipts of the last decade, deriving in large part from movies in the *Rambo, RoboCop, Lethal Weapon,* and *Die Hard* genre. Men are manly men in these tough-guy movies; hence women (insofar as they show up at all) are womanly women. This is the backlash at work: the more things change, the more frightened people get and the harder they hold on to the old ways, exaggerating them to such extremes that these movies have all the verisimilitude of action comic books.

There is at least one series of movies, however, that does acknowledge change—the *Terminator* films. *Terminator 2,* the fourth-highest-grossing movie of the last three years (*Home Alone* being number one), is a virtual catalog of attitudinal changes in our culture, particularly as they pertain to the relationship between the sexes. In fact, a mother-son relationship is at the heart of this film. Sarah, who has been visited by a man from the future, knows that her son, John Connor, is destined to save the world from domination by evil machines—unless the machines get to him first. Unfortunately, the mental health establishment doesn't give much credence to Sarah's prophetic vision of the future and has locked her up as a crazy person. Since that leaves her son at the mercy of those who would kill him, Sarah is plotting her breakout from the asylum, and just in the nick of time, too, because the evil Terminator man/machine is heading his way.

Fortunately, a good Terminator (in the well-developed form of Arnold Schwarzenegger) has taken John under his protection, putting his superpowers at John's disposal. Like the valiant hero that he is, John wishes to use those powers not in his own behalf but in his mother's, and he orders the reluctant Terminator to help him rescue Sarah. Thus far the movie sounds like the most conventional of male action-adventure fantasies. A young hero, who looks about ten, is going to save his mother and then the world. But Sarah (in the well-developed form of Linda Hamilton) is no helpless female awaiting her Superman. With her lean, muscled physique, her years of hanging out with the Green Berets in Nicaragua, and her knowledge that the future of the world depends on her actions, she's a powerful warrior. After John and his Terminator help her to escape in a hail of bullets, she is furious. "You cannot risk yourself even for me," she tells him in a blistering tongue-lashing. "You're too important."

"I had to get you out of that place," he pleads.

And then the unkindest cut of all: "I didn't need your help. I can take care of myself."

At this point the strangest thing happens. John Connor looks away from his mother and his eyes fill with tears. We are meant to notice this, for the Terminator comments on it, asking, "What's wrong with the eyes?" It's like watching the swan song to an ideal of masculinity that has become totally obsolete, in the middle of a movie that nonetheless continues to celebrate it. Still, the hollowness of "Take care of your mom" stands exposed—for at least one brief moment. How painful to have to concede that women no longer need men to save them.

Perhaps that's why Lois Lane's savior, Superman, died in 1992: he was a symbol of what one cultural commentator called "the death of the all-American hero as he has been defined for much of the twentieth century." He had to go, because "In the post–cold war world where America's role as superpower is . . . shifting in substance and tone, what need is there for the old macho derring-do of Superman?" But he also had to come back. Surely his return to life less than six months later was not just a marketing strategy but a sign—of the intensity of our longing for the old hero myths, however irrelevant they may be to modern life. Backlash and nostalgia are merely the flip sides of the same phenomenon. And both come to the fore when a culture is undergoing fundamental change.

The Myth of the Male Role Model

In his book *A Choice of Heroes: The Changing Face of American Manhood,* Mark Gerzon writes: "Men today consume certain images of manhood even though the world from which they are derived may have disappeared." As discussed, it's probably *because* that world is in the process of disappearing that these hero images are consumed with such avidity, such a desperate desire to hold on to them. The remarkable success of the male action film genre, the proliferation of a veritable arsenal of weaponry in our toy stores, video arcades, and home video games, the bodybuilding mania of deskbound middle-class men—all these phenomena speak of a longing to recapture a heroic male past in an age when that kind of heroism is at best irrelevant. As one personal trainer describes the appeal of bodybuilding: "To be honest, you can consider yourself part of the warrior class without ever putting yourself in danger." Pop culture has responded to the irrelevance of traditional concepts of masculinity by reinstating them with a vengeance.

Pop psychology has done something rather similar in its response to the declining institution of fatherhood. In 1970 single-parent families—the single parent almost always being a mother—made up only 12.9 percent of those with children under eighteen; in 1980 the proportion grew to 21.5 percent; and in 1991 it was 28.9 percent. Now that men seem to be disappearing from the family unit in ever greater numbers, the women who are left behind to raise the children are being told that their sons are in dire need of male role models.

With men no longer being men in the old sense of the word, they have become "male role models"; no longer clear about what it is to be masculine, they "model" masculinity; confused about their identity as men, they have "male sex-role identities"; no longer functioning as fathers, they are "father figures."

"Missing Dads," "Life Without Father," "Mothers, Sons Going It Alone: Single Women Agonize Over How Their Boys Will Become Men," "Rise in Single Parenthood . . . Reshaping U.S."—this is just a sampling of recent newspaper headlines. Alarm bells are sounding throughout the nation over the phenomenon of the absentee father. And with good reason—though not the reasons that are usually given by either well-meaning newspaper writers and their psychologist and sociologist sources, or by "family values" preachers like Dan Quayle. The single most terrible thing about female-headed households is their poverty. "Almost half of all female-headed families with children under 18 live in poverty, and the median family income for two-parent families is three times that of female-headed families," according to an article in *The New York Times*. More than two-thirds of children under age six living in such households are poor.

There's no question in my mind that for most heterosexual women and their children, generally speaking, life with a man is better than it is without (provided the man isn't alcoholic, drug-addicted, violent, or abusive). The families of these absentee fathers need their paychecks, and certainly most of the women in these families long for male companionship, for love, for commitment, for practical help around the house and with the children, for someone with whom they can share both the joys and hardships of everyday life. Women and children alike want men and need men for all sorts of benefits, material and emotional, and numerous studies support the idea that children of both sexes do better, psychologically and intellectually, when there are two parents actively involved in their care.

That's not the story that comes across in the popular press, however. There we are told that the phenomenon of absentee fathers is most alarming not so much because it results in poverty and loneliness, and all the problems deriving from those forms of deprivation, but because it denies young boys the "male role models" they need. Thus we blame social ills on the individual, scapegoating the absentee father and often the single mother as well, rather than seeing both as victims of a social system that gives inadequate support to families while paying lavish lip service to "family values."

"Who was going to show my son how to walk [like a man]?" a woman agonized in one article. "Fathers protect, they provide, they initiate into adulthood, they bring the standards of the outside world to bear on their children," says the author of another (ignoring the fact that it is men who commit most of the crimes in the world, as well as in their own homes). Psychiatrist Frank Pittman, who scolds the "politically correct" for their mistaken belief "that a mother [is] able to show a male child how to be a man," tells us categorically that "in families where the father is absent, the mother faces an impossible task: she cannot raise a boy into a man. He must bond with a man as he grows up."

How profoundly this notion of male role models has insinuated itself into our culture, to the point that just about every divorced, separated, widowed, or unmarried mother of sons is likely to be anguishing about how to get one of these for her boy! Even the fact that her son is doing just fine without one will not deter her, for any behavior that isn't downright macho may seem to her to signal a full-blown crisis in her child's gender identity. On my way to the elevator the other day a young neighbor confided that she was concerned about her eight-year-old son, and she wondered if I could recommend a therapist, preferably male. I knew the boy only slightly but couldn't imagine what she was worried about. He was a quiet, slightly reserved youngster, but self-assured and reasonably forthcoming for his age, as well as polite and appealing. Matthew and I had often exchanged pleasant greetings and chitchat in the lobby. So what was the problem?

"Matthew's a very good kid," she told me. "His teachers like him, he does well in school, he gets along with the other kids, but—I don't know how to say this—yesterday he came home crying because a bunch of toughs from the class ahead of his ganged up on him. They called him 'a fruit' and other things I can hardly repeat."

"What did he do?" I asked.

"He ran home."

"That seems wise," I commented. "He was one small boy against a group of bigger boys. What are you worried about?"

"He won't fight. He doesn't like rough games. He prefers being home and reading and building things."

"Well, what's wrong with that?" A question I might have not asked under different socioeconomic circumstances, where fighting might be more of a basic survival technique, but one that seemed appropriate for a young matron on the Upper East Side of Manhattan with a child in a prestigious private school.

"It's just that he might be different if he had a father. But he barely knows Sid. After we separated Sid virtually disappeared from our lives. He spends all of his time racking up hundreds of billable hours at his fancy law firm. So I keep thinking Matthew needs a male role model," she said.

Perhaps Sid could be induced to spend more time with his son, I suggested—not because I think Matthew needs more male companionship in his life but because I see she does. "No, no," she protested, "I don't want him to have a driven, workaholic role model."

What about her father? "An alcoholic, and abusive on top of that," she replied.

Any brothers? "My brother is a playboy. He hates women and he hates kids and he probably hates himself." And so we went through the list. Ultimately, I had to ask her, as I have so many others, what she meant by a male role model. The distant, closed-off, unknowable-to-himself-as-well-as-others male? The successful, driven, workaholic male? The macho, angry, abusive male? The womanizing, promiscuous, unable-to-commit male? And so forth. Is *any* male better than none?

But this is begging the question. Despite the lack of viable "male role models" in a given individual's life, there certainly are many good men in this world, who could be held up to any young child as exemplary. The more fundamental issue is the very notion of a male role model as something that a young boy needs in his life if he is to become a man. Though this notion is simply the latest trendy psychological panacea for a host of societal ills, it's taken as gospel. Like so much that we believe in so unquestioningly, it comes to us, in its latest incarnation, via Freud, with the theory of identification; and in recent years this psychoanalytic construct, which *is* simply a construct, not a fundamental truth, got retooled, by the social learning theorists, into another construct, which we call modeling.

Identification

According to Freud, it is through the working out of the Oedipus complex that boys and girls achieve their appropriate masculine and feminine identities. Sexual identity in Freudian terms is a question of learning to desire the opposite sex, and of a fundamental conviction that one is a male or a female; it is not a social role. For the boy, achieving this sexual, gendered identification means incorporating the qualities of a powerful rival, and becoming what one fears—an act that is primarily defensive in nature: "The male child develops a strong emotional attachment to his mother but comes to fear his father's retaliation against him for this attachment. Specifically, the son comes to fear that his father will castrate him . . . [as someone has castrated his mother]. The son deals with this fear by becoming like his father through an identification process called identification with the aggressor." Boys identify with the aggressor to become the aggressor, rather than the object of aggression, according to this theory. For Freud, masculinity is achieved by separating from Mother, and, in the act of identifying with Father, denying the feminine within the self so as to avoid the female's terrible fate of castration.

Oedipal theory notwithstanding, anybody who has lived with a four-year-old boy can tell you that his love for his mother does not result in his being afraid of his father—unless his father has given him good reason to be. The Freudian scenario makes little intuitive (or logical) sense. If Father seemed a forbidding, dangerous person, how would fear enable a small child to make the psychological leap from an identification with a loving mother to an identification with a castrating father? If, on the other hand, Father was what we all hope fathers to be—not just strong and firm but kind, nurturing, and gentle—would the child's failure to fear that loving figure preclude his being able to identify with him, and thus to achieve a satisfactory male identity?

There is very little in the psychological literature to support the notion that sex-typed traits are passed on from father to son. Moreover, boys seem to have no trouble arriving at a masculine identity with or without a father around, and it is now believed that they arrive at their sense of themselves as male as early as age eighteen months, considerably before the Oedipal stage. Even the fear of homosexuality, which is the subtext of many of the discussions (like the one with my neighbor) about boys needing a father to develop a properly masculine identity, seems unwarranted. The steadily building consensus on homosexuality as a biologically influenced, if not determined, trait should alleviate that fear (until that day when we understand that homosexuality is nothing to *be* feared). So should the many studies of homosexual and lesbian parents, which have shown no evidence of higher rates of homosexuality in their children than in the population at large.

In short, boys do not need to "learn" a gendered, sexual identity. They are born male, and from that will follow the gendered and sexual aspects of their masculinity. For better or worse, what they do acquire over time, not so much in the Oedipal period but in the latency and adolescent phases, is a social definition of masculinity, an understanding of how to take their place as men in the existing social structure. Enter the male role model.

Modeling

Like the identification theory, the concept of role models seems to me to be a way of recentralizing the marginalized father. In Freud's day Father had lost his position in the household because the recent phenomenon of the Industrial Revolution meant that he simply wasn't there much of the time. By making the father the central figure in both his son's and daughter's developmental dramas, the Oedipus complex gave the children back to him—which may help to explain why such an improbable theory spoke so eloquently to its time and eventually won so many converts. Now that fathers are not just off in the workplace but out of the family unit altogether, with over 10 million households (out of a total of 35 million) headed by single parents, mainly women, along comes the theory of the male role model to tell those women that their sons are doomed to mere humanity, as opposed to manliness, without the guiding influence of a man.

The modeling theory gives fathers an even more active part to play in the developmental drama, at precisely that moment in time when they're playing less of a role than ever. No longer is it sufficient for Father just to be a masculine presence whom the young boy, desiring his mother, fears, then learns to identify with because of that fear. Now Father is to actively teach his son, via example and instruction, what it is to be a man. Or if he's not teaching his son, he is to be a mentor or "male mother" (in Robert Bly's terminology) to someone else's son.

If no such teacher is on the premises, as is the case for millions of boys in families where fathers occupy little or no place in the lives of their children, then it seems that these boys are doomed to some deviant, neutered, sissified, or otherwise inadequate form of masculinity, unless their mothers can press a teacher, clergyman, coach, Boy Scout leader, father, brother, uncle, or other family member into service as a male role model. Many women, indeed most single mothers of sons, among them my neighbor, live in fear of what will happen if they are unable to find a suitable candidate.

MALE THERAPISTS AND THE MALE ROLE MODEL

In middle-class families like my neighbor's, the amulet against this fear is the male therapist.

"A male therapist," as she says, "like the one in *Ordinary People*. Someone strong but gentle, firm but caring."

"In other words," I translate for her, "someone male who has those female qualities you don't value in yourself? Why go to a therapist?" I ask. "Why can't you be the role model your son needs? Why can't you be the one to show him that one parent, man or woman, can own all the qualities that it takes to be a human being in the world we live in?"

After all, what does it tell a boy about his mother, and about women in general, if a man has to be brought in to take charge? And what does that tell him about how he's going to treat women later in life? Why not show him that women can nurture *and* lead, can be loving *and* competent, can be figures of authority *and* compassion? Unlike the new "add-ons" that often do conflict with the masculinity society expects of men, these are not mutually exclusive qualities, and they are precisely the qualities that women have already had to develop for use in the outside world.

Certainly I have seen these qualities in hundreds of the women who have passed through my office over the years, many of them struggling with doubts about how to raise boys on their own. If women would bring into their homes the same qualities they've had so much practice using in the workplace, or if they would simply deploy the complete range of competencies that is involved in full-time mothering today, instead of "dumbing out" when their sons reach a certain age, they could be completely adequate role models if necessary—as it increasingly often is, however much we might wish otherwise.

Fear of Effeminacy

Unlike Matthew, whose mother seemed to me to be panicked over nothing and who has done just fine without therapy, some boys (with fathers as well as without) do need help, and I am certainly not averse to recommending male therapists for them, as there are many fine ones around. Male therapists are believed to be the treatment of choice by families fearful that their boys are turning into mama's boys or sissies. Hence the phone call I received some years ago from the mother of a young boy who had been a playmate of my daughter Judy, when they were in preschool and kindergarten: Could I refer her to a male therapist for her son?

I remembered Joey as a lively and interesting little boy, but now that he was eleven, Nancy explained to me, he was having a lot of problems. When he was left to follow his own interests, math and science as well as music, he seemed happy enough, but only a couple of the other boys at his school shared those interests. He was therefore by himself much of the time, which worried his parents.

Joey's father, Mack, wanted him to get involved in activities that would help him to develop a wider network of friendships, and a more overtly masculine persona. Previously a rather remote figure in his son's life, Mack had been mobilized by his alarm at Joey's growing social isolation and had embarked on a campaign to get Joey to go out for baseball so that he could make new friends. Maybe if he went out for some all-boy type of activity, Mack reasoned, his classmates wouldn't see him as such a sissy. Joey wasn't interested, as Nancy explained to me, "because he's a little overweight and can't run very fast, so he's afraid of what the other kids will think." But Mack persisted, dragged Joey out to the park several weekends in a row to pitch balls to him, then took him to a practice game on a Saturday afternoon—with the result that when the two of them came home that day, Joey was sobbing. He had gone straight to his room and hadn't left it, even to eat, as of late Sunday afternoon, when Nancy placed her call to me.

The final straw for Joey, it turned out, had been his father's exasperation with him. As Joey ran across the field, clumsy and slow, Mack lost his cool and said to him: "For Chrissake, you look like some fat girl, everything flapping."

Discouraged by his inability to effect the desired changes in his son's life, and guilt-ridden over his own display of cruelty, Mack had now decided that Joey needed therapy. Nancy concurred with him that the therapist should be male. She was as eager as Mack to get Joey into therapy, because she felt he was too dependent on her for everything, and that this had resulted in her becoming extremely short-tempered and losing the feeling of closeness she had previously had with him. My suggestion was that they call Steven S., a young colleague of mine who years before had been my student. I knew Steven to be a very empathetic, emotionally connected person, and a wise, thoughtful therapist.

Three months later Nancy called and asked if she could come talk to me—"professionally, of course."

"By yourself?" I asked.

"Yes, Mack and Joey are still seeing Dr. S., and Mack and I are also seeing Dr. S., but he won't see me with Joey and Mack. Dr. S. is wonderful, but I feel like I need some help myself now." I told Nancy that if it was all right with Dr. S., then I'd be happy to have her come in.

A week later Nancy showed up in my office and explained the problem. "I don't know what's wrong with me. Dr. S. says that Joey and I are too close and that's why Joey is unhappy, but it seems to me that Joey is only unhappy when Mack is pushing him to do sports and that sort of male stuff. Also he says Joey is fat because of me, but when I try to watch Joey's diet, then Dr. S. and Mack jump on me and tell me I'm overinvolved.

"Dr. S. wants Joey and Mack to spend more time together. Well, I want that too. I've been pushing for that since Joey was a baby, but Mack was always too busy with his job. Now that Dr. S. says so, Mack's been taking time off from work and spending all his free weekend time with Joey too. Last Friday night he took Joey to the movies and left me home! They said it wasn't a woman's picture. What does that mean? Some macho, violent thing, I'm sure, and I don't think Joey even enjoyed it, but at least they're finally doing things together."

Now she started to cry. "Dr. S. says Mack and I need couples work, so he's been seeing the two of us, but I always come out of there feeling dumped on by both of them. I like Dr. S., he's smart and Mack likes him too, thank heavens. I don't know what Joey thinks because Joey doesn't talk to me anymore. But I'm sure he's helping Joey."

This was beginning to remind me of that old joke "The operation was a success, but the patient died."

"Am I crazy, or what?" Nancy asked. "If you tell me this is the way it's supposed to be, I'll be quiet, I promise. I just want what's best for Joey." I told Nancy that I would talk to Dr. S. and find out what was going on. Then she and I would meet again.

"Nancy was in to see me," I said when I called Steve. "She says you're wonderful, but she's miserable."

"Well, yes, I guess she is," he said, "but it can't be helped. It's a typical case of the overinvolved mother and underinvolved father, and the kid's been caught in the middle. Naturally, he's become a mama's boy. I just shifted things around. But she's having a hard time giving up her overfunctioning."

"Whoa, you're losing me, Steve. Talk to me in descriptions, not labels."

"Well, it's a scenario you've seen many times before. Nancy does everything for everybody. She talks for them, she organizes everything, she plans their social lives, she drives the boy everywhere, she waits on them hand and foot. She's a typical Jewish mother—and they're not even Jewish. With her around nobody even has to articulate their own emotions. When they first came into therapy and I asked what the problem seemed to be, neither Joey nor Mack said anything, so Nancy leapt right in and told me all about what everybody, not just herself, was feeling."

"Was she right?"

"Well, actually she was. . . ."

"So, let me understand. Are you assuming that if only Nancy didn't do everything for them, Mack and Joey would be responsible, well-rounded people? Don't you think it's possible that there's something of the reverse going on—that she "overfunctions" as a mother because Mack "underfunctions"? And that Joey is really a daddy's boy, because if he were his mama's boy he might be doing a little functioning on his own? I'm not talking about his learning to play baseball, which seems to be Mack's main focus. Nancy strikes me as a much better role model for the things that are going to matter to Joey in his life."

Not long into this discussion, Steve began to reflect on the parallels between Joey and himself. "I think what happened is that I got too emotionally caught up in this family. As you know, my father died when I was about Joey's age. And I guess I just wanted to make sure that Joey got what I never had after that—a father. I think I can use a little supervision on this case."

When Steve came in to see me we talked about the necessity of getting past the old stereotypes of therapy—that a boy has to be rescued from his mother if he is to develop his masculinity. The unidimensional Mack, responsible to his job but with very little life outside it other than what Nancy orchestrated for him, was not necessarily an ideal for Joey. Nancy needed to be invited back into therapy with her husband and son, where they could explore the important contributions each made to the family and, since Nancy was feeling overburdened, could perhaps contract for a more equitable distribution of responsibilities. "You got stuck on the Freudianized notion that a boy has to choose between his father and mother. Joey has two parents," I said to Steve. "Now they need help in being two equal parents."

I also suggested to Steve that he go back to talk to his own mother and recharge some of those valuable empathic qualities he had learned from her, which had made him such a good therapist.

Once he saw the role his personal history had played in his work with this family, it didn't take Steve long to get back on track. He'd been right to think that Nancy was doing too much. Still, the answer, he now saw, did not lie in nullifying the value of what she did for the family, but in getting Mack and Joey to do things too. Otherwise her anger over what she felt to be their exploitation of her would continue to grow, alienating Joey even further, at just that time in his life when he particularly needed the emotional support she could give him. With Mack's help, insofar as he was able, she needed to teach Joey to do more for himself. Being taught by a woman is not emasculating; failure is. The emphasis on baseball (a sort of automatic response in families worried about effeminacy in their boys) was therefore abandoned. Joey will never be an athlete. He's not built for it, and neither is his father, who carries at least as much extra weight as his son. In fact his disappointment in himself, projected onto his son, was probably a factor in the unfortunate way he'd handled the scene on the baseball field.

The last time I spoke to Steve he had closed the case. Mack and Joey were swimming regularly at the Y, and both had shed a few pounds. Mack was being a better role model by doing more around the house, and he and Nancy were both working on getting more cooperation from Joey. Nancy and Joey had resumed their old closeness, but Joey, thanks to new extracurricular involvements in the orchestra and a computer club, had also made new friends and was less dependent on either of his parents for companionship.

Steve had helped them all by seeing to it that no relationship was sacrificed for another. The father was respectfully validated without denigrating the importance of the warm, empathic bond between mother and son. And once Mack stopped pressuring him into being something he couldn't be, Joey started feeling good about himself. No longer a "soft" boy in the eyes of his father, he was just a boy with his own interests, which he was now being encouraged to pursue.

This was a very happy ending. Too often, however, therapists of both genders get caught in a kind of doing-business-as-usual trap, which pathologizes the mother-son relationship in order to re-engage the father in the life of his family. No regard is paid to what each parent has to offer, the result being that the son misses out on the emotional comforts he is accustomed to getting from his mother, which his father doesn't value, or doesn't know how to give him.

What Do "Male Role Models" Model?

Nancy is typical of the numerous women (including many of those characterized by therapists as "overfunctioners") who have stepped in to fill vaccuums left by the fathers of their children—sometimes in very surprising ways. Ironically, the lack of male involvement in family life has resulted in women's taking on role-model responsibilities in the very heart of the male character-building establishment: the Boy Scouts. Founded in 1910 by Sir Robert Baden-Powell, a highly decorated British army officer, the Scouts were dedicated to the task of making "big men of little boys," for which purpose they called on volunteers who were "REAL, live men—red-blooded and right-hearted men—BIG men." By 1974, a woman was suing the Boy Scouts over their refusal to open their doors to female scoutmasters, but the Scouts won that suit in 1987, only to capitulate the following year, thanks to a favorable ruling on another woman's effort to bring this battle into the courtroom. By the end of 1991, there were nearly 1,400 female scoutmasters, more than double the number from the year before, and over 3 percent of the total. Why?

"This is a recognition of what's going on with families. . . . Lots of households are headed by women and there are lots of instances where men aren't available," Bryan Archimbaud, a spokesman for the Greater New York Councils of the Boy Scouts, was quoted as saying in an article entitled "Master Is a Woman." Indeed, much of the growth in urban membership in recent years—in New York, for example, from 65,000 in 1986 to nearly 110,000 by the end of 1992—has been attributed to the willingness of women to participate.

Apparently, women can teach not only the same skills—knot tying, wood carving, and fire starting—that men can, but the same values too. "I know a lot of parents who cherish the idea of a positive male role model as scoutmaster," the article quotes another executive from the Scouts as saying. "But with the ideas we're teaching, does it matter who is teaching them? Family, responsibility to yourself and your community, cleanliness of mind and body. They are human ideals. . . ."

Would it be better if men were doing the teaching? Certainly for overburdened mothers who already have quite enough to occupy their time, between job and family responsibilities, it would be better. But is it better for the boys? Ask them. They may long for adult male companionship, as many of them certainly do, since they are so deprived of it at home, but apparently they're realists. Neil Davis, one of the children interviewed for the story, voiced his opinion: "A woman's better. . . . The men quit too early. The women stay with it." Along with all the other "male" qualities that women have had to cultivate to suit their changing responsibilities, women can now model "stick-to-it-iveness" too.

The search for male role models is often misguided, but it can sometimes be destructive as well, insofar as it can be translated into an unquestioning acceptance of the hero ethos. For when we talk about fathers "bringing the standards of the outside world to bear on their children" or being "the arbiters of the child's acceptability in the world they represent," which is the conventional description of what fathers are expected to do, what we really mean is that we want them to enable us to continue to produce the kind of male who is physically strong and brave, emotionally cut off and remote.

Middle-class families tend to reject some of the cruder manifestations of the cult of heroism. Generally speaking, they don't want their boys going off to fight wars (one of the reasons the armed forces are overwhelmingly drawn from the ranks of the poorer members of society), and they know that physical strength isn't going to get a boy very far these days, so they may not be interested in the outcome of schoolboy brawls on the playground. But the competitive spirit is very much alive.

Fear of Failure

"A man does a better job of putting his sons on the road to success." That was how Rona explained to me why she had turned over her nine-year-old twin boys to the guiding hand of their surrogate father, Allen, whom they called Pops. Although he was not the legal guardian of Aaron and Eric, or the husband of their mother, Allen had become Rona's live-in lover when the boys were about three and a half and had quickly assumed primary parenting responsibilities for them. It was he who made the initial phone call to me. He wanted to make an appointment to bring in Eric, he explained, because while Eric was identical in looks as well as abilities to the high-achieving Aaron, he was not living up to his potential.

"Aaron is a good athlete, an excellent student, very popular, and I think Eric is jealous of his brother."

"How does he show that?" I asked.

"He just doesn't do anything. If Aaron gets there first, that's the end of it. He won't compete. If Aaron joins the Boy Scouts, Eric won't. If Aaron goes out for track, Eric won't, even though he used to be at least as good at it as Aaron. This behavior started a couple of years ago, and we keep waiting for him to outgrow it, but it's only getting worse. We're at the end of our wits with this boy."

I agreed to see Eric and his parents, but insisted on seeing Aaron too, and Allen reluctantly acceded. When they came in I was struck by what a handsome family they were. Rona, a successful soap opera star, was a strikingly beautiful thirty-eight-year-old woman, Allen a tall, slender, distinguished-looking sixty-three-year-old man, the boys the very picture of well-scrubbed, all-American affluent youth as they sat quietly together, with none of the jostling and fooling around I had come to expect of nine-year-old boys. They looked like a magazine-perfect family, and indeed it turned out that Rona and her sons had posed for a number of magazine fashion spreads.

Allen immediately took control of the session. "I'm not sure why Aaron has to be here," he said. "He's doing fine. As a matter of fact, he's missing track practice right now, which is a shame, since he has a good chance of making it to the regional finals if he works hard."

"Why do you feel he's not part of the problem—or for that matter part of the solution?"

"Because he's not his brother's keeper. I've told him that repeatedly. That's why we separated them. They go to different schools now."

"What went into that decision?" I asked, looking directly at Rona in an effort to engage her, but Allen answered.

"They were too close. It wasn't good for either of them. When Eric started to lag behind, Aaron was always trying to bring him along, and Eric was getting too dependent on Aaron."

Since no one else had said a word yet, I now tried to engage the boys by asking neutral questions about their different schools, but succeeded in eliciting only monosyllabic answers and a lot of "I don't knows." Both of them looked repeatedly at Allen to make sure they were giving the "right" answers. The tension in the air was palpable.

Next I turned my attention to Rona and asked about the history of her life with the boys before Allen came along. She had been a rising young film star when the twins were born, married to a man whose own acting career seemed at a dead end. Sean had done much of the child care during the first year so that Rona could keep working, in both New York and L.A., but then he got a lucky break, became a huge hit, and went off to Hollywood, never to return.

"Do you ever see your dad?" I asked the boys.

Aaron: "Sure we do. In the movies."

Eric: "No. We go to California every summer for a week."

Rona: "I think of Allen as their father. He's the one who takes care of them, who's always with us when we need him. Sean was out of here like a shot as soon as his career took off."

Rona was still very bitter about Sean, feeling that had she not had to abandon her bicoastal life in order to provide her children with some stability after he left, she would have become as big a star as he was now, instead of being "stuck" (as she saw herself) in the backwaters of the soaps. "It's a man's world," she said, "and women always get the short end. So I'm glad I have sons, and I'm glad they have a daddy to show them how to get by in life."

When Rona met Allen he was the producer of a show she was in. A very strong, supportive presence, he soon became indispensable to her both on and off the set. "I was in heaven when we first began seeing each other. I just knew I could count on him to take care of me and my boys. But it took me a year to get him to move in with us. Believe me, I worked at it!" Not that Rona was the only one to benefit from the arrangement.

Allen had recently left a marriage of twenty-five years and was in the midst of a long and nasty divorce. The two sons from that marriage were in their twenties, both of them school dropouts and serious drug abusers. Bitterly disappointed in his sons, Allen explained their problems in conventional terms: his wife had babied and spoiled them. But to his credit he also shouldered his own share of the blame, explaining that he had been too involved with his work to be there for his boys when they needed him.

For Rona and Allen the fit was perfect: she needed a father in the family, and he needed to be a father but to do it right this time. For the boys the fit was less than ideal: they lost a mother and gained a male father substitute who had too big a stake in their success, and in his own. They were Allen's opportunity to redress the past.

For a while things seemed to go well. Eric and Aaron were exceptionally bright, engaging children, whose natural competitiveness with each other Allen encouraged, to the point where they began to have frequent fights. Though they remained close, the fighting was a constant source of tension in the family, and somewhere along the line Eric seemed to have opted out. As he told me in the only session I had alone with the boys, "There was no use in competing with Aaron because one of us doing it was enough. So I stopped." Indeed, he had stopped doing much of what he was expected to do. He put up a struggle about getting up and dressing himself each day, complained about having to go to school, cried easily when pushed into participating in anything against his will, refused to go out for sports despite having shown signs of being an excellent athlete, and so forth. By the time I saw him he had become a sad, lonely, withdrawn child, his loneliness much exacerbated by his enforced separation from Aaron.

What I saw over the course of the first several sessions I had with this family was that issues of success and failure had taken over their lives. Because of the highly competitive business they were in, and because of the particulars of their individual histories, this was all that mattered to Allen and Rona. Who was up, who was down, who had gotten a role, who had failed to get a role, who had been mentioned in the gossip columns, who had been ignored, who had gotten good reviews, who bad ones—this was the stuff of their daily conversations. In fact, that's why they had come to me. Having seen my name in a number of newspapers and magazine articles, they felt I was the therapist for them. Every time I was quoted in print it confirmed to them that they had come to the right place. Rona once said to me, "I know you're very successful, but on a scale from one to ten how successful would you say you are?" With Allen the success issues went beyond the professional to the personal. Aaron and Eric had to turn out well to validate him as a father.

After four sessions, I made the following intervention speech: "You came into therapy because of a problem with Eric. But the way I see it, the problem is not Eric's. He declined at the age of nine to perform to the impossible standards set by your family. He was wise to do so. The constant emphasis on who's up and who's down has made everybody in this family tense and anxious. Allen shows his anxiety by trying too hard to make the boys prove him a success as a father. Rona shows her anxiety by abandoning her sons emotionally because she feels a man can give them a better shot at a successful future. Aaron shows his anxiety by performing to Allen's standards, out of love and appreciation admittedly, but in the process he has lost his relationship with his brother. He's not his brother's keeper, to be sure! Only Eric doesn't play the game. We need to listen to the message Eric is giving."

That was the reframe—to depict Eric not as a miserable failure but as the bravest one in the bunch, the only one who had enough character to stand up for what he needed. He needed his mother back in his life and was willing to play the recalcitrant crybaby failure if that's what it took to get her. He also loved and missed his brother and needed to know that he could compete with him without the stakes being so high that one or the other of them was always going to be up or down in Allen's favor.

Rona began to cry halfway through my speech, while Allen remained very quiet. When I finished, Rona sobbed. "I want to be their mother. I really love them both, but I don't know how." In subsequent sessions I learned that she herself was the daughter of an alcoholic mother, and as a basically motherless child knew very little about nurturing or being nurtured. The dominant figure in her youth was her father, a wealthy, powerful man she had idealized, as she also idealized her two older brothers, who like their father had gone on to become immensely successful in their professions. Much of the work we did in the remaining several months of their therapy, then, was focused on reinforcing her rather vague sense of herself as a mother, helping her learn how to deal with her sons' emotional needs.

Allen, a very intelligent man and at heart a caring one, found it hard to hear what I was saying about the kind of pressure he'd been putting on the children. But over the course of a number of sessions, it gradually sank in. What I worked on with him was a redefinition of what constitutes success as a parent, and an understanding of how to measure it—not by the children's achievements but by their contentment and satisfaction with themselves. In this case the message was made more palatable by the quite noticeable change in Eric's demeanor as soon as the pressure on him eased up.

PETER PAN ACCORDING TO ROBERT BLY

Closely allied to the male role model, and invoked with equal frequency, perhaps because it can be just as difficult to find, is something called the father figure—or just plain Father. Our culture has a near-obsessive interest in reclaiming and rehabilitating the reputation of this missing person. Even if he is, as Robert Bly has written about his own father, alcoholic, unsupportive, and emotionally remote, he is to be embraced and forgiven (while Mother is left in the cold). Indeed, Jungian analyst James Hillman, one of the leading thinkers of the men's movement, has gone Bly one better. In *A Blue Fire* he pays something resembling tribute to the "destructive father," because such a father "smashes the son's idolatry" by virtue of his negative traits, "teaches [the son] that failing belongs to fathering," and "awaken[s] moral resolve . . . by provoking moral outrage at [his] bad example." Imagine a comparable tribute to mothers!

Having been incubated in the relatively small world of men's groups, the cult of father hunger is now making its way into the popular press, into movies like *Boyz N the Hood,* not to mention *Field of Dreams* and the *Godfather, Star Wars,* and *Indiana Jones* trilogies, all of them father-son stories, and into television sitcoms, where a perversely unrealistic two-thirds of the single-parent households were headed up by men during one recent season, while only three shows in recent memory, *Kate and Allie,* the short-lived *Valerie,* and the even shorter-lived *Hi Honey, I'm Home,* have depicted single women raising sons.

Nowhere, however, has the father-son theme been more elaborately celebrated than in *Hook,* the 1991 rewrite of that old classic *Peter Pan,* which is a remarkable departure from the source. Though it wasn't written by Robert Bly, it might as well have been.

One look at the differences between *Hook* and *Peter Pan* tells us much about the changes in the culture between then and now. In the original *Peter Pan,* both the 1911 J. M. Barrie book and the 1960 Mary Martin movie (filmed from the Broadway play), there's absolutely no sign of "father hunger" but a great deal of longing for mothers. Surprisingly, since what most of us probably remember of the story is the blithe, eternally young spirit of Peter Pan himself, even the most casual rereading of the book reveals, on almost every page, the focus on Mother. Father—Mr. Darling, the only father in the book—is a rather silly, petulant, self-important fool who ends up exiling himself to the kennel to repent for the error of his ways. Mother—Mrs. Darling in particular, as well as Wendy, her stand-in, and the concept in general—is supremely important. Peter brings Wendy to the Neverland precisely because all the lost boys need a mother. And my, how she works at her mothering, and how the boys, even including the ambivalent Peter, adore her for it! "A lady to take care of us at last," one of them cries when she first arrives. Soon she is reading good-night stories to them, tucking them in, doing their cooking and darning, and protecting them from the pirates, who are so envious that Hook conceives a scheme whereby he will capture all the boys, make them walk the plank, and force Wendy to be *their* mother.

Many adventures and many years later, Wendy decides it is time for her and her brothers to go home, to fly back through the window she is sure their mother has left open for them all this time. How can she be so sure? "If you knew how great is a mother's love . . . you would have no fear." For that is the way of the world: "Off we skip like the most heartless things . . . which is what children are, but so attractive; and we have an entirely selfish time; and then when we have need of special attention we nobly return for it, confident that we shall be embraced instead of smacked." So attractive is this vision of the eternally patient, loving Mother that all the lost boys—except Peter, of course—decide they would like to go home with Wendy, to be adopted by Mr. and Mrs. Darling. There in the Darling home their adventures end, Mrs. Darling having consented instantly to the adoption, Mr. Darling a bit reluctantly (for his permission was not asked and he'd been made to feel a "cypher" in his own house; but as soon as all the boys assured him that they didn't think he was a cypher, "he was absurdly gratified and said he would find space for them all").

The Steven Spielberg story couldn't be more different. Father is the central figure in *Hook,* not Mother. Robin Williams, who plays Peter, retrieved from the Neverland and grown up to be, well, actually, a pirate (in mergers and acquisitions), is now married and the father of two children, whom he rarely sees because he's too busy making millions of dollars. These children need a father. What do they need him for? In the words of his wife: "Your children love you. They want to play with you." But, alas, he never shows up for playtime. He misses his son's baseball game and conducts business on his cellular phone during his daughter's performance in a school production of (what else?) *Peter Pan.*

When the children are abducted by Captain Hook, who is still carrying a grudge against Peter, and who wins their favor by promising to be the father they don't have, Granny Wendy (don't ask!) tells Peter: "Only you can save your children. Somehow you must go back. You must make yourself remember." Remember what? She shows him a picture of the wild child that he once was, creature of imagination and freedom, before he became a money-crazed businessman with a cellular phone as his main companion in life.

The movie is a hopelessly confused mess, which I describe in such detail because it seems so accurate a reflection of the current confusion about men and manliness in general, fathers in particular. Fathers need to abandon their adult selves to return to their childlike selves, reclaim their imagination, their wild child within, but they also need to be responsible, fatherly, caretaking. They must be heroic, they must be free spirits, they must play with their children, they must save their children. And so forth. Hard to read its multitude of messages, hard to sort out the add-ons from the core, just as it's hard to make sense of the mixed messages that all men are receiving these days. But one message comes through at all times: the importance of Father. "Only you can save your children," the voice of wisdom has told Peter, and the entire movie is about his becoming worthy to be the father his children need. Alas, if it's only the father who can save his children, as the experts are telling us today, then millions of households are at terrible risk.

At the end, after the lost boys have taught Peter to have an imagination again, after he's learned to fly by thinking his happy thought—"I'm a daddy"—and after he's been able to "touch" his children and thereby free them, it's time to take them back home. But first they have to learn to fly, like him. To do that, he tells them, they too have to think a happy thought. In the Mary Martin movie it's the thought of Christmas that enables them to fly; in the book it's the addition of fairy dust that does the trick; in *Hook* the little girl simply thinks "Mommy," and the little boy "My dad," and off they go!

What a timely, topical transformation Steven Spielberg has wrought. Like Bly, he apparently believes that the lost boys of the world want Dad, when what they really want is Wendy (Mom). Or so I believe. Not because Mom is intrinsically any better suited to parenting than Dad, but because, for a variety of socially and culturally mandated reasons, she's there for her children in a way that Dad isn't.

It used to be that the absence was an emotional one. Mom, after all, was responsible for the "expressive" role in family life, for conveying affection, comfort, nurturance, warmth, for maintaining interpersonal relationships; Dad had the "instrumental" role, concerned with problem solving, discipline, achievement. (As the father in the movie version of *The Great Santini* put it, in a drunken reverie addressed to his wife, "You do my caring for me. Deal?") Both did their jobs, for better or for worse. But now many dads are absent, not only emotionally but physically and financially as well. If Mom has also backed away, out of concern that a failure to do so may compromise her son's masculinity, he may be a very lonely— indeed "lost"—boy.

The crisis only escalates at adolescence.

FOUR

The Adolescent Years: Establishing—and Enforcing—Masculinity

If neither foes nor loving friends can hurt you,
    If all men count with you, but none too much;
If you can fill the unforgiving minute
    With sixty seconds' worth of distance run,
Yours is the Earth and everything that's in it,
    And—which is more—you'll be a Man, my son!

—RUDYARD KIPLING

DEVELOPMENTAL TASKS FOR TEENAGE BOYS—AND THEIR MOTHERS

There is fairly broad consensus in the therapeutic and analytic communities about the major developmental tasks confronting the male adolescent: he is to establish a firm, unambiguous sense of his own sexuality, and he is to prepare for the final separation from his parents, most particularly his mother. The latter task is of course related to the former, for the belief is that a satisfactorily masculine sexual identity can be fully achieved only through that separation. Mother's "task" is, more than ever, to get out of the way; she usually complies, however ambivalently, for adolescence is such a vivid signal of her son's incipient manhood that the taboo against closeness takes on new force.

Thus, as a boy enters adolescence at about age twelve or thirteen and begins going through its physical changes, even a woman who has until then resisted her husband's warnings and ignored the dictates of the culture is likely to pull back from her son, out of a newly aroused concern for his masculinity. Not wanting him to be "soft" or "effeminate," she will now begin to guard against any kind of emotional expressiveness between herself and her son. Moreover, since one of the worst accusations that can be leveled against a mother in our Freudianized age is that she is "seductive," evidence of her son's burgeoning sexuality may cause her to be equally wary of any physical demonstrations of affection, lest she arouse his sexual feelings—or her own (despite the fact that mother-son incest is extremely rare, and never more so than at this age). As a friend of mine put it, describing the uneasiness she began to feel in the presence of her teenage son, "When they put that sweet little boy into my arms fifteen years ago it never occurred to me that one day this big strange man would be walking around my house in his underwear."

The fear of "contaminating" her adolescent son with her own femininity, of compromising (or, alternatively, exciting) his sexuality, can cause a mother to effect a very abrupt withdrawal. Indeed, it is sometimes so abrupt that it is experienced by the boy as abandonment, especially if there is some specific event that alarms the parents and thereby convinces the mother that she has been harming her son by her continuing closeness to him. At this stage of life, any kind of deviation from peer behavior can set the process in motion, whether it's something as significant as an admission of homosexuality or as trivial as a refusal to go away to camp or take part in a class excursion. If a girl doesn't want to go on a class trip, most parents don't make much of it; but if a male child doesn't feel ready to leave home and go off with his peers for a few days or weeks, the parents think they have a big problem on their hands and are almost certain to make matters worse by their panicked reaction.

However they handle the immediate situation, you may be sure that the mother will feel that she is to blame. And once convinced that what she is doing is harming her child, she will no doubt try to stop doing it. Hence her withdrawal from him, which can be very painful.

Not that the boy will express his loss, or even necessarily understand that loss is what he's feeling. This is an absolutely taboo subject among boys; even the most "deviant" knows that he may not engage in a discussion of his feelings about his mother with any of his peers. But it does sometimes get articulated in therapy, if the questions are posed carefully enough.

"Why are you so reluctant to go to camp?" I'll ask. "Dunno." "Do you think you'll get homesick?" "Nah." "Do you think something bad might happen to you there?" "Nope." "Is there anyone whom you can talk to about this problem?" "No." "What about your dad?" "He wouldn't understand." "Your mom?" Long silence. "Why not talk to your mom?" "She never listens to anything I say anymore." "But she said you used to be very close. Why did that change?" "I don't know." The sudden welling up of tears in the eyes of both mother and son lets me know I've hit home. "When did your mom stop listening?" "When my dad said I was getting to be a mama's boy and that I had to go to camp this summer."

The suffering caused by this estrangement is often enormous, for both mother and son, and it occurs, to varying degrees, in almost all families with adolescent boys. For the child it's particularly painful, since adolescence is probably the most emotionally vulnerable of all the stages of life. Flooded with confusion about the changes occurring in his body, uncertain whether he'll ever be worthy to take his place among the men of his society, anxious about whether he'll ever be able to attract a member of the opposite sex, swimming in emotions he thinks he's not supposed to be having, he can only interpret his mother's withdrawal as a lack of love, or disapproval of the sexual feelings he's sure she has guessed at, or even physical revulsion—boys this age are often obsessed with their cracking voices, their bad skin, their body odors. ("Stinko" and the like are common nicknames they give one another.)

And the inner drama is only half of what's going on with him. Having spent the last several years free to alternate between his different selves, reverting to little-boyhood when it suited him to do so within the privacy of his own home and the safe embrace of his mother's arms, then strutting his stuff in the schoolyard, he's now faced with making an irrevocable exit into the public, male world. The Jews mark this time with the bar mitzvah at age thirteen, after which the boy leaves the upstairs gallery of the synagogue, where once he had sat with all the women and children, to join the men downstairs. Other groups in our society do not have formal rituals to signify this stage in a boy's development, but their expectations are equally clear, the pressure they put on the boy equally strong.

Now is the time he must prove he's a man. Everyone is expecting him to, including his formerly indulgent mother. Not only does his mother withdraw from him, she may even defer to him at this stage, which can be just as upsetting. Out of fear of emasculating him—a boy shouldn't take orders from women, after all, especially a boy on the cusp of manhood—she turns him over to his father for discipline: "Your father will deal with you when he gets home" are words more likely to be spoken at this stage than at any earlier time. If there is no father, or the father won't play the expected role, she may either let her son run wild out of a reluctance to exercise authority over him ("It's hard for him to take direction from women," she'll explain with barely concealed pride. "He's too independent") or go in search of some other male who can step in and be the "father figure" she thinks he needs. She may also "dumb out"—asking him for help with mechanical things even if she's perfectly capable of dealing with them, telling his younger brother to go to him for help in dealing with the other kids at school, conveying in a multitude of ways that she believes herself to be weak and incompetent because she's a woman but sees him as big and strong and able because he's a man.

Often the result is an escalation: the more a boy's parents expect of him, and the prouder they are of his accomplishments, the more he may try to prove himself, holding himself to ever higher, more unrealistic standards. Alternatively, if he can't or doesn't want to live up to their expectations, he may attempt to prove his masculinity in destructive ways—sexual promiscuity, drug and alcohol abuse, delinquency, school failure, even violence.

By age fourteen or fifteen a boy doesn't just want to prove he's a man, he wants to show he's Superman. He's strong, he's tough, he's wild, he's reckless. Or if he's not, he may identify very strongly with an athlete or rock star or some other cultural icon who can act out all that stuff for him. Perhaps he'll form his own garage band, a wonderfully efficient way for an adolescent to rebel without doing anything much worse than perpetrating a lot of dreadful noise on his parents and neighbors. Or perhaps he'll work at bodybuilding, drive too fast, do drugs, brag about his sexual exploits (real or imaginary), get into fistfights with other boys—or worse.

Power and status become all-important to him, however power and status are achieved in his particular socioeconomic group. Affluent, well-educated families tend to value scholarship, if only as a ticket to professional success, so for their boys the highest form of achievement is to get accepted at a good college. From grade school on, they will have heard messages about the importance of this goal, and the pressure intensifies dramatically in the early teen years. Families who live in crime-ridden, impoverished areas, with little access to the education and skills they would need for social mobility, are likely to value physical rather than intellectual aggression, and their boys may aspire to glory in the sports arena, the battlefield—or the streets. Boys from blue-collar families are likely to earn their manhood through the physical strength required to run heavy machinery or work on a construction site.

All this is an oversimplification, of course, but the underlying notion—that boys from all ethnic and economic groups are pressured to compete, be aggressive, gain status and power, and do it at the expense of those against whom they are competing—holds true throughout Western (and Westernized) society today. Members of the middle class may feel that they've come a long way because their boys no longer have to flex their muscles to prove they're men, but these kids still have to achieve power and status, and they still have to cut off their feelings in order to do so. If that weren't the case, thousands of affluent young and middle-aged males wouldn't be paying hundreds of dollars apiece for wilderness weekends the whole point of which is to try to reconnect with those feelings.

How well I know this, not just from my practice, but from my personal life as well! Like all parents, I wanted the best for my son, and I thought "the best" for a boy with such potential meant that he should *be* the best.

A Room of His Own

When Michael was thirteen, his father and I decided to fix up the third-floor attic space of our house as an apartment for him. Without asking him whether he would like to move up there, we simply assumed he would be thrilled at our acknowledgment of his new status in life. A space all to himself, where he could have total privacy, where he would be free to do his homework and follow up on his many other interests without interruption from his younger sisters—this was something both his father and I saw as the ultimate luxury we could offer our newly bar mitzvahed young man. How smug I was in my pleasure at being able to give my child what I myself had never had—a room of his own.

We never thought to question what that room might mean to him. We never wondered whether the quiet of that attic space, so removed from the sounds of his parents and siblings down below, so distant from the give-and-take of family life, might have cut him off from us at just that vulnerable moment in the teen years when we should have been with him. And certainly, despite my extolling his new room's advantages as a quiet place where he could spread out and work, we never dreamed it might be interpreted as pressure on him to perform. Still, when I look back, I can see why Michael might have taken it that way; indeed, I can see that, if only unconsciously, we meant it that way. We were immensely proud of Michael for his achievements, and eager to do what we could to facilitate them. Just as we applauded his every award, prize, and honor, so we were now paving the way for further ones.

Michael used his room well. An excellent, responsible student, he spent most of his time there when he was at home, exactly as I had thought he would. If our hope in giving him that room was to remove any obstacles to his stellar performance, we were more than gratified by the results. At school Michael was a winner. At home he was becoming what I thought teenage boys were supposed to be—remote, moody, distant—so I chalked up his attitude to adolescence. Perhaps, I thought at the time, that attitude accounted for his failure to exult over his various successes, his puzzling reluctance to share them with us. Only recently, more than three and a half decades after Michael moved upstairs, during what I now think of as the years of his exile from our family life, did I ask Michael himself. By not telling us about his achievements, he said, he hoped to scale back our expectations, to reduce the pressure he felt we were putting on him. As for the privacy we thought was such a gift, what I see now is that we cut Michael off from his family. Though it was only much later, he says, that he began to have a sense of what he had missed, and he was never aware of feeling lonely up there, the picture I keep seeing in my mind's eye is Michael lying on his bed, eavesdropping enviously on the sounds of his siblings and parents downstairs.

Once again I had bought into the social norms: the boy was to achieve, the girls to relate. Michael, under so much pressure from his parents, not to mention the usual peer pressures, bought into them too. Without parental support it's very difficult not to, as the travails of one our best-loved literary creations make clear.

Rebel with Cause

For a comprehensive look at all that ails a garden-variety male adolescent in crisis, there's still nowhere better to turn than *The Catcher in the Rye,* J. D. Salinger's 1951 book about sixteen-year-old Holden Caulfield. Having been kicked out of four schools and institutionalized in what was probably a mental hospital at the time he tells us his story, Holden could hardly be said to be a typical teenager himself, but he does exemplify, albeit in extreme form, the inner conflicts that torment a typical boy of his age. Sex, moral values, religion, parents, peers, personal identity, the masculine ethos, the future—Holden has questions, doubts, fears, and ambivalencies about all of them.

Pencey Prep, the school from which Holden has most recently been expelled, is an all-male boarding school with conventional male middle-class values. What these values amount to, according to Holden, is drinking, making money, getting girls, and at least pretending to a desperate concern for the fate of the home football team.

Seen through Holden's eyes, the experiences he has during the days immediately before and after his expulsion are testimony to one boy's inability to make the leap from being a child—trusting, loving, emotionally connected—to being the kind of man his culture values, the kind of man Pencey has been molding young boys into since the nineteenth century, as its ads proclaim. Holden, in short, is a dismal failure at conventional masculinity.

Perhaps his most basic problem with manhood is that he has not succeeded in achieving the emotional cutoff that is celebrated in the Kipling poem: "If all men count with you, but none too much . . ." Everybody counts with Holden, and far too much, especially his dead brother, Allie, his younger sister, Phoebe, and his mother.

Girls in general are a major problem for him, for he has remained open to them—to their feelings, their charms, their vulnerabilities—in a way that is unacceptable in mainstream masculine culture. He's just plain smitten with the whole lot of them, and he's always falling in love, he explains, because girls are always doing little things that capture his heart. Far from having learned the requisite macho attitude toward them, which requires at least a surface display of indifference and contempt balanced by a desperado's lust, Holden likes, admires, and respect girls and women—girls his own age, little girls, his mother, other boys' mothers, nuns, and so forth.

Unlike the other boys he knows, who brag of sexual "conquests" (regardless of whether they have made any), Holden has a skittish sort of gallantry toward the opposite sex, which makes him unable to exploit and plunder, or even to pretend that he does. The problem as he sees it is that he never feels sexy with any girl he doesn't really like. Moreover, if he does really like and want a girl, he always takes her seriously when she tells him to stop: "You never know whether they really *want* you to stop, or whether they're just scared as hell . . . Anyway, I keep stopping." For Holden "no" means "no." Hence he's still a virgin—a condition less unusual for a sixteen-year-old boy in 1951, but no more likely to be admitted to then than now.

As for the other attributes of masculinity, there, too, Holden is lacking. Son of a rich corporate lawyer, whose existence is barely alluded to in Holden's account of his life, brother of a successful Hollywood writer with a fancy car in his garage and a gorgeous girl on his arm, student at a tony prep school where everyone is college-bound, Holden is supposed to be headed toward an Ivy League college, and then down one of the usual paths to success available to bright upper-middle-class WASP boys. He's balking, however. He despises all the prep schools he's attended, and doesn't think any more highly of the colleges for which they are training grounds. Nor is he enthusiastic about the life and career possibilities that open up for the typical Ivy Leaguer, which seem to him to amount to little more than making a lot of money and looking important. This is a young man who seems to have no use for owning "the Earth and everything that's in it."

The only future Holden can imagine for himself is as some kind of rescuer of the helpless. Being a lawyer might be okay if it would mean you could save innocent people's lives, he thinks, but since that's not what lawyers do, he'd rather be "a catcher in the rye"—standing at the edge of a cliff, watching over thousands of little kids playing a game in a rye field, and catching anybody who started to go over the edge (a career choice inspired by a misremembering of a Robert Burns poem).

Holden's not conventionally brave—in fact he's pretty much a coward by his own reckoning—though he does have a sort of cockeyed courage that gets him beaten up a couple of times in the course of his narrative. He has no desire to prove himself on the battlefield, and though he's a passionate reader, he has no use for the macho poses of Ernest Hemingway, one of the most popular and highly regarded writers of his time. He's utterly indifferent to sports, as his weary comments on the big annual football game between Pencey and Saxon Hall make clear. Indeed, Holden finds virtually all conventional enactments of masculinity absurd bordering on contemptible, and his descriptions of those who participate in them reveal them in all their hollow ridiculousness. There's the fellow in the dorm who always emerges from his shower wet towel in hand and ready to be snapped at other people's asses; the guy who likes to demonstrate his manliness with his painful, bone-crushing handshakes; and the young man on a date who's putting his companion to sleep by recounting every play from the pro-football game he'd watched that afternoon. Holden has no use for any of the male rituals his contemporaries use to consolidate their shaky identities.

In fact, about the only conventional male adolescent attributes that Holden seems to share with his "better-adjusted" peers are a love of fart jokes, skittishness about homosexuals and homosexuality, and a persistent anxiety about his hormonal makeup.

It's hard to say how Holden came to be so alienated from his culture, or what will happen to him in the future. But I have some hunches. From the many incidental remarks he makes about his mother—her nervousness, her insomnia, her headaches, her inability to enjoy herself, his concern for her, and hers for him—it's clear that he's very emotionally connected to her. Indeed, he's so connected that he can enter imaginatively into her experience, which is saying a great deal for the average self-absorbed adolescent of either gender, but particularly for the male. As he packs his bags to leave Pencey he comes across his brand-new ice skates, and a vivid mental image of his mother going into the store to purchase those skates wrenches his heart, for he knows what high hopes she has for him, what pleasure it would have given her to imagine her schoolboy son wearing them, and how disappointed she'll be to hear he's no longer *in* school.

Holden actually likes his mother. After an encounter with two nuns who win his heart, he tries to imagine his mother and a couple of other women he knows doing what they do, standing outside department stores collecting money for the poor. The other two he can't picture, but his mother, he thinks, has the kind of goodness that makes such a picture plausible. He worries about her—she's nervous, she smokes too much, she doesn't sleep at night; he knows she's still in pain after losing a son to leukemia four or five years before; and he feels bad about the pain his own actions will inevitably cause her.

In short, I believe it is Holden's closeness to his mother that accounts for his distance from and disdain for conventional male attributes. But it need not have made him such a dropout from life, for boys can prove wonderfully resilient about affirming their own identities, even in the face of a hostile environment, if they feel supported by their parents. The problem, then, is not the bond between Holden and his mother but the apparent severing of that bond in the wake of Allie's death.

Like his mother, Holden is still in mourning for his brother. From the fact that he always speaks of his mother as a rather remote, suffering, ghostlike figure, we can infer that he is almost certainly in mourning for her as well. What seems to have happened in the Caulfield family, which is a common occurrence after a death (or divorce), is that the parents withdrew into the private world of their own suffering, leaving their children adrift. Thus, it is probably the loss of their mother that explains the intensity with which Holden and his sister, Phoebe, have turned to each other for affection. In Holden it also resulted in an emotional fragility so extreme that it landed him in a mental hospital. Ultimately, a restoration of their former closeness could help heal him, but this will happen only if Mrs. Caulfield is able to let go of her grief for her dead son and attend more carefully to the living one.

It is surely the universality of Holden's feelings that accounts for the four decades of enduring popularity enjoyed by this book. Boys identify with Holden because he describes and evokes feelings they themselves have had to suppress; girls relate to him because he admits to such feelings, unlike the boys they know. After all, by the time most boys reach Holden's age, the "big boys don't cry" ethos has not only dulled their feelings but for all intents and purposes obliterated the words in which they could be expressed. So if you ask a boy how he felt when he saw his mother weeping as she put him on the bus to camp, it may be that he quite literally doesn't know what you mean, or how to answer. "Feel?" He'll look blankly at you. Feelings have become a foreign language with their own, now alien, vocabulary, in which women are fluent and men are deaf and dumb.

I have observed this reaction for many years in the consulting room, but only recently learned that there is a word for it: "alexithymia." Psychologist Ronald F. Levant defines it as "the inability to identify and describe one's feelings in words," which he describes as the result of men's socialization in denial, their being "trained . . . to be out of touch with their feelings."

Sooner or later, usually by the end of the teen years, this incessant denial will spell the death of feeling.

ADOLESCENCE AS PATHOLOGY

As a family therapist I can tell you that male children in adolescence are assumed to be well functioning when they are athletic, do reasonably well in school, and show signs of leadership qualities and bravado while remaining basically attentive to authority. That they may also be detached, uncommunicative, and emotionally sealed off is seldom perceived as a problem. Indeed, in a variety of ways we demand that cutoff and, as mothers and fathers, do what we can to ensure it. We do this out of love for our sons—we want them to fit in, to be accepted, to succeed, and thus, we think, to be happy. But twenty years of looking at the results in the consulting room have convinced me that the costs are too high.

Ranging from mild depression, irritability, and sullenness to violence and suicide, these costs are seldom recognized for what they are. Indeed, we have an entire mythology of adolescence, a veritable symptomatology of male (and to a lesser extent female) behavior, to account for them, to explain them away. "Typical teenager," we say, in response to a remarkably wide range of antisocial and self-destructive behaviors, some of which might better be acknowledged and dealt with as real problems.

Our current view of adolescence as a form of pathology relies heavily on the work of the earliest theoreticians of this developmental stage, who deemed it a time of *Sturm und Drang*. In 1904, Freud protégé G. Stanley Hall produced a monumental two-volume tome entitled *Adolescence: Its Psychology and Its Relations to Physiology, Anthropology, Sociology, Sex, Crime, Religion and Education*. Its overall thesis was that the development of the individual recapitulates the development of the species, with adolescence corresponding to that transitional period in human evolution when the dictates of instinct were being supplanted by those of civilization. Hall's overwrought account of the "adolescent turmoil" afflicting young people has colored much of the work that has been done since then, from Anna Freud and Erik Erikson to Peter Blos, all of whom see adolescence as inevitably a time of great turbulence. During adolescence, Hall tells us, every step of the path toward adulthood "is strewn with the wreckage of body, mind, and morals."

> There is not only arrest, but perversion, at every stage, and hood-
> lumism, juvenile crime, and secret vice. . . . Sex asserts its mastery
> in field after field, and works its havoc in the form of . . . debauch,
> disease, and enfeebled heredity, cadences the soul to both its nor-
> mal and abnormal rhythms, and sends many thousand youth a
> year to quacks, because neither parents, teachers, preachers, or
> physicians know how to deal with its problems. Thus the founda-
> tions of domestic, social, and religious life are oftenest under-
> mined.

While obviously dated, Hall's theory, and the purple prose in which it was expressed, have left their mark on our collective psyche. "To be normal during the adolescent period is by itself abnormal," was Anna Freud's reworking of Hall's views more than half a century later. Teenage boys, we tell ourselves today, are *supposed* to be moody, withdrawn, mercurial, driven half wild by hormonal urges they may not be able to control; they need to reject their mothers, rebel against their fathers, put childish (and girlish) ways behind them, sow their wild oats, conform to and compete with their peers, excel, achieve, and test their mettle continually.

The Sanctification of the Insatiable Male Sex Drive

> Boys of seventeen aren't thrilled about much besides their muscles
> and their victories against everyone else's brains and bodies.
>
> —Rosellen Brown
> *Before and After*

Because they are male, teenage boys have to be aggressive, and they have to use this aggression to prove themselves, not just intellectually and athletically but sexually as well. So goes the conventional thinking. In this way our mythology of adolescence elaborates yet another of our cultural mythologies, our belief that male sexuality is by nature, and irrevocably, aggressive.

"Boys will be boys," one of the lawyers told the jury by way of a defense in the case of four Glen Ridge, New Jersey, young men accused of sexual assault on a retarded girl. Exactly the same rationale was cited by residents of Lakewood, a Los Angeles suburb where a group of teenage boys calling themselves the Spur Posse scored "points" for each of their acts of sexual intercourse, some of which, according to the girls in question, were achieved by force. "Nothing my boy did was anything that any red-blooded American boy wouldn't do at his age," the father of one eighteen-year-old member of the "posse" was quoted as saying. Glen Ridge and Lakewood have both been described as pleasant, middle-class communities, which presumably do not intend to foster attitudes of violence against women. But these attitudes are in part an inevitable outcome of our culture's inability to distinguish between normal male sexuality and aggression, between potency and brutality. The teenage boy who murdered his girlfriend in Rosellen Brown's haunting novel *Before and After* describes to his parents the provocation that led up to his terrible act:

And then, she's getting all wound up, she even blames me for, like, taking care with her. For using—only a wimp would, you know, think ahead like that, and—I don't know, it was all too—sort of, too controlled for her. You know what I mean? She made it seem like she only respected somebody who would—like, just force her. So I said, "Are you looking for a caveman, you want some guy to yank you around by your hair? You like the idea some hairy ape knocks you up and doesn't even give a damn what he's doing?" And she goes, like, "Yes. Yes, that's what I want, and that's sure not *you*." Which ought to make me proud, I suppose, but, boy, not then. It made me feel like a turd right then.

Jacob's lover and ultimately his victim is a working-class girl with a crude but, alas, highly recognizable vision of the kind of man she wants—a "virile specimen," as one of the Lakewood "scorers" was described by his father. The son of sophisticated, sexually liberated, and enlightened people, Jacob aspires to something beyond "caveman"-style masculinity, knows that using a condom and being considerate of his lover should not be held against him, knows in the thinking part of himself that he's no less of a man for his gentleness, but is nonetheless so much a prisoner of his culture that he feels all the "shame and impatience and dishonor and sexual humiliation" she intended him to feel.

After her repeated assaults on his manhood, while he is still in a state of rage, "ashamed and angry and disgusted and—like, so many different things I couldn't see straight," she strikes out at him with a car jack and he grabs it from her and bludgeons her to death with it. As products of the same culture that shaped Jacob, we readers are sympathetic to him, we know how such an act of violence could have occurred, we feel the pain of his humiliation, we understand that a boy (or man) must not be undermined in this way. Indeed, his father thinks the jury will understand too, that this account will be his salvation in the courtroom: " 'You'll be all right, Jacob . . . If you tell them exactly that—every word of it—you'll be fine.' " He's probably right too, for this is a society in which the "Fuck you" we hear on the streets every day is the perfect expression of the link we implicitly make between sex and aggression. As for "boys will be boys"—that's an acceptance speech, not a statement of fact.

BELIEF IN THE UNKNOWABILITY OF THE MALE

Jacob's parents are, of course, stunned when they first hear the news of what their son has done. But as his mother looks for some way of comprehending it, she comes up against the realization that she doesn't really know her son anymore. And yet they are a close and loving family, as families go. How did it happen that she lost track of him? It happened because in this family, as in most families, there is the expectation that teenage boys will become distant and unknowable. Indeed, we step aside to make sure that they do. Reflecting on the limitations of her knowledge of her own son, Jacob's mother looks back: "Seventeen years of infinite painstaking attention, intimate, consuming, slacking off as it had to around when? Eighth grade or so—a spotty dedication to the details after that. Not wanting to crowd him. Not asking more questions than she had to."

No, we don't ask too many questions, and we don't push for answers to those we do ask. The attention *has* to slack off, we tell ourselves. Thus: "Where have you been until four o'clock in the morning?" we may venture. "Out." "What were you doing?" "Nothing." "Who were you with?" "A bunch of guys." Chances are, that suffices. We're almost glad of this show of independence, pleased that our boys have been accepted by the gang, proud of their prowess, relieved that they no longer seem to need us. The occasional stubborn mother who pushes too hard is likely to be admonished by the father: "Leave the boy alone." What potency in those words: "the boy." With our teenage girls, however, we behave quite differently. My daughters could never have gotten away with that kind of stonewalling; I wouldn't have allowed it. But if Michael had closed the door on me and wanted to be alone, I would never have intruded. I now think that parents in general, and mothers in particular, must not pull back in this way. It's no favor to our sons if we do.

Often, of course, in the teenage years just as in the earlier phases of our sons' lives, we don't recognize that it is we who are doing the withdrawing. There's a reciprocity to this dance of withdrawal that has been going on for so long, and there's our firmly held and culturally mandated belief that it is the inexorable destiny of the adolescent male to move away from his parents. If for some reason he doesn't—if he's not ready yet to make that move, or if he is comfortable and happy enough within his family circle not to see the necessity of making it—we become very alarmed. And then we are likely to force the issue, with results ranging from disappointing to disturbing to disastrous.

The Myth of Male Autonomy

> Most current theories of male development are about a "self," not a "self-in-relation." Yet . . . it becomes clear that men . . . are fashioned by an event that is profoundly different from that fashioning women: the disconnection from the *relationship* with mother, in the name of becoming a man.
>
> —Stephen J. Bergman, M.D., Ph.D.
> "Men's Psychological Development: A Relational Perspective"

Autonomy, separation, differentiation, individuation—these terms are tossed about rather promiscuously (and interchangeably) whenever adolescence is being discussed. If infancy is the time of the "first individuation," when the child begins to be aware of himself—or herself—as a separate being, adolescence is frequently described as the time of the "second individuation." But at this stage, with regard to the individuation experience, the genders are thought to diverge (insofar as any thought at all is given to females).

Erik Erikson, whose eight stages of psychosocial development focus mainly on the male experience but do take note of certain gender differences, tells us that for a boy the adolescent developmental task is the forging of an autonomous self. "Identity versus role confusion" is the issue he must resolve, hence the adolescent "identity crisis." Only after his identity is consolidated, in early adulthood, is he ready for intimacy. Whereas for a girl, according to Erikson, the process is different: intimacy and identity are inextricable, and neither can be fully achieved until marriage and motherhood, when "the peculiarities of the man to be joined and of the children to be brought up" bring her to the full-fledged realization of who she herself is.

While Erikson professes to believe in a sort of different-but-equal view of the sexes, the Bowen "differentiation of self scale," which is a measuring instrument devised by family therapist Murray Bowen to assess psychological maturity, pays no such lip service to the spirit of democracy. Those at the lower end of the scale (who will be mainly women and girls) are emotionally attuned to others—as though being fully "differentiated," hence fully oneself, must necessarily mean shutting out others. Those at the upper end (mainly men and boys) do not live "in a 'feeling' controlled world" but in a world where cognition rules emotion—or, as Kipling put it, where "all men count with you, but none too much" as you are running your "sixty seconds' worth of distance." Female identity, our culture is telling us, is forged by the girl's relating *to* others; male identity is the boy's ability to differentiate himself *from* others, from the "context of a personal or shared relationship with others." And the former is a less fully realized identity than the latter.

Another way of expressing this, in the words of Peter Blos, one of the leading modern theoreticians of adolescence, is that the adolescent girl remains "far more preoccupied with the vicissitudes of object relations than the boy." (Colloquially speaking, "object relations" are our relationships with the important people in our lives.) The boy is not only more oriented in general "toward control of and dominance over the physical world" rather than "object relations," but is quite specifically charged with doing the work of withdrawing from the mother "object": "There is no doubt that he has little, or only conditional, or no use at all for mother and sister, indeed, for the female sex generally." If he remains tied to his mother, Blos seems to be saying, there is something wrong with him and we may fear for his psychological health: "The sidestepping of this phase-specific task invites all kinds and degrees of sexual maldevelopment."

In short, the standard neo-Freudian account of adolescent male identity formation is that the boy, having earlier made the Oedipal bargain of giving up his desire for his mother in exchange for the promise that he will someday be like his father—and thereby gain possession of a "girl," and a lot of other masculine perks, just like the ones "dear old Dad" has—now faces the difficult job of consolidating that identity. But since from birth on most boys spend more time with their mothers than with their fathers and therefore know them better, masculine identity formation must be an indirect process. It will consist less of identifying with and imitating Dad than of disidentifying with and becoming *unlike* Mom (or unlike those qualities of Mom's that are quintessentially "female"). Hence, much of a boy's energy in his adolescent years is spent in denying his mother—both his connection with and his similarity to her. Given the culturally sanctioned view of masculinity, this is what we expect—indeed, demand—of our boys, all in the name of autonomy.

Aside from the fact that such a process leads inevitably to misogyny, there's something wrong with a concept of autonomy that requires one to become unlike, or like, someone else. Surely genuine autonomy can be achieved only by learning to be true to oneself. In our eagerness to foster autonomy in boys, I believe we have lost track of what it really is. To my mind no better definition exists than that proposed by psychotherapist Arno Gruen: "Autonomy entails having a self with access to its own feelings and needs."

I think we are now at a turning point, where we can begin to question not just the usual definition of autonomy but also the social construct that values disconnection and autonomy as prerequisites for success, and success as the chief prerequisite for achieving male identity. We need to challenge the valuation of that identity, to question both the desirability and the inevitability of that "achievement."

Do we really think that there is something inherent in male psychological development that *must* lead to the kind of manhood embodied in the Kipling poem? That the devaluation of the feminine to which boys are exposed from their earliest days will not lead to contempt for women? That the power imbalance between men and women will not impress upon a boy the desirability of identifying with the dominant sex?

How can we fail to understand that if a boy lives in a culture that depicts women and girls as "mired in relationships," as "pawns of the ebb and flow of the emotional process," in contrast to men and boys who soar free of involvements that would interfere with their manifest destiny—then his parents, mother and father alike, will of course choose to set him free? Even, alas, when that "freeing" feels more like abandonment than liberation.

It is our continued insistence on a different developmental path and a different destiny for boys that creates the Kiplingesque male who is still the prevailing cultural ideal. The long-term results, I believe, are lost boys, lonely men, lousy marriages, midlife crises, and worse (see Chapter Six).

The immediate result, for the adolescent, is that he is going to have to say goodbye to his mother. Any lingering closeness between them must be put to an end. If he doesn't do it first, she will almost certainly do it for him. "I know it's important for him to separate from me," she'll say, explaining why she now makes a point of being away from the house when he gets home from school, or why she's sending him to boarding school or camp, or why she wants him to spend more time with his father. If he seems happy the way he is, so much the more reason to effect a change.

As my friend Marsha said about her fourteen-year-old son, Evan: "He's too comfortable here. How will he ever be able to grow up and leave home?" Women who are raising sons on their own are particularly vulnerable to this concern.

When Things Are Going Too Well

After an initial period of intense mourning following the death of Evan's father some years before, Marsha had enjoyed the happiest of relationships with her young son. When he reached adolescence, however, all manner of vague worries about whether he was developing normally began to assail her. Evan had always been a charming, sweet youngster, by nature sunny and agreeable. At fourteen he was a tall, clumsy, affectionate young man who still kissed his mother and even her friends good night, quite unself-consciously. He wasn't moody or reclusive, he had an active social life, he did well in school. All of Marsha's women friends envied her this delightful paragon of a son. But Marsha worried that he wasn't male enough. She wasn't referring to anything physical: his voice had deepened, there was an appropriate fuzz over his upper lip. Nor did he seem backward with girls: he enjoyed their company and even seemed to have had crushes on a couple of them.

But Marsha just couldn't get over her sense that something was wrong. Whenever I spent an evening with her, I noticed that she now stiffened when Evan bent to kiss her good night, and soon I realized I was seeing less and less of him as she began sending him to his uncle's for a bit of male bonding. Given these puzzling signals from his mother, not all of which were conscious on her part, Evan became less happy and more irritable with her, verging on rebellious. Sometimes he would "forget" to call her after school if he was going to be home late. No doubt sensing her discomfort with him, he spent as much time as he could hanging out with his friends or playing assaultively loud music in his room. Once he seemed to be experiencing what Marsha thought of as normal adolescent angst, her worries disappeared. Presumably he was now uncomfortable enough at home that she need not worry about whether he would be satisfactorily launched into the world.

There's nothing dramatic about this story; I tell it only because in its very lack of drama it seems so typical.

When Not Being Able to Cry Means Going on the Attack

On the continuum of problems caused by a mother's pulling back from her adolescent son, Evan and Marsha are at the benign end. The damaged relationship between Ira and Louise, however, seemed potentially much more dangerous.

When Louise called to ask for a consultation about her seventeen-year-old son, Ira, she voiced a long list of concerns, the most urgent of which was that she feared he might become violent with her. After ascertaining that he had never actually followed through on his threats in the past, and that she was not in any immediate danger, I made an appointment to see her and whatever family members were willing and available the next morning.

When the receptionist announced their arrival, I was almost surprised to see that in addition to Louise and her two daughters—young women who had moved out of the family home a year before—Ira, too, was in the waiting room. Many young men his age would have refused to come, out of fear that this acknowledgment of a connection to their family would be construed as dependency. This was a hopeful sign, his rather hulking, menacing presence notwithstanding.

Ira displayed all of the earmarks of the sullen, rebellious adolescent, his long, unkempt hair, torn jeans, and dirty sweatshirt a striking contrast to the appearance of his sisters and his mother, who were neatly and conventionally dressed. As the three women took turns recounting the events that had convinced Louise to seek help, Ira paced anxiously around the room, radiating hostility. It seemed that two days before, after a long period of escalating tension between mother and son, punctuated by numerous rage-filled outbursts on his part, there had been a particularly frightening episode. Louise accused Ira of being unwilling to live up to his commitments (specifically his oft-repeated promise to look for a job), and he became so angry that he stormed out of their apartment and stood on the pavement below, yelling up to his mother that he wanted to kill her. Not knowing what else to do, she had called his sister Karen, who found him still there, ranting and raving, when she came running over from her apartment nearby.

"She's never known how to talk to him," Karen broke in by way of defending Ira's explosive behavior.

"But he must know I love him. I would let myself be skinned

alive if I thought it would help him," Louise declared—an alarming statement insofar as it suggested a profound sense of guilt about the quality of her mothering, which was presumably based on an equally profound disappointment in the way her son was turning out. As indeed proved to be the case when Louise recounted the history of their relationship.

She had raised Ira on her own after her husband walked out on her when the girls were six and four and Ira was a newborn. With no financial support from her husband—indeed, not so much as a post-card to indicate his whereabouts—Louise had been forced to assume full responsibility for her young family. For years they had been a very close family, the children looking to one another for love and companionship while Louise worked long hours to provide for them. Ira had been a rather solitary little boy, closely attached to his sisters, with few friends or interests outside the family circle. The children took such good care of one another that Louise had been a rather laissez-faire mother, comfortable in the knowledge that they were able to function effectively on their own. This was just as well, since she had very little time to give them.

When the girls were in their teens they became involved in school and social activities, leaving Ira somewhat adrift. He then turned more and more to his mother for the emotional connection he was now lacking. By the time he was fifteen she had begun to worry about him—surely it wasn't normal for a boy to spend so much time with his mother—and to put many new pressures on him to perform. "I felt I'd really let him down as a mother. Otherwise he wouldn't have had so much trouble making friends and wouldn't have done so poorly in school. So I decided it was now or never if I was to make a man of him."

By a frantic immersion in what she thought of as good mothering, Louise was determined to undo the past, to make sure her son didn't turn into the same kind of deadbeat his father had been. He should work harder to succeed in school. He should go out for after-school activities. He should meet people. He should get a haircut. She nagged, she bribed, she cajoled, she even called his teachers. A not particularly bright, athletic, or outgoing boy, socially awkward and solitary by nature, Ira wasn't capable of living up to her new expectations. The pressures had intensified still further when both of his sisters moved into their own apartments the preceding year, leaving him without any of the support he'd been accustomed to getting from them when he needed to make Louise back off. At the same time that the pressures were increasing, so was his feeling of pain. He was a young man experiencing too many losses. He'd already lost his father, then his two sisters, and with them much of his sense of competence in the world. To be losing his mother as well was one loss too many.

Not surprisingly, Ira felt crushed by Louise's disapproval. "Do you think you are a disappointment to your mom?" I asked.

"Sure I am," he said. "She tells me every day what a mess I've made of my life."

Faced with Louise's endless complaints and corrections, Ira had responded with confusion and paralysis. This reaction only escalated his mother's efforts to shape him up, until finally Ira dropped out of school and became exactly the loser she had feared he would be. He didn't go to classes, he didn't get a job, he simply vegetated in his room. For her part, Louise withdrew all emotional support. "Ira is very dependent on me. Every day when I leave the house he asks me when I'm coming back, and most of the time I tell him 'late,' because I know it's wrong for him to be spending so much time with his mother."

I felt we needed an intervention that would change the basic notions that had been formed in this family. As long as Louise saw herself as a bad mother, she would continue to work overtime to undo the damage she thought she had caused; and as long as she engaged in her frantic mode of mothering, Ira was going to see himself as a failure. "Louise," I said to her at the end of our first session, "I think it would help if you would stop working so hard at being a good mother."

"You mean at being a *mother*," she was quick to correct me.

"No. You'll always be a mother. I mean a good mother. You're trying too hard to help Ira shape up and be a mensch."

"So what should I do? Leave him alone to rot like his father?"

"Just try to sit back and enjoy him," I insisted. "You've done your job, and now it's up to him."

In the weeks that followed, by sheer force of will Louise kept herself from nagging. At first Ira responded by volunteering to do a few chores around the house—not necessarily what Louise was hoping for, since her vision of what she wanted for her son did not include women's work. Next he found a job, and that pleased her very much. Soon he had made a friend at work, was spending less time with his mother, and had begun to talk about getting his own apartment. At their last session Louise asked ruefully, "Why is it, just as they get to be nice, they leave you?"

Ira and Louise were fortunate they began therapy before he acted out any of his violent impulses. When I first met him he seemed very threatening. He had become so confused by the shift from Louise's easygoing, affectionate style of mothering, and her sudden withdrawal from him, that he was almost crazy with loneliness. In boys, that kind of extreme dependence is mixed with so much shame and discomfort that it often results in eruptions of anger—the only socially sanctioned way of expressing feelings. I see this as the male version of hysteria. Psychiatrist Jean Baker Miller explains its workings: "It is particularly common to find men acting most aggressively when they feel vulnerable, hurt, frightened, and alone." This occurs when "there is no context of assurance that [they] will be respected or well cared for if [they] make a direct, honest expression" of their feelings. A seventeen-year-old young man interviewed on a daytime television talk show about why he abused his girlfriend put it this way: "Some people cry. If you can't cry, you strike out."

As often happens with mothers and teenage sons, the feelings of dependence that Ira expressed to Louise had alarmed and alienated her, rather than eliciting her care. She thought they got in the way of his becoming a man, and saw them as a sign of her own failure as a mother. But the appropriate response to excessive dependence is not withdrawal; that will only escalate the boy's distress. Ira's extreme vulnerability at this point in his life could only be alleviated by "more mother," not less.

Far from being authentically autonomous, boys (and men) are hooked into the demands of the culture, not their own inner reality. The occasional "crazy" kid like Ira, who does express something of his neediness in violation of the cultural norms, is likely to pay a heavy price in parental disapproval. For the boy this can mean great suffering. If not expressed as violence toward others, as Ira was threatening, that kind of pain may be turned against the self.

When It's Not All Right to Love Your Son

There's no violation of the social norms more upsetting to most parents than homosexuality in a boy—and no parental rejection more painful to a boy than the horror so many express upon first hearing such news. When seventeen-year-old Harold and his parents, Anna and Jose, first came to see me, six months had passed since he had tried to kill himself, shortly after revealing his homosexuality to his family. During those six months he and his parents had seen a social worker for counseling. Apparently there had been considerable improvement in Harold's state of mind, but now Mrs. K. was taking a job in another state, and Anna and Jose were worried because he seemed depressed again. Jose made the initial call to me.

When the three of them arrived, Jose informed me that, despite my request to see all of the family, the other two children were not coming. The older son was working, and the daughter was too young to have to listen to "all this." I decided that challenging this Puerto Rican father at so tentative a stage in the therapeutic process would serve only to antagonize the family, so I consented to see the three without further comment.

Anna, a serious-looking woman, sat with her coat on, her hands in her lap, and her eyes cast down. Jose perched on the edge of his chair, feet planted firmly on the floor in a ready-to-start position. Harold was a neatly dressed, delicately built boy with smooth skin and shiny, longish hair. He sat meekly by his mother, with a vacant air, looking at no one, as his father gave a recitation of the events of the last six months, culminating in his pronouncement that the therapy they received "had worked." Harold had returned to school after the brief hospitalization following his suicide attempt, was expecting to graduate with his class despite a number of absences, and had even won a partial scholarship to college.

"So," I asked Harold, "does that mean you are less depressed?" Shaking his head, whispering, Harold answered, "No."

"I'm afraid he's going to do it again," Anna broke in for the first time.

Jose, wearily: "I told you and told you to stop worrying."

"Why do you think Harold was so unhappy?" I asked Jose. "What's your idea about why he would try to kill himself?"

With the air of a man who has had to tell this story too many times, Jose explained: "He has an identity problem. Like, on one occasion he told me that he wanted to be a girl. At that time it was hard for me to accept this, but now I do. He's still my son and I love him, see? Whatever he is, I want him alive. So I have told him I would accept him. Accept the fact that he's that way."

We now explored the question of how they accounted to themselves for Harold's homosexuality. Though both Jose and Anna had gotten the message through the previous therapy that no one is to "blame" for a boy's homosexuality, it was clear from the direction the therapy had taken—the effort to involve Jose more actively in his son's life, to loosen the bond between Anna and Harold—that there had been a contradictory double message: It's no one's fault that Harold is gay, but perhaps he can still be "rescued" if only Jose will step in and Anna will step back. Jose was trying valiantly to hold on to both messages. Jose readily admitted that until the crisis with Harold he had left childrearing pretty much to his wife. As he remarked in a defensive tone, assuming that I would be critical, he had worked two jobs to support his family; but now he felt guilty for not having been there enough for Harold, with the result that Anna had been there "too much," had perhaps had too great an influence on the boy.

"Were you and Harold very close?" I asked Anna.

"Yes, always. Because when he was born he was sick. Since he was a little boy he was always with me. He used to help me a lot around the house and sometimes I think . . ." She trailed off. Clearly, Anna did still see herself as the cause of Harold's homosexuality, whatever the overt message of the earlier therapy had been. While therapy had helped Jose to an acceptance of Harold that went beyond lip service, Anna was less forgiving, of either herself or Harold. Mother and son were still locked in the unhappy, uneasy distance by which Anna was trying desperately to undo her past errors.

The estrangement between Harold and Anna had begun a year ago. "It was when I told my father that I planned to be a nurse, and he said that was a girl's job," Harold recounted. "So I told him I wanted to be a girl. He slapped me. After that she [pointing to his mother] wouldn't talk to me—never again. Just like that."

Although it was certainly important for Harold to gain the support of his father, which had been the goal of the previous therapy, it was clear that the sudden loss of support from his mother, which had been at least tacitly sanctioned, was a devastating blow. Harold was still depressed and possibly not out of danger. He needed Anna back in his life. On this premise I made the following intervention: "Anna, I think part of the problem right now is that you blame yourself so much that you're afraid to love your boy. You're afraid that somehow your love has damaged him, so you don't show him how deeply you care about him, and that seems to hurt him very much."

"He thinks I don't love him?"

"That's what he thinks."

"It's not true."

Harold, breaking in and starting to cry: "You don't show it." This was a revelation to Anna, and food for much thought.

The strategy I adopted in our subsequent sessions was to renew the bond between Harold and his mother on the assumption that Harold had not tried to commit suicide because he was homosexual, or even because his father didn't accept him, but because he felt he had lost the primary relationship in his life. By re-establishing the bond between mother and son, I felt I was improving the chances for both of them to regain their self-esteem. Anna needed to realize that the intimate relationship she had enjoyed with Harold did not have to be viewed in a negative light. Her competence as a mother had contributed to his high achievement in school, his good manners, his devotion to his family (which was readily seen in later sessions when his brother and sister were present). Continued closeness with her son would not damage him but would reinforce in him the sense of empathy and sensitivity and the capacity to nurture that would serve him well in the future. Certainly those qualities would help him in his chosen career.

If I had continued with the direction of the previous therapy, which attempted to shift Harold out of his mother's and into his father's sphere, I would have risked reducing Anna's already radically diminished self-esteem, and this in turn would have been destructive to Harold's. After all, implicit in a mother's sense of herself as a poisonous influence on her son is her profound disappointment in him, her vision of him as damaged goods, which will be very painful to him. Conversely, pride in her accomplishments as a mother—meaning pride in him—will make him feel good about himself.

The relief that all three felt at Anna's return to her mothering role was palpable. Jose, whose hard work and good example to his children were also validated during the course of this therapy, seemed particularly grateful.

Without urging from me, all five members of the family attended several of our following sessions. The last of our sessions together occurred one week before high school graduation day. Harold was graduating with honors and preparing to leave for college. He had a summer job as an orderly on a hospital psychiatric ward. His family was teasing him with "Better be careful or they won't let you out."

Anna joined in the teasing by saying to Harold, "Well, you got something from me anyway. You can go away from home because you know how to do your own laundry. That's more than I can say for your brother." Everyone laughed.

THE DIFFERENT DYNAMICS OF MOTHER WITHDRAWAL

From birth on, as we have seen, a boy's mother is engaged in the process of pulling back from him. Certainly there are bad mothers in this world who withdraw—or who were never there in the first place—for all kinds of less-than-altruistic reasons. They're so caught up in their own problems that they don't have the emotional energy to give to a child; they're too addicted to alcohol or drugs to care for him; they're passing on the legacy of their own abused or emotionally deprived childhoods; they're giving in to a husband or lover's jealousy of the mother-son relationship; they're fearful of men, hence of any manifestation of maleness, which causes them to be rejecting when the boy reaches a certain age; they're using the boy to take out their anger on men; and so forth. There's also withdrawal into the private world of grief after a death or a divorce.

But beyond these reasons are the many and more typical ones that speak of love, not neglect, of a mother's eagerness to prepare her son for what will be demanded of him in life. We have seen the following thus far:

- *Desire to protect the boy from social censure,* by making sure he does not become known as a sissy or a mama's boy because of his bond with or similarity to her. This motive plays a part in most or all of the following.
- *Buying into the notion of difference*—the belief that certain attributes are male, others female, and that a woman could contaminate her son if she were to pass on her own qualities to him.

- *Avoiding the grief of projected loss*—the belief that "a daughter's a daughter the rest of her life, but a son's a son till he gets him a wife." If a woman accepts this, she may remain at a distance out of the desire to protect both her son and herself from the pain of the inevitable break to come.

- *Female lack of self-esteem*—the feeling of being inadequate to the job of raising a male child, of being incapable of modeling any of the qualities he needs to become a man. Another version of this is the self-obliteration of the "sacrificing" mother, who lives through her sons but never allows them to know her as a person.

- *Fear of exercising control over a male child,* out of the belief that for a woman to do so would be inappropriate, and potentially emasculating.

- *Male "ownership" of the boy*—the notion that the boy belongs to his father, and that a son is a woman's gift to her husband (and sometimes to her father as well).

- *Elevation of the boy*—the raising of the boy to a position superior to his mother's, which can result in a very lonely child perched up there on his pedestal.

- *Dread of homosexuality,* since homosexuality is thought by many to result from too close a relationship between mother and son.

- *Belief in the unknowability of the male*—hence a decision to bow out of a son's life, particularly at adolescence.

- *Fear of being a sexually seductive mother*—again, a concern that takes on new urgency at adolescence.

Most if not all of the above intensify the older a boy gets. In their varying ways, and to varying degrees, all seem to me to be forms of abandonment, yet all of them are enacted with the best of intentions, in the service of masculine development.

There is yet another form of abandonment that kicks in with special force at adolescence—the relinquishing of the boy to his peer group. Mothers and fathers alike go along with this, with the fathers having a special stake in it, out of their faith in the potency of male bonding, their trust that the peer group will serve as the launching pad that enables a boy to make his final separation from his family.

BELIEF IN THE SOVEREIGNTY OF THE PEER GROUP

It is an article of faith with most of us that the values maintained by a boy's peer group must be allowed to prevail in his life. For adolescent males it is especially crucial, because the male bonding that occurs at this stage of life can help boys consolidate their ever-tenuous sense of masculine identity. So goes the popular thinking, and many parents are so convinced of the necessity of allowing a boy to find himself through his relations with his peers that they resign from their child's life prematurely. "Everyone's doing it" carries considerable weight coming from the mouth of an adolescent boy, much more than it does from a younger boy, or from a girl at any age.

What Price Acceptance?

When my secretary gave me the message that Marjorie Grant had called to say that she had a dire emergency on her hands, I got back to her immediately. I remembered the Grants—housewife mother, construction-worker father, six-year-old daughter Sally, and eight-year-old son Georgie—from a series of sessions we had had some years before when Sally had been diagnosed by their family pediatrician as psychosomatic. Several months of treatment, during which Marjorie was discouraged from taking on too much responsibility, and husband George was encouraged to take on more, had helped alleviate some of the most severe stresses in their family life, while relieving Sally of all her symptoms. With Sally's return to health, George had declined further therapy for his family.

"Oh, Mrs. Silverstein, I'm so glad you called," Marjorie wailed when she heard my voice on the phone. "We're in real trouble. Georgie has been picked up by the police. He's out on bail now, but he's done a terrible thing." Since she was crying too hard to be coherent, I agreed to see them that very evening. When they came in I saw that Sally had become a lovely, competent fourteen-year-old, and that Georgie, whom I remembered as a bright, active cheerful child, was now a miserable, frightened-looking boy of sixteen, small and slight of build, trying hard to project an air of menace rather than panic.

After the obligatory round of greetings and exclamations at seeing one another again, we sat down and I asked what was going on. The formerly silent George, still playing an active role in his family as he had been urged to do in the therapy eight years earlier, was the first to reply—with a harangue rather than an answer. "I don't know where we've gone wrong. We've given him everything. I work a double shift so my family never has to do without. But maybe he's just no good." Meanwhile, Marjorie had begun to cry, and Georgie never lifted his eyes from the floor.

"Can you tell me what happened?" I asked again.

"I don't know. Ask Georgie." But Georgie only shook his head and continued to look at the floor. Sally started to say something, but I stopped her. Finally George got up and moved menacingly toward his son. "Talk, dammit!" Again Georgie said nothing.

Finally Marjorie began to recount the family history to date. After therapy, she said, things had gone well for a number of years. She and Sally had become close once she ceased to smother her with attention and anxiety; George and Georgie had developed a pleasant relationship once George made an effort to spend more time with his son; and both children had been doing fairly well in school. When Georgie was around eleven, however, he became self-conscious about his small size. She reassured him that that was nothing to worry about—"I told him, look at your father, he's short, and he operates that huge crane; you don't need to be big to be tough." With her support, he was able to tolerate the teasing of his classmates and to feel relatively content with himself, while spending a good deal of time with his mother and sister. Marjorie continued to give him sensible advice whenever he felt uncertain about how to handle his uneasy situation, and he readily confided his fears, which were many and quite legitimate, given the macho ethos of the working-class neighborhood they lived in.

That relatively tolerable state of affairs lasted until what Marjorie described as Georgie's first real crisis, when he had just turned twelve. Three older boys accosted him on his way to school, stole his lunch money, and beat him rather badly. When he came home in tears and tatters, she cleaned him up and put him to bed. George was furious when he heard about it—at Marjorie for "making a sissy out of the boy," at George for being a sissy. He then began giving Georgie boxing lessons and teaching him how to work out with weights, while Marjorie, badly frightened by the beating Georgie had taken, stepped aside almost entirely and encouraged her husband in his determination to take charge. Now she began to make a point of being out of the house when Georgie returned from school, so that he couldn't come complaining to her.

Perhaps emboldened by his new muscles, Georgie began to keep company with a group of boys about whom Marjorie had very mixed feelings. Of course it pleased her to see her son accepted, but it worried her too, for they were boys with a reputation for trouble. She went along with the situation, however, because Georgie was so glad to have found some friends, because Georgie's father approved—indeed, he sometimes gave the boys rides to the local mall—and because she hoped it would make Georgie less vulnerable. "I know that short guys have a harder time proving they're men," she explained, "so I just tried to stay out of his way and not interfere with his life."

At this point in his wife's narrative George grew impatient. "Get to the point."

"Two days ago," Marjorie continued haltingly, "we got a call that Georgie had been arrested together with four other boys. It seems they robbed and beat an old man. We were able to get Georgie out on bail because it was juvenile court."

Unable to control his rage, George got up and began yelling at

Georgie again. "Why? Why? That's what I want to know. Don't we give you everything?" he ranted, pulling handfuls of money from his pocket and hurling them at his son. "You want money? Here's money, you little bastard!"

By now Georgie was weeping silently.

"Stop sniveling. Act like a man."

I decided to intervene. "Wait a minute," I said. "Why shouldn't he cry? He's got a lot to be upset about."

Once father and son were able to calm down a bit, I began to help them talk about what it meant to "act like a man." We spent several sessions talking about that, which involved getting them to expand their definition beyond physical size and strength. Simultaneously, I also encouraged Georgie and his mother to discuss the beating he had received several years before, so that he would be getting feedback from both his parents about their expectations of him. "She was disappointed in me that I didn't fight back," he told me, and this statement enabled her to clarify her reaction.

"Oh, my God, no, I never knew you thought that. I wasn't disappointed, I was scared, I was worried for you, I didn't want you to get beaten up again. That's why I was all in favor of your father teaching you to fight."

Georgie, however, had projected onto his mother his own sense of shame—an emotion that is to varying extents experienced by every boy on every playground. Thus he had interpreted her withdrawal as disappointment and disapproval, and her tolerance of his new friends not as a perhaps necessary evil in their working-class neighborhood, but as a loss of interest in him, an unwillingness to protect him any longer. "I figured she didn't care what I did anymore so long as I didn't go running to her to tell her about it. She just didn't seem to want anything to do with me after I got beat up." Feeling that she considered him a coward, he withdrew in hurt and anger. The inner dialogue went something like: "She doesn't care about me. So I don't care about her." And then it got generalized to the next level as well: "I don't care about *anybody*."

Thus the loss of connection to his mother, and the necessity to deaden the pain of that loss, resulted in Georgie's losing his connection not just to his own feelings but to other people's as well. Moreover, nobody was telling him that fighting was wrong, or sympathizing with him when he got hurt. The implicit message from his mother, and the explicit message from his father, was that he had to fight back. The two of them thereby reinforced the messages he was getting from his peer group, that aggression is a necessary part of masculine life. Hence his ability to participate in a violent act.

"What were you thinking about when you helped rob and beat up the old man?" I asked him.

"I wasn't thinking," he said. "They did it, so I did it too."

For Georgie, as for so many boys and men, the only feeling still available to them, once they have jettisoned all those that are deemed inappropriate, is anger. To quote Jean Baker Miller again: "Fear, horror, sadness, isolation, and especially pain and hurt . . . are turned into aggressive actions" and experienced as anger, because the actual emotions "cannot be known or expressed for what they are."

Therapy helped George and Marjorie to stand by their principles and encourage their son to say no to peer pressure. Once he knew he could opt out of the culture of violence and delinquency that surrounded him and still be accepted by his parents, the temptation to run with the gang faded away. For Marjorie such acceptance came readily, as she had always been unhappy about Georgie's friends. For George, a conventionally masculine man who lived and worked in a macho culture, it was harder, but out of the desperation he felt over what had happened, as well as his genuine love and concern for Georgie, he realized he had no choice but to redefine his expectations of his son.

Peer Pressures Versus Paternal Authority

In their eagerness to see their son accepted by his peers, Marjorie and George had virtually blinded themselves to the reality of what those peers demanded as the price of acceptance. Their eyes opened only when Georgie was arrested.

Some parents see the price quite clearly but believe so strongly in the necessity of a boy's being one of the gang that they allow the price to be paid. In the Barr family, the parents were at odds with each other on this issue: the mother was indulgent of her sixteen-year-old son's use of marijuana—"I don't want him to feel alienated from his friends"—the father was adamantly against it. Both were acting from love, but neither had effectively communicated that love to their child.

Initially the problem was described as a power struggle between father and son, with the mother caught in the middle. "I'm terribly worried about Frank," Sandra told me when she called. "His father found marijuana in his room and is threatening to turn him in to the police unless he swears never again to use it, which Frank is refusing to do. I'm worried about Jack too. He has a heart condition and I've never seen him so upset." Sandra saw their struggle as "arche-typically Oedipal," the son needing to overthrow the father, both of them thus unable to compromise. (She seemed unaware that the classic Oedipal scenario requires the boy to claim his manhood by joining with his father, not defeating him.) Tensions were running so high that it was only when Sandra packed her bags and threatened to walk out on both of them that they agreed to come into therapy.

When the three of them arrived in my office, I saw a handsome, middle-class family. Jack was tall, even-featured, conservatively dressed; Frank was similar in appearance but wearing a bomber jacket, torn jeans, and unlaced sneakers; and Sandra, nearly as tall as both, had on simple but expensive-looking casual clothes. Jack's version of the problem was in some ways similar to Sandra's—a power struggle. "I've lost control in my own family. He"—gesturing toward Frank—"doesn't give a damn about what I say and she"—indicating his wife—"thinks that's just fine. 'It's only grass,' she says, 'and all the kids are doing it.' Well, it's not fine with me!"

For Sandra the important issue was Frank's developing masculine identity, which she saw as threatened by his father's demand for obedience. Like drinking beer or going to a prostitute for one's first sexual experience, doing drugs is in some circles a male rite of passage. Thus Sandra felt that she had to sanction his drug use by way of supporting his masculinity.

"I'm confused," I said to her. "Do you agree with Frank that it's okay to smoke marijuana?"

"No, but . . ."

"Do you think it could be dangerous to him, either legally or physically?"

"I guess so, but . . ."

"Well, is your position clear about this?"

"No, it is not!" Jack broke in to declare, bursting with self-righteousness at what he perceived as my coming over to his side against his wife and son.

No one in this family had discussed the possible consequences of marijuana use. Questions about its safety had gotten lost in what Frank, Jack, and Sandra all believed to be the obligatory power struggle between father and teenage son.

So now I challenged Jack: "Have *you* talked to Frank, or for that matter to Sandra, about what your concerns are?"

At this there was a long, awkward silence, followed by a great deal of hemming and hawing. Finally, clearing his throat and turning toward his son, Jack said, "I never told you this because I never wanted you to know that I did drugs too. But I grew up in the sixties, so . . . I smoked some pot." In a voice that grew steadily fainter Jack went on: "I did other things too, hash and LSD. Everybody was doing it. That's what I told myself—as though everybody doing it made it okay. Eventually I did one bad trip too many, and I stopped. Some of my pals didn't." Flushed and almost shaking, Jack finished his account. "One died, another one has been in and out of mental hospitals for the last twenty years."

Sandra was dumfounded by this information, and by the show of emotion on her husband's face. Even Frank, sullen and withdrawn like so many boys his age, looked impressed. He was moved enough by the depth of his father's concern for him that I felt sure this would be the beginning of the end of their impasse over the issue of drug use. But there were more fundamental issues to be addressed.

We used subsequent sessions to talk about Sandra's and Jack's own family histories—how they helped to explain why Sandra had bought into the idea that real men should be "strong, silent types" like her husband and son, and why Jack had chosen to deal with his son through confrontation and anger, rather than through a discussion of the very real fears he had for him.

Change did not come readily to this family. I had to challenge every gender stereotype they had—which was difficult, since that was the one thing all three of them agreed on. Masculinity, they concurred, was something hard won and easily undermined. Sandra was particularly tied to the notion that women who make demands on their sons, who try to discipline them or get between them and their peers, will impede their progression toward manhood. It was only when I asked her if she was willing to allow her son to put himself in jeopardy to prove that he was a man that her position began to shift.

"What about drinking and driving?" I asked. "What about diving off a fifty-foot cliff? What about playing Russian roulette? How much risk does he need to take to prove his masculinity? How far will you let him go before you decide to speak to him about your concerns?" Sandra had to learn that at sixteen her son still needed some protection against his peer group. He needed to know that his parents worried about him, sometimes with good reason, that his mother was not going to let him risk his safety in the name of his masculinity, and that his father was not setting limits as a way of proving his own masculinity. Recast this way, many of the discipline issues that loom so large in families with teenage boys are much easier to resolve, and peer pressures can be put in perspective. The supposed sovereignty of the peer group must never be allowed to override the judgment of the parents.

AUTONOMY AND SEPARATION, RIGHTLY UNDERSTOOD

As I was thinking through some of the issues addressed in this chapter, I watched my sixteen-month-old granddaughter, Molly, say no for the hundredth time that day. And I remembered another day, many years ago, when my two-year-old son announced to me, "I'm old enough to say no if I want to." "No" is the child's announcement of his separateness from us, and it's a word parents hear often, from the time of their child's earliest efforts at speech.

Thus I have to laugh at all the energy that goes into worrying about whether our children, boys or girls, will be able to "separate" from us. The process of separation starts at birth, and all healthy organisms do it automatically; they don't need our help. Indeed, it would be difficult to stop the process even if that were what we wanted to do. But we don't—children must and will separate from their parents.

Achieving autonomy, however, is a different process, if autonomy is defined as "having a self with access to one's own feelings." There are dozens of opportunities each day for validating a child's sense of himself, and thus allowing him to come into the fullness of his autonomy. When we allow a boy to cry, for example, that's one very basic way of validating him. It seems to me that he's as entitled to his pain at twenty-two as he is at two. But any boy much beyond the early stages of adolescence is going to be looked at suspiciously, perhaps even brought into therapy, if he's caught crying. The justification we use for our attitudes is that we have to save the boy from himself and make sure he doesn't become an outcast. We need not worry: peer pressure will see to it only too well that most boys don't cry, betray undue sensitivity, or in any other way deviate from the straight and narrow course of masculinity. As for the occasional boy who has received enough validation from his parents to be completely himself, even if it does put him at odds with his culture, he's not going to be a misfit. He's going to feel good about who he is, to function very happily in his own skin without any of the expectations about male- and female-appropriate behavior that dominate everybody else.

Ultimately, what is at stake is the freedom to act authentically, on the basis of one's own beliefs. In the Bette Midler movie *For the Boys*, we watch a woman's fatherless son be taken over and all but turned against his mother by her professional partner, who inculcates in him all the traditional masculine values. Because she feels she can't model what a boy needs to learn, she allows this to happen. The climactic scene reunites mother, son, and father figure on a battlefield in Vietnam, where the young man, who is the commander of his platoon, confesses to his mother that he knows the war they're fighting is meaningless. She tells him she can use her connections to get him out, but he says no, he could never do that, because it would break Father Figure's heart. Shortly afterward, he and the rest of his company are blown up. Our boys, driven by the demands of their culture, act from compulsion. Though the consequences are not usually fatal, very often they're deadening.

If a boy's sense of identity is founded on denying his feelings, on being like somebody (e.g., his father or the other boys), or unlike somebody else (e.g., his mother or all other females), then he will never become truly autonomous.

Nonetheless, he will separate from us, as he must. The hope is that he will not, in the process, become cut off—from either himself or us.

FIVE

Leaving Home: The Young Man's Rite of Passage

"Grown-up" . . . should have some meaning for a
boy other than "gone away."

—BARBARA EHRENREICH
The Hearts of Men

The separation for which we begin training our sons at birth begins
to loom large in the high school years. For some it can seem a veritable abyss, threatening to distance them from all love, comfort, se-
curity. Hence the indefinable, unassuageable nostalgia of the
adolescent male. Again, it is J. D. Salinger's *Catcher in the Rye* that
best communicates what for most boys goes unspoken.

At seventeen, Holden Caulfield looks back on childhood visits to
the Museum of Natural History, explaining that what was great
about that museum was that you could always count on everything
in it to stay the same. No matter how many times you went back,

you could always see the same Eskimo catching the same two fish, the same birds flying south on the same migration. What we hear in Holden's evocative description is the longing of a boy on the verge of what seem like overwhelming transitions—the longing to freeze time, to stave off the inevitability of movement, change, and loss. He wants certain unspecified "things," which we can readily guess at, to be preserved, just as surely as the creatures in the museum's glass cases are.

Ultimately, *The Catcher in the Rye* is about loss; indeed, the very last words in the book are about how much he misses everybody. Holden differs from his peers in his ability, and willingness, to express feelings of loss. But from birth on, most boys in Western society are on a trajectory intended to culminate in leavetaking—and loss. This is not the same as the leavetaking girls do. Boys and girls alike are expected to leave the parental home and eventually to make marriages and families of their own, of course. Only boys, however, are expected to make the kind of final break implicit in our belief that "A son's a son till he gets him a wife, a daughter's a daughter the rest of her life." Nowhere is this more true than in the United States and Great Britain, where it has become part of the cultural heritage.

JOURNEY FROM THE MOTHERLAND

As a nation made up largely of immigrants and of citizens whose ancestors were immigrants, the United States has been marked in its very soul by the experiences of those millions who set off from faraway lands to make a new life here. The pattern was for the men, who were usually in their teens or twenties, to come first; once settled, they would send for their wives and children, if any, and sometimes their siblings and parents as well. England's hundreds of years as a colonizer of lands thousands of miles away have had a similarly profound effect on its men, who were (and are) trained in the self-reliance that enabled them to run the British Empire by being sent off to the harsh rigors of boarding school at a tender age. Indeed, since we were once a British colony ourselves, our national character is twice marked by expectations of displacement, exile, and loss.

Whether they left their homelands to escape persecution or to seek their fortunes, whether it was duty, fear, ambition, patriotism, or a sense of high adventure that drove them, the men who had this experience all understood that it was the mark of a man to be able to set forth alone on a great journey, to push on to new frontiers. The cost—the pain of separating from loved ones—was simply the price that had to be paid.

Women, I suspect, paid this price much less stoically. One of my earliest memories, dating from when I was seven, was of being on a boat in Hamburg harbor with my mother, my two brothers, and my sister. As desperate tears streamed down her face, my mother waved goodbye to her parents on shore. My father had preceded us to this country by seven years, and now that he had finally sent for us, she faced the certain knowledge that in joining him she was leaving her parents forever. Overwhelmed by the emotions of the moment, I, too, began to cry, only to be shushed by my mother: "Stop your crying," she said bitterly. "*You* have nothing to cry about. You're not leaving your mother." She never saw her parents again.

Though few people who now live in the United States or Europe will ever have to say such farewells—the farewells even of recent immigrants are in the past, not in the future—the way we raise our sons suggests we are preparing them for precisely that fate. It's not just Robert Bly calling for the "clean break from the mother," or Sam Keen declaring, "To grow from man-child into man . . . he must take leave of WOMAN and wander for a long time in the wild and sweet world of men." No, there is nearly universal consensus that a boy must go out on his own, and that he must do it at the culturally mandated age, which is eighteen. Ready or not, he is to make his exit—to college, to the army, to marriage, to full-time employment. Otherwise, he is not a man.

The belief is so ingrained a part of our culture that we forget how arbitrary it is. In many other countries, including much of Europe, young men may choose to continue living with their parents until they marry, without any diminution of their manhood. Who better to speak to this issue than Italian-born soap star Antonio Sabato, profiled in *People* as *General Hospital*'s "newest throb," who lives with his parents in Los Angeles and claims to enjoy it: "I could be 30, and if I'm not married, I would still live at home," he says, perhaps a tad defiantly, out of recognition of how counter this is to the values of his new home. "It doesn't make you a man to live on your own. That's an American thing." In Spain, many a mother would be insulted if her son moved out before getting married, no matter how long he remains single.

The fact that most eighteen-year-olds in this country are not able to support themselves and will be reliant on parental help for many years to come; that in an era of decreasing wages and rising unemployment, 54 percent of eighteen- to twenty-four-year-olds were living in their parents' home in 1992; that the many college and graduate school students who do live away from home are often the least independent in that they rely the most on financial support from their parents; that more men than women are living with their parents—none of this seems to have made much of a dent in our collective psyche. Reality has not intruded on our expectations. We still expect a leavetaking, even if financial dependence renders it largely symbolic.

Perhaps because it is only symbolic, we seem to entertain ever higher expectations about the psychological component of the separation—hence the readiness to heed the call for the "clean break from the mother." Though their message may seem new, Bly and Keen and other men's movement gurus are simply reflecting the time-honored assumption that emotional ties to Mother—"apron strings," we call them—will get in a boy's way, will prevent him from developing suitably manly qualities of independence and self-reliance. Thus, the grief that mothers (and some fathers) feel over a young man's turning away from them is exceeded only by their concern if he doesn't.

In most families, it's sometime during the high school years that the psychological preparations for the "clean break" begin in earnest (if not always in full consciousness). Both parents and child have to be made ready.

The Self-Fulfilling Prophecy

When Irene and her son, Zeke, came in to see me, having been referred by a school counselor who was concerned about Zeke's rapidly falling grades during the past year, both seemed more upset by the recent deterioration of their formerly close relationship than by the decline in his academic performance. But it was Zeke, an unusually articulate, expressive boy, who redirected our discussion away from school and toward what was really on his mind: "I just kind of think that my Mom and I are having a really hard time recently," he said, as I questioned him about what he thought the problem was. "We used to have a really neat relationship, and that changed this year. Now we're always at odds with each other."

"That's true, but I don't want it to be that way," Irene said plaintively. "Zeke's fifteen now. In three more years he'll be gone, and this is not what I want him to remember. But these days I just seem to get angry and crabby a lot and to take it all out on him. Everything will be fine, and then some little thing will set me off and I'll be really pissy."

Gone, I thought. *He hasn't even begun his sophomore year in high school, but in his mother's eyes he's almost out the door. She's already thinking about how he'll "remember" her, as though memory will be all that's left to them after he "leaves."* Was her anger a way of jumpstarting what she saw as the inevitable process of separation? I asked her to describe to me what she meant when she said "everything will be fine."

"It feels like when I say something, he understands and responds, and when he says something, I understand and respond. There is an even flow of communication."

"And at those times you're feeling comfortable and at ease with each other?" I asked, looking to Zeke for confirmation.

"Yeah."

"So who gets worried first that things are going too well?"—in response to which both of them looked blankly at me. This was a question I knew would take them by surprise. But I wanted to plant the idea that these sudden bad moods of Irene's might be serving a purpose.

"Well, let me rephrase that: Who's usually the one to break the even flow of communication?"

"Me," Irene said, thoughtfully, "but I don't know why."

Changing the subject, I asked about the family history, which was recounted during the course of that session and the next. When Zeke was only two, Irene divorced his father and moved to New York, leaving her ex-husband, Lloyd, and all the rest of her family behind in Oregon. There had been hard times in those early years, even some time spent on welfare while Irene went back to school, but eventually she earned her law degree and now had an excellent if underpaid job as a public defender. Though Lloyd was supposed to provide a modest amount of child support, he paid erratically, if at all. Zeke's contact with his father was limited to two weeks in Oregon every summer. Their relationship had been amicable in years past—in Zeke's words, Lloyd is "really, really nice"—but his last visit to his father, who had remarried a few years earlier, had apparently had some bad aftereffects.

"I think it was a catalyst," Irene told me, choosing her words carefully. "It kind of allowed something to surface that may have had an impact on what's been going on with Zeke's schoolwork this year."

Not long before he made his annual visit, Zeke had learned that Lloyd's always irregular payments had dwindled to nothing. The check he kept saying was in the mail never arrived. Once he got to

Oregon, Zeke looked at his father with new eyes, and didn't much like what he saw. What had previously appeared to be gentleness now looked like passivity, and his easygoing nature like submissiveness, beneath which Zeke thought he could detect a silent but ineffectual anger. "Pretty much anything my stepmother wants, he does," Zeke said with contempt. Indeed, he seemed to Zeke to be at the beck and call of everyone in his environment—his new wife, his stepchildren, the people he worked for, and Zeke himself.

Irene felt Zeke's poor performance in school that year had something to do with his disappointment in his father. "I'm never going to be like him," he had declared shortly after returning home from the visit. "I'm going to make up my own mind about things and nobody is going to tell me what to do."

Zeke's attitude toward Lloyd dovetailed only too neatly with Irene's; both of them now became wary of any signs of resemblance between father and son. For Irene this concern translated into a determination that Zeke become someone completely different from his laid-back father. She began to wonder if she'd made Zeke too dependent on her—as though closeness meant dependence—and to worry incessantly about whether he'd do okay on his own, though he was still more than three years away from college age. Her way of dealing with these anxieties about his capacity for independence was to pressure him about his grades and to insist that he take on more responsibilities around the house. At the same time, her newly volatile temper got in the way of the easy give-and-take that had characterized their relationship until then.

For his part, Zeke began to resent not just his mother's new pushiness, but also her sudden irritability and irrationality, which he of course did not recognize as an unconscious distancing mechanism. Zeke balked, and soon his grades were lower than they had ever been, his contribution to housekeeping duties nil. As he explained to me: "I'll be going along doing real well and then she gets down on me for some little thing and I say to myself, 'What's the use?' So I don't do anything."

It seemed to me that these two had gotten locked into an escalating cycle of response and counterresponse: Zeke doing a passive-aggressive routine on his mother out of his newfound determination not to be "submissive," not to take orders from anyone; Irene growing ever more distressed at his resistance, which she saw as endangering his future. The "be-independent-do-what-I-say injunction" she had given him that fall was backfiring, and the passive aggression with which he countered it seemed to be generalizing to other areas of his life.

In our next session I decided to test my hunch about Zeke's behavior by exploring his attitude about school. "Do you find that you do better in subjects taught by teachers you like?" I asked.

"Mm-hmmm."

"And could you tell me what kind of teacher you don't like?"

"You know," he said, "the ones who try to force things out of a student, as though we're in a prison and they have the key and if we don't do what they say they'll punish us."

"So what's your usual response to that?"

"I get mad."

"And?"

"And—nothing. I don't feel like doing what they say. Maybe I'll do it, but I'll be late, or I won't finish it or something."

"That's just like your dad," Irene said, a flush of anger visible on her face. "Whenever things didn't go his way, he just ceased to function, didn't keep his commitments, walked away from his responsibilities."

"No way! That's not at all what I'm doing," Zeke retorted. "I just don't like to be bossed around."

I interrupted. "It sounds to me as though you're doing a little standstill number. On your teachers at school, and on your mother at home. Is that how you get to feel that you're not being submissive? That you have some control?"

"I guess. . . ."

"Well," I said, knowing my words would upset him, "that's a

very male way of fighting. More like Dad's than Mom's, I would guess, since what you both tell me is that your mom has a bad temper, while your dad avoids conflict. And that's how some men express their anger—indirectly, not directly." Zeke was clearly uncomfortable with this comparison, but he was listening, so I went on. "There are really two ways you can express anger against a teacher who you think is being unreasonable. One is to do what you're doing—to do the opposite of whatever it is she wants you to do. But since you always have to be doing the opposite, that locks you into a certain kind of behavior just as much as if you did what she said; it doesn't give you any real freedom. The other way would be to say, 'You can't make me fail no matter how difficult you're being. You have no control over my performance.' "

During the rest of the session we talked some about Zeke's dreams for his future. Since he was interested in law school as a route to a possible political career, he agreed that it would be in his best interest to improve his grades.

The following session began on a tense note. Mother and son both looked grim. Irene announced, "We're pissed at each other now."

"Who got mad at whom first?" I asked.

Irene and Zeke, simultaneously: "He did." "She did."

His mother had been late again, Zeke explained, and since she'd been late to every session, he finally said something to her about it. But he had only been "a little bit mad," he said, whereas she "went ballistic" the minute he criticized her.

"I guess I did overreact," Irene conceded.

"Does that happen often?"

"Often enough."

"If you blow up at Zeke whenever he expresses any criticism, even a legitimate criticism such as the one he made today, you leave him without any outlet for his own anger, and I think that may contribute to the passive-aggressive number he does."

Looking very unhappy, Irene said quietly, "I know, I know, I'm sure you're right. It's just I get so scared of his anger. So I get angry first and then he gets that hurt puppy-dog look on his face and I worry myself sick over him."

"Why? What are you worried about with him? He seems pretty together to me."

"I worry that he'll be unhappy."

"And? Is that the worst?"

"That's definitely the worst. But the second worst, which isn't far off, is that after he leaves home he'll never want to see me again. It's like I only have three more years to fix things between us and then he'll be gone."

We were back to the idea of Zeke's leaving, which seemed to haunt Irene. "I don't know where you got that notion," I began.

Irene: "That it ends at eighteen?"

"Yes. . . . Do you have the same notion," I asked Zeke, "that at eighteen you're going to disappear out of your mother's life? That you'll be finished with each other?"

"I didn't used to. But I'm starting to feel like maybe that is going to happen. Like maybe she'll treat me—not badly, exactly, but as an outsider."

Irene, puzzled, and trying to make light of it: "Like I'd pretend not to know you if I passed you on the street?"

"No, but like you'd not really do any more parenting."

Every once in a while the unadorned truth gets spoken. An extraordinarily bright, verbal, perceptive boy, Zeke expressed his fear, and helped his mother to express hers, about what both saw as the monster in the box: their impending separation. By bringing the monster into the light, they were able to tame it. Over the course of our next few sessions, both came to see that they need not ever be "finished" with each other. They were free to reject the conventional wisdom that boys cannot have as deep and enduring a connection to their parents as girls do.

It had taken three different but overlapping and synergistic sets of responses to turn an open, bright young boy into a passive-aggressive, refusenik teenager: (1) Irene's anxiety about their separation. The anticipatory distancing she then effected was her way of minimizing the pain of that loss three years hence, and of trying to toughen him up so he could function alone. (2) Zeke's reassessment of his father's behavior, which made him determined not to be similarly "submissive"—a particularly unacceptable quality in males. (3) Irene's fear of Zeke's open expression of any anger, which left him with few alternatives. He could not fight openly with his mother because, as he put it, "she always gets madder than me," and because he was reluctant to hurt her.

Had they not come into therapy, these two were set on a course that would have made all their fears about separation a self-fulfilling prophecy. Irene's angry outbursts, unconsciously motivated and thus puzzling even to her, would have served their dual function—to end their previous closeness so that neither of them would feel the pain of their eventual separation, and to drive Zeke as far away as he could get, both geographically (no doubt to a college or job on the opposite coast) and emotionally.

By expecting our sons to cut off from us, we make sure that they do. And there is surely no more commonplace a form of male cutoff than the passive aggression Zeke used with Irene. Millions of girlfriends, wives, and ex-wives will attest to that.

Stigmatizing the Stay-at-Home

Reinforcing our cultural heritage as a nation of immigrants, and more influential by far than the men's movement gurus, is the mental health establishment. With its notion of appropriate stages through which we all (ideally) pass, it has given new weight to the idea that the young man must put his parents behind him. Erik Erikson believes that's the only way of achieving a satisfactory resolution of the adolescent identity crisis. Similarly, psychiatrist Daniel Levinson sees the necessity of "numerous separations, losses and transformations" during this "early adult transition" on the road to

"Becoming One's Own Man." As Carol Gilligan says, summing up the work of developmental psychologists like these: "Development itself [has] come to be identified with separation."

Conversely, failure to achieve the goal of "greater psychological distance from the family," especially if it results in the boy's failure to leave home, is viewed as a form of pathology. True to the spirit of this Lone Ranger developmental ethos, family therapist Jay Haley published a book that was highly influential in the field. *Leaving Home: The Therapy of Disturbed Young People,* was written for the express purpose of giving fellow therapists practical techniques to help families through the difficult "leaving home transition." Most of the "disturbed young people" in this book were males, and they were so severely disturbed—drug addicts, recovering suicide attempters, schizophrenics—that they had been institutionalized, then released into their parents' care. With all the focus on facilitating a departure, too little consideration is given to the possibility that getting sick, or getting into serious trouble, may be a young man's only means of being able to come home again, and perhaps a sign that he needs to *be* home.

Unfortunately, the mental health field has managed to convince us that there is something wrong with any boy who is not ready to "leave the nest" on schedule. But human development is vastly more complex and variable than that of the birds who inspired this metaphor.

COLLEGE BOUND—OR BUST

Underlying the vague uneasiness we may feel about Bly's "soft men," Keen's "WOMAN"-driven men, and the psychologists' borderline mental cases is our very real fear that the boy who does not leave home at the proper time is going to be a failure in life. That was the not-so-subtle subtext of one of our most popular and endearing coming-of-age films, 1973's *American Graffiti*. Four boys spend a long summer night cruising the streets of a town in Southern California looking for action, sex, love, and the meaning of life. Two of them are about to go off together to a fancy college in the East—the very next day, as it happens; the third is a sweetly humpy hot-rodder who works in an auto repair shop; the fourth is a nerdy loser type who hangs out with the other three.

Curtis, one of the college-bound, is having second thoughts about leaving home. He has a variety of rationales for not leaving, which we hear him trying out on each of the many people who ask him about his plans during the course of that long night: "I'm not sure I'm the competitive type either," he confides to a teacher who has just recounted his own failure to stick it out at an East Coast college. "Why should I leave home to find a home?" is a line he has apparently used a lot, since various characters in the movie quote it to each other. And then there's "I don't know what the big hurry is. Maybe I should stick around here and go to the junior college until I figure out what I want out of life," and so forth. Whether Curtis is frightened of the challenges that he'll have to face in college, sad at the prospect of missing his parents, sorry to leave his hometown, apprehensive about life in the East, or what, we are never told. To plumb a young man's fears would perhaps be too great a violation of all our unspoken taboos. We don't want to know why he's reluctant to leave. In lieu of any specifics, there is a free-floating sense of anxiety about the future. Curtis's parents, also taboo, are never seen, or mentioned, until the end of the film, when we see him saying goodbye to them at the airport, after he has found the courage to make his offscreen decision to go.

At the fadeout of the farewell scene, each young man's yearbook picture appears on screen with a brief summation of his destiny: the hot-rodder and the nerd are both killed within a couple of years, the first by a drunk driver, the second in Vietnam; Steve, who had looked forward confidently to college and tried throughout the film to talk Curtis into joining him there, decides at the last minute to stay home to be with his heartbroken, possessive girlfriend (the ties that bind!), and ends up selling insurance in Modesto, California.

Curtis is a writer living in Canada—a man who has gone far in every way. The moral is clear: Cut those ties and soar.

And so we have generations of men looking and longing for their lost connections, angry, isolated, and sometimes even dangerous. Most don't do anything dramatic, however. They simply become simultaneously needier and more remote on their journeys to success.

Michael on His Own

The summer after our son, Michael, graduated from high school was a hard one. He was eighteen, headed for the college of his choice in the fall, and, after several summers of working at typical teenage jobs (cashier in a burger joint, ice-cream-truck driver, etc.), he finally had a "real job" as an assistant in a research laboratory. We were very proud of him. With his high school diploma, his grown-up job, his admission to a first-rate university, and a girlfriend, he was clearly a finished person. Thus whatever distance had developed between us seemed appropriate.

We had rented a cottage at the beach where the girls and I were to spend two months that summer. Michael and his father, our two workingmen, were to join us for weekends. Fred came out every weekend, Michael hardly ever, and then only with his girlfriend.

I remember thinking there was something wrong with this, thinking that I should be home with Michael, since he would be leaving so soon. But I always put my unease down to my own problem with letting go, and reassured myself that a summer spent alone with his father was the best possible preparation for the new phase of life he was now entering.

Anyway, Michael didn't seem very happy when he was with us, so I didn't push it. He was always withdrawn and quiet, and I interpreted his behavior as impatience with family life, eagerness to be gone. That he might have been lonely, or even angry at my having left him that summer, never occurred to me, certainly not then. I missed him terribly, but I had read my Philip Wylie as well as a great deal of Freud and I was determined not be an intrusive, controlling,

emasculating mother. Thus I never questioned him about his behavior, which I thought was a kind of psychological leavetaking that
would serve him well when it came time to make his actual departure. Why didn't I realize that it was I who had left, taking with me
his two sisters?

At the end of the summer Fred and I drove Michael to Boston to
school. I remember that trip vividly: the men both very quiet, me
chatting nervously away, trying to reassure all of us that this was an
exciting and happy event. By the middle of the trip I had run out of
chatter. Nobody spoke much from then on. When we finally arrived, we said hurried and strained goodbyes. Fred and I drove back
home in sad silence.

Recently, Michael wrote and asked me if I had been aware of how
lonely and unhappy he was in his first few years at college. No, I
wasn't. My fantasy was that he was having a wonderful time, enjoying intellectual and social opportunities his father and I never had.
His grades were excellent, he made new friends whom he brought
home during the holidays, he seemed to me to be having just the
kind of college life I had pictured in my mind's eye. Being so successful, surely he must be happy—so I would have reasoned, had I
ever even thought to wonder. The remoteness, the coolness, and
the long silences that continued to characterize his behavior whenever he was with his family I continued to rationalize as the attitude
appropriate to a newly independent young man with his own, now
separate, life. I wouldn't have dreamed of questioning him about it.

Even if I had had any inkling of his unhappiness, I would probably have been reluctant to try to discuss it with him, again out of the
conviction that "mother hovering" would be harmful. A momen-
tary blip in his developmental progress is how I would have described the problem to myself, something he had to simply hang
tough to get past; surely talking wouldn't be of much use—might
even be counterproductive, by blowing a small thing out of proportion.

Now I would do things very differently. Years of experience in the consulting room have taught me that the closed-off look I see on so many male faces is not boredom or indifference, nor a developmental inevitability, but is often, rather, a way of concealing pain. I think now I could see past the remoteness, past all the external signs of successful adjustment—the good grades, the new friends, the upbeat notes home—and dare to ask my male child about his feelings.

"You look unhappy. Is something wrong?" I might begin. If we didn't have the habit of talking about feelings (as Michael and I certainly did not at that time), he would probably respond by putting me off—either politely ("Everything's fine, Mom") or not ("Mind your own business"). But I would persist, if only in expressing my own feelings: "Seeing you looking this way upsets me, so I need to know what's going on with you. Maybe you don't want to share all the details, but please at least give me a general idea of what's wrong. I think it might help you to talk to me, and I know it would help me." After that, it's up to him. I would want him to feel welcomed into my confidence, not invaded by my insistence on knowing about his life.

Sometimes this sort of approach works, sometimes it doesn't. It almost doesn't matter whether the boy talks. He has the right not to, and the mother has the right to say what she feels. More, I think mothers have an obligation, that it would be the grossest neglect of their children for them to remain silent out of some mistaken notion of appropriate boundaries. All children, male *and* female, need to know that someone is concerned about them, ready to hear them out, sympathetically and nonjudgmentally, on the basic assumption that they are entitled to their feelings, whatever they are. And make no mistake: the message will get through, even if it goes unacknowledged.

There's a poignant little scene in Robb Forman Dew's novel *Fortunate Lives* where a mother tells her Harvard-bound son, who has been growing ever more distant from his family in that last summer at home, that they're going to miss him when he's gone. By this juncture in the narrative we've seen numerous instances of Dinah trying to negotiate a proper balance between intrusiveness and caring, and we know how fearful she is of overstepping the line with David. Since this is a kid who once snapped at her, in response to her question about what he wanted for dinner that night, "I don't know why you need to know *everything* about my life!," she has good reason to be apprehensive. In fact, David is withdrawing from everyone that summer, not just his family but his friends and his girlfriend, Christie, who is the only one who seems to have any insight into the defensive nature of that withdrawal. In a moment of rage she calls him on it: "You're getting ready, aren't you, not to care about anybody? Won't that make your life easy? Won't you be *free?* You can just go away with your great, fucking *brilliance,* and your . . . *superiority.* . . ." To which there is no satisfactory reply from David, because he can't allow himself to understand what's happening to him.

Nor is there much of a response to his mother's impulsive little gesture of affection, which is met first with silence, then by a flip, hurtful remark about empty-nest syndrome. Taken aback by his cruelty to her, Dinah doesn't realize how very much David needed to hear her words. This will become clear only in the final pages. But at that moment he is unable to respond in kind, to tell her that he'll miss her too, for "he was far too endangered to say such a thing. She had no way of knowing that he was full of alarm on his own behalf. He had no practice at leaving behind every familiar thing in his life."

Fearful of rejections and dismissals such as the one David leveled at his mother, most parents opt for silence. Often they justify it with the rationale that they don't wish to be intrusive. But there's a difference between intrusiveness and caring. "Are you doing your homework? Are you sleeping with your girlfriend? Are you eating properly?"—questions like those are intrusive. They're accusations, not questions, statements that say, implicitly, "I'm worried you're not living up to par." They're not appropriate to a college-age son. "Are you unhappy?" however, is both appropriate and to my mind necessary if there are visible signs of trouble, for many a boy that age is indeed feeling "endangered." He should know there is someone he can turn to for help at those times.

Having asked the question, I would be prepared not just for stonewalling—the usual response—but for the possibility, however remote, that I might get a real answer: "Yes, I'm miserable. I'm dying of homesickness. I want to quit school." I hope that I would then have the courage not to panic, but to suggest, "Well, if you're that unhappy, perhaps you should come home for a semester. Let's talk about it." In fact it's unlikely that a boy would take his parents up on such an offer, because the cultural stigma against it is too great. But the knowledge that he could come home should he choose to, that his parents would not think it a disgrace, or a sign of severe mental problems, if he did, would help to get him through a difficult time.

Too often, however, our boys feel there's no way out. Perhaps that's one reason for the high rate of emotional breakdowns and suicides among young men—more than five times the number of suicides in their female counterparts.

Ethan at Home

Sometimes a boy faced with the obligatory leavetaking is as clear as a bell about what he wants, but chances are his parents don't want to hear him. That was the case with Ethan, a seventeen-year-old boy in his last year at a good private school. He had procrastinated all year long about filling out his college applications, unswayed by endless amounts of parental persuasion, bribes, threats, and nagging, until in a fit of desperation his mother had filled them out herself. Now he had only to sign them, and even that he had declined to do. In fact, when she presented them to him for his signature he went to bed, turned his face to the wall, and refused to speak to either of his parents, or to leave his room, from that moment forward. All he would say was he didn't feel well. Hence Edith and Neal's distraught arrival in my office several days later—alone. "I'm afraid he just doesn't want to grow up," Neal said. "He's almost eighteen and still acts like an irresponsible kid." But in fact, until this year, he had done well in school, and except for his present inexplicable behavior, was "a good kid."

After ascertaining that Ethan seemed to be in no immediate danger, for he was eating the meals Edith brought to him on a tray, talking on the phone to friends, and getting a normal amount of sleep, I made the following suggestion: "Tell Ethan that it seems obvious to me that he is not ready to go away to school, but that I don't understand why he has chosen such an odd way to say no to his parents."

"Do you think that's what he's doing?" they asked.

"I don't know. I can only guess, without seeing him. So tell him I would like to help him find a better way of saying no, and that if he wants to he can call me. Give him my number, but don't say any more about it. Just casually leave my card by his bed."

I was counting on what I knew about seventeen- and eighteen-year-old men. There's no permission in our culture for them to postpone the leaving-home rite of passage. To say, "I'm not ready to go" is virtually an impossibility. For a young man who is determined not to leave, the alternatives are covert maneuvers, such as the procrastination Ethan had been successfully deploying for many months, or sickness, the one he was deploying now (or really drastic actions like suicide attempts). "What sickness do you think he might have?" I had asked Edith and Neal, who were torn between their natural desire that their son should be healthy and their reluctance to accept the possibility that his taking to his bed had nothing to do with a physical ailment: "Mono?" one of them ventured, tentatively.

The message I asked Ethan's parents to give him was intended to reassure him that I was not necessarily going to become their ally in trying to pry him loose. Edith was willing to give it a try, but Neal was dubious: "I think it's just another way of indulging him," he said. "Maybe I should tell him to get out and get going. Sometimes you have to throw a kid out."

"Would it be so terrible if he spent a little more time at home?" I asked. "If maybe he worked for a year or two, grew up some?"

A hardworking man who had scrimped and saved to give his son the college education he never had, Neal was fearful that that scenario would be the end of college for Ethan. When we yearn to see our children enjoy our own thwarted dreams, it is a double disappointment when they refuse. He agreed, however, to give Ethan some space in which to make a decision.

A week later they were back in my office in a panic, again without Ethan. "We did what you suggested," Edith recounted. "That is, I did. Neal won't have anything to do with it, or with Ethan for that matter. When I told Ethan what you said about his not being ready to leave home and the rest of it, he said, 'I don't need help to say no. No, no, no, no! I am not going to college!' So what do we do now?"

"What do you want to do?"

"Well, we can't just throw him out, can we? But that's what Neal wants to do," Edith said, appealing to me for support.

"No, of course not," I obliged. "Why would you?"

Neal felt that tossing his son out on his ear was the only way to make a man of him, but I suggested that having reached his own decision about such an important matter, Ethan had already taken a big step toward growing up, which needed to be respected. The only thing remaining to be done was to negotiate an arrangement that would honor everyone's needs—Ethan's need to remain at home for some additional time, and Neal's and Edith's need to see that he didn't lapse into the kind of future Neal foresaw for him: "I know what he plans to do," Neal told me. "Lie around the house all day and have his mother wait on him hand and foot when she gets home from work." I agreed this was not acceptable. Therefore, Ethan was to be told that he must show up in my office, with his parents, at 5:00 P.M. on Friday of the following week, for discussions that would lead to a satisfactory settlement.

He did. He was sullen and sulky, but he was there. Neal was silent and angry. Edith twittered around trying to make everyone comfortable. I began by addressing Ethan: "You surprised your parents by making such a big decision by yourself. That took courage."

Ethan allowed that indeed it did, given how hard it was to say no to his father. That was the beginning of six sessions' worth of discussion, three with all three members of the family, two with Ethan alone, and one with Edith and Neal alone, at the end of which they had devised the following plan: Ethan would finish his senior year of high school as well as he could, trying to make up for his increasingly lax academic performance of the preceding months. He would also take his SATs over, since he had done poorly the first time. All this was with the understanding that he was not planning on going to college but was willing to please his father by keeping his options open. The postgraduation part of the plan, which surprised me very much but seemed acceptable to all three of them, was for Ethan to remain at home and earn his room and board, plus $50 a week in spending money, by doing the household cooking, cleaning, and marketing.

Since Edith was a very nurturing mother who liked to do all those things for her boy, and both parents were protective of what they saw as Ethan's shaky masculinity, I had my doubts about a plan that called for him to take on such a "feminine" role. But Ethan convinced me and his parents alike that these were skills he felt he would need before he could go out on his own. The plan worked very well for six months, with Edith even learning to enjoy the experience of coming home after work to a clean house and a freshly cooked meal.

At the end of six months, however, she called to say she had lost her houseboy. He was now paying room and board and working on a construction site. "Hard work," she reported him as saying, "but it beats housework." We both laughed. Six months later she called with another progress report. Ethan had decided he was interested in engineering and had applied to the local college, which he could attend while continuing to live at home. She was thrilled.

"How about Neal?" I asked.

"He's pleased but he doesn't understand why Ethan doesn't want a college life."

"That was his fantasy," I reassured her. "Ethan obviously has his own."

Throughout the time I had contact with his family I was committed to honoring Ethan's choices, and thus to helping him achieve genuine autonomy, which is the only kind of "manhood," or maturity, that matters. Unlike Ethan, however, few boys get to make a choice. Whether eased out, kicked out, escorted triumphantly to college, or bade a hero's farewell on the way to training camp, they go, often before they're ready, as soon as it becomes economically viable for them to do so.

An Alternative Rite of Passage

College is the preferred middle-class way of separating from home. But if college is not an option, for whatever reason, there are other routes, other ways of establishing manhood. Sometimes, unfortunately, they involve getting into trouble—or "getting a girl in trouble."

From Son to Father

One day I hailed a taxi in front of the Ackerman Institute for Family Therapy. The driver, one of the old-fashioned New York cabbies, immediately launched into conversation.

"You a therapist, lady?"

"Ummm," I replied noncommittally, hoping this was not an invitation to a free therapy session on what I had looked forward to as a quiet ride downtown.

Without missing a beat, however, he went on. "I've got six kids,

God bless 'em. They're pretty good kids too. Three went to Brooklyn College, two got good jobs right out of high school. It's Nickie, my youngest, I'm worried about. Nick is nineteen, almost twenty." He glanced back to see if I was listening. I nodded very slightly. "But I don't understand kids these days." Long pause, during which he waited for some sign from me.

Undeterred by the silence, he went on: "Anyway, the kid wants to get married. It seems his girlfriend is pregnant. His mother is heartbroken. What do you think? You're an expert. Should the kid have to marry the girl because he got her pregnant?"

There I was, trapped. But before I could even say anything he continued. "It's funny, because of all the kids, Nick has always been the toughest. We used to call him Nickie the Bull." He laughed. "You never saw such a tough kid. You know, every day, a bloody nose, a black eye. And every week a new girl. Always screwing around, you know.

"Now he knocks up this chick and all of a sudden he thinks he should do the right thing and marry her. My wife—she's crying all the time. Nickie's her baby. She does everything for him. Everything. Waits on him hand and foot. Always has. So I always say to her, 'Next thing you know you'll be washing his ass' (you should pardon the expression). Anyway, what would you do?"

I mumbled something noncommittal in the back seat, while getting my money out in preparation for a quick getaway.

He continued: "I tell her it's okay. He'll settle down. It'll make a man of him. She babies him too much, you know."

I paid my fare, giving the poor man too big a tip, never saying a word. As I exited he was shaking his head resignedly. "Women . . ."

In a family that grades masculinity by the number of battles a boy fights with his peers and the number of conquests he makes in the bedroom, it's certainly no surprise that he would oblige with the requisite amount of swaggering in adolescence. When it's the youngest boy in the family, the "baby," who may have inadmissible yearnings to maintain his privileged position with his mother, the swaggering may be even more extreme, as a means of assuaging his painful anxiety about whether he's truly manly. Thus he will have a very well developed masculine self on the outside, masking frightening feelings of dependency on the inside. The result: a strong need to prove himself. And what better way of showing he's a man than by getting a girl pregnant, doing the "right thing" by marrying her, and thus negotiating the separation from mother—without ever having to be on his own? He may not get all that he's bargaining for, however (and his wife almost certainly won't).

To a boy in Nickie's situation, marriage probably represents delivery on the Oedipal deal: that if he makes a suitably manly identification, he will someday have a wife (read "mommy") of his very own. To his girlfriend it must seem the chance to get a husband for herself and a father for her unborn child. Instead she's likely to have two babies on her hands. In fact, her husband may be the more demanding of the two, since boys in families that place a high value on masculinity often get shortchanged of the emotional nurturing they need, and thus keep on demanding it forever after. In Nickie's case it might seem as if he had "too much mother," not too little. However, what some would call a close relationship between mother and son, citing Nickie's father's words—"she babies him," "she does everything for him"—sounds more like dependence than intimacy to me. Nonetheless, that kind of caretaking will be what Nickie has learned to recognize as love, and what he will expect from his wife. When the effort to take care of house, husband, and children begins to overwhelm her and she can no longer deliver on that expectation, then their battles will begin.

A HOLE IN THE WORLD

Sometimes "not enough mother" means none at all. A very dear friend and neighbor of mine died young, leaving four children behind—including six-year-old Daniel, who had been the apple of her eye, and three younger ones. Deeply affected by the loss of his mother, Daniel had become a troubled, difficult child by the time his father remarried, and he was never well accepted by his stepmother. I fell out of touch with the family soon after the remarriage, then moved several times, and was thus astonished some years later to answer my doorbell and find Daniel standing outside. At eighteen, he had left home and by some mysterious process found his way directly to me.

Though I doubt Daniel was even aware of his longing for his mother, it was surely his memory of my connection to her that made him seek me out at that terribly vulnerable moment in his life. I was as close as he could come to her. Nothing, however, could redeem his loss. As Richard Rhodes says in his memoir, which begins with the death of his mother when he was thirteen months old: "At the beginning of my life the world acquired a hole. That's what I knew, that there was a hole in the world. For me there still is." And there was surely such a hole for Daniel too.

I often remember Daniel and the sad afternoon we spent together when I think about young men leaving home. Like him, many of those who must go out on their own for the first time at that age will find themselves reliving the early loss of their mother, though they almost certainly won't understand that that is what they are feeling. In most cases, of course, their mothers did not die when they were little, but they did distance themselves in the culturally mandated fashion, and that too is a loss, as we are only beginning to understand. As products of the same culture, the boys would not only have accepted but encouraged this distancing, often without any conscious sense, or memory, of loss. But old griefs have a way of resurfacing when familiar supports disappear, as happens when a child leaves home. Then the illusion of connectedness is gone, and he realizes he's really on his own. The realization can be devastating, especially if the connection was tenuous to begin with. If he is also facing the possibility of new losses, he may find life all but insupportable.

Ashton at the End of the Earth

Ashton was one of the most charming, likable young men I ever met. A sophomore at a prestigious Ivy League university, he had the kind of good looks one rarely sees outside of the movies, a fine and subtle mind, and a thoroughly engaging way about him. He came to see me during his Christmas vacation, at the suggestion of his girlfriend, to whom he had confessed feelings of unreality and sadness.

"I don't understand why I should feel this way," he said by way of introduction. "I've got a great life." And by his account, he did. He went to a great school, was known as a "great guy," had a relationship with a terrific girl, who was his first serious love, and had no monetary worries whatsoever.

"What's wrong with me? I sit in class and it's like I'm not there. I'm just watching someone who looks like me sitting there. And I feel like crying a lot," he added, so softly I could barely hear him.

"And do you?"

"No."

"Why not?" At which he looked at me as though I'd lost my mind. "What do you do to keep from crying?" I persisted.

"I run. Sometimes I run two, three times a day. Sometimes I get up at night and I run."

"And that helps?"

"It helps while I'm running. Sometimes I have this fantasy I'll start running and I'll run and I'll run until I reach the end of the earth and I'll keep on running, right off the edge."

Now I began to be seriously worried about this young man. The incidence of suicide in male students during the college years is very high, particularly in the more competitive schools such as the one he attended, and Ashton struck me as a prime candidate.

Then we talked some more, about his fear of losing his girlfriend, who was supposed to have come home with him for the Christmas holidays but had decided at the last minute to go to her own parents', saying she needed more "space." "So she's in Maine with Mummy and Daddy and Santa Claus," he reported in the flip manner he used to deflect any expression of concern or sympathy. "She's got space and I'm spacing out."

At that point I became even more worried, for I knew that in young men the loss of a first love can reactivate the pain of earlier losses, which is why young men tend to be much more devastated by the pain of first love than women are. As I was about to learn, Ashton's early losses had been very early indeed, and all but total.

"Who else have you told about your feelings?" I asked, hoping that he had some network of support to fall back on if he and his girlfriend broke up.

"You."

"What about your parents?"

"What good would that do? I can hear it now. 'Dad, I think I'm flipping out.' 'Flipping out?' [Imitating his father's deep voice.] 'You know I hate slang. Speak up, boy. You need more money?' "

"Your mother?"

"Ah, yes, my mother. Let me see. 'Mother, I think I'm going crazy.' 'No you're not, darling. You just need to relax. Why don't you fly down and spend a few days at the house in Palm Beach?' "

"That's it?"

"That's it. End of conversation. Back to running."

Ashton was the youngest of four brothers in a socially prominent New England family. As the youngest by some eight years, however, he had been very much on his own, while the other three constituted what he called a "secret society" to which he had no access. Nor did he have much access to his parents, for, as "Mumsie" once explained in an excess of candor, he had been a midlife "surprise," and his father, having barely tolerated his wife's attentions to the first three, ran out of patience with the birth of the fourth. "I just couldn't disappoint him any longer," she told Ashton, so he would understand why she had given in to her husband's demand that she keep him company on his quite extensive business travels, thus essentially abandoning her son. And he did understand: "I'm a very understanding type," he told me in his wry way.

Ashton was left with a nursemaid (later a housekeeper) and a driver, until at the age of fifteen he begged to be sent to boarding school, thinking that there he might find the companionship he lacked at home. His father agreed with alacrity, for the usual reason: he thought it would make a man of the boy. But "it felt like another secret society, and I didn't know the password. I never felt like I belonged there either."

Deeply alarmed by now, I asked Ashton to bring his parents in the next day, which was his last day before returning to school. He only laughed.

"Don't laugh," I said. "This is important. You can tell them anything you want. Tell them simply that you're in trouble."

"I'm in trouble, all right. But it is my trouble and I'll handle it by myself."

I backed off, out of fear that, in a panic, Ashton would indeed run off the edge of the world—commit suicide—and out of a desire to respect the huge investment he had made, indeed had had to make, in notions of individualism and personal responsibility. But I insisted he come see me at 8:00 A.M. the next day, making an elaborate point of the fact that I was squeezing him into a very overcrowded schedule, and telling him how much I hated getting up early. That way I felt confident that the good-guy, responsible persona he had cultivated would see to it that he show up. In the meantime, I made phone calls to colleagues in the town where he went to school, looking for a suitable therapist to pick up where I was leaving off. When he arrived the next day, I gave him the name of the therapist I had found for him and asked his permission to call his parents to tell them about our plan. Perhaps because my sense of urgency was a challenge to his habitual flipness, he agreed, with surprising docility, to both of my suggestions. His parents, when I called, were exactly as he had described them.

A few weeks later I received the customary thanks-for-the-referral letter from his therapist, so I knew he had followed through. Two years later I saw an announcement of his wedding (to the woman he had wanted to marry all along) in *The New York Times*. So all seems to have worked out well.

A hole as big as the one in Ashton's life, however, has a way of never filling up, and of looming even larger in the middle years, the age of the so-called "male menopause." Young men like Ashton, who go out into the world without ever having mastered the losses from their early years, are the ones who have to be watched carefully when they reach midlife, lest they put a bullet to their heads.

REPARATION AND REPARENTING TIME

When a boy leaves home before he is ready, without having gotten what he needed, he may appear to the world to be someone who has grown up, but he is always going to have an inner sense of sadness and deprivation. For most, fortunately, the emptiness will not be as profound as it was for Ashton; his family was extreme in its distancing. For virtually all, however, there is going to be some feeling of loss, which will be different in both kind and degree from what girls feel, because of the different demands we make on boys. Sometimes that loss can be mediated in later life. Therapy is one way of doing it, especially if the man is willing to take the emotional risk of bringing his parents into the process and trying to repair the relationship. Even if they're dead, the very fact of his being willing to take on the task of re-examining his relationship with them can be healing.

Every once in a while, however, a man may get the opportunity to go home and get reparented. The trick is to see that as a blessing, not a curse—a hard thing to do in this culture.

Home Again

When Alison called in a panic, I remembered her and her husband, Barry, as a young couple whom I had last seen about seven years be-

fore, when they were in their early twenties. At that time Barry had
been reluctant to take on the responsibilities of marriage, feeling
that he first needed to prove himself professionally in order to demonstrate to Alison's highly successful father that he was worthy of
her. Since Alison thought he was plenty worthy already and was
eager to get married, the task of therapy had been to get Barry to
see that he was marrying Alison, not her father—a task in which we
all succeeded. Now they were married and the parents of a five-year-
old daughter, Alison explained on the phone, but the troubles on
Wall Street had hit home. Barry, like many another hotshot trader
who had gloried in the bull market of the eighties, had lost his job
a year ago and was now utterly demoralized. Alison feared for their
marriage.

The immediate dilemma that was facing them, Barry explained
when they came in a few days later, was where to live. Their lease
was almost up, which was just as well, since they couldn't afford
their apartment on Alison's salary alone. Barry's widowed mother
had invited them to live with her and offered to take care of daughter Jennifer during the day, while Alison worked and Barry looked
for work. Alison's parents had extended a similar invitation, though
with her father still working and her mother busy on the golf course
and the charity circuit, there would need to be some kind of after-
school arrangements made for Jennifer. Alison longed to return to
the comfort of her parents' big suburban house, while Barry wanted
to go home to his mother, even though she lived in a small two-
bedroom apartment.

Still fighting that old battle with Alison's father—or, more accurately, with himself and with his own father, a manual laborer of very
modest means whom he regarded as a failure—Barry couldn't bear
the shame of accepting "charity" from his well-to-do in-laws. "Alison actually expects me to live under her father's roof. To face him
at the dinner table every night. But I can't do it. I'll live on the
street first. She can take Jennifer and go home."

To Alison it was the same old story. "You see how stubborn he is," she said. "You helped us before. Now help us again so Barry will see that this is just his foolish pride."

Certainly that was part of the story. For Barry as for most men in this culture (if not all), his sense of himself as a man is tied in with his ability to compete, and the geography of his world is bound by the twin poles of failure and success. During the last several decades, when most bright, hardworking, ambitious young men of Barry's color and class could be assured some measure of success, this way of looking at the world was viable. Thus, it's no surprise that many of them have found it excruciating to have to adjust to the economic realities of the nineties.

Compounding the sense of failure Barry had over the loss of his job was the humiliation of accepting help from a man who had once thought him not good enough for his daughter, even though those feelings had long since changed. With all that he was facing, Barry was in no frame of mind to be able to understand that Alison, too, had needs, and that after a very difficult year she was now looking forward to going home and having her parents take care of her for a while.

After helping Alison and Barry to listen to each other, I told them, "You each have feelings that are valid. That's why you're having such a hard time making this decision. Go home and talk about it together. You'll come up with a solution as long as you recognize the validity of both sets of needs, and the possibility that, being different, those needs may bring you into conflict at the moment."

A week later they returned with the following plan: Barry and Jennifer would go to Barry's mother's, for a period not to exceed six months, while Alison went to her parents' for what she referred to as "rest and relaxation." At the end of six months, if Barry still didn't have a job, they would re-evaluate their situation.

When they first proposed this idea, I was concerned, because of what I remembered about the issues that had come up for Barry during the therapy seven years before. Specifically, I was worried that Alison's willingness to leave him and go back to her father's house might make Barry feel threatened, reawakening old feelings of abandonment from the year he turned sixteen. That was the year his father became an invalid after a serious construction-site accident, and his mother had had to all but turn her back on her children in order to care for her dying husband. From then until he and Alison began going together, several years after each had graduated from college, Barry had been, by his own description, a lonely, often driven man, working hard to put himself and his younger sister through undergraduate school, then studying for an MBA at night while holding a full-time job. But the same sad family history that made me apprehensive for Barry also suggested to me that now might be a good chance for him to get some of the reparenting he seemed to need, an opportunity for some reparation time with the mother who had been forced by circumstance to neglect her son.

Two months later Alison called me: Barry had a new job. Her parents, eager to see the young couple back on their feet, had offered to make the down payment on a house that Barry and Alison would carry from then on—an offer that Barry had agreed to accept. They were about to move in, and were very excited about getting back together. Having used their hard times as an unexpected opportunity to get what each of them needed, they—and their marriage—were much the better for it. Now that they had both touched home base, they were more than ready to resume their adult life together.

"ONLY CONNECT!"

It's very rare for a man to get the chance to repair old losses as Barry did. Instead, he must deny the regressive longings that all of us feel, to varying degrees, at occasional junctures of our lives. The leaving-home juncture is obviously a critical one, when children of both sexes are likely to feel such longings, particularly for their mothers, who are generally the source of their first and most intense emotional connection. But eighteen-year-old boys are expected to have outgrown their need for Mother.

If we accept eighteen as the automatic, arbitrary age for separation, we create a lot of frightened kids. If we push them out before they're ready, they may grab at various kinds of pseudo-adulthood—joining the army, making instant marriages, or simply going out, quite miserably, on their own. Alternatively, they may find dramatic ways of returning, like illness, nervous breakdowns, suicide attempts.

The intense form of male bonding that occurs in fraternal organizations is another possible way of overcoming the emptiness and loneliness that young men feel when they leave home. Anthropologist Peggy Reeves Sanday quotes one typical college student's comments to that effect: "When I left home I was both glad and scared to be independent of my parents. . . . Although I was noisily proclaiming and celebrating my new life as a free agent, I needed a family substitute, a tight social situation where I could count on emotional support. The fraternity provided me that support."

Often, alas, the brotherhood of men means hostility to women—hence the subject of Sanday's book, *Fraternity Gang Rape*. Much of the attraction of the brotherhood, which is evident in the elaborate initiation rituals required of each pledge, is the way in which it enables these young, vulnerable, unsure males to be "reborn" into the fraternity of men and thus "cleansed" of any dependence on Mother. Needless to say, such dependence will feel particularly shameful and troubling at this age. Hence the need of the brothers to "use their rituals, other brothers, and women to gain control over infantile desires."

Emotional invincibility is what they are seeking, and "the inner, despised female" is the obstacle to that goal. The phenomenon of gang rape, which a number of researchers now feel is an increasingly common practice in fraternities and other exclusively male enclaves, represents an extreme response to the insecurity—and resulting misogyny—of men's lives. Obviously, it is not standard practice among men, and as such is outside the scope of this book. But I think the psychological needs that fuel it *are* standard.

A more commonplace means of responding to the unassuaged, unacknowledged need for Mother is to replace her, with a new mommy (a wife). When I watch any of the movies or television shows depicting young people in their late teens and their twenties, that's what all the young men seem to be doing—trying desperately, by way of their frantic coupling, decoupling, and recoupling, to find Mother again. Everything about these shows is related to connection, as though nothing else matters—in which case perhaps we should recognize that the way we raise our boys results in feelings of loss that may never be overcome.

Look, for example, at *1996, Melrose Place, Singles, St. Elmo's Fire,* and *Bodies, Rest and Motion*—a representative sampling of the recent "twenty-something" media output. One episode after another of the sitcoms depicts lonely young men yearning for love, trying to fill an emptiness of which they (and the writers who created them) are no doubt unaware. As for the movies—*New York Times* film reviewer Caryn James said about this genre, " 'Mommy!' might be the unspoken rallying cry behind the slew of films about people in their 20s and early 30s." Indeed, the opening pan of *Singles* comes to rest on graffiti proclaiming "Mother Love." Did the filmmakers know what they were doing? Who can say? But whether consciously or unconsciously, they are expressing something powerful about the culture they live in. The final scene depicts the entire city of Seattle as an elaborate communications grid on which people strive ceaselessly to make connections. Between opening and finale, we watch a charming array of anxious, discombobulated young people as they go through their elaborate singles contortions. Ultimately, however, it's always the males who appear needier.

Ultimately, it's always the males who *are* needier. We raise them to be heroes, and the prevailing cultural mythology is that these valiant adventurers succumb to marriage only because of the wiles of the women lucky and skillful enough to capture them. The truth is very different.

SIX

Men in
Relationships

"What's wrong with his heart, exactly?"
"The usual thing, ma'am. It's tired and stiff and
full of crud. It's a typical American heart, for his
age and economic status et cetera."

—JOHN UPDIKE
Rabbit at Rest

Having been raised to be a hero, what does a boy do in his adult
years? In the words of the epigraph to *Rabbit Is Rich,* the third in
John Updike's quartet of novels chronicling the malaise of the Middle American male: "At night he lights up a good cigar . . . and
shoots out home. He mows the lawn, or sneaks in some practice
putting, and then he's ready for dinner." That's true enough of
Updike's protagonist, Harry "Rabbit" Angstrom, high school basketball star turned Magipeel kitchen-gadget demonstrator in *Rabbit, Run,* Linotype operator (thanks to his father) in *Rabbit Redux,*
Toyota salesman (thanks to his father-in-law) in *Rabbit Is Rich,*

and semiretired golf-playing Florida snowbird (thanks to his wife) in *Rabbit at Rest*.

Certainly part of what Updike is telling us is that there is no suitable arena in which a grown-up Rabbit can continue to prove himself a hero. Once off the basketball courts of youth, he's lost, always pining for the place "where they remembered him when," the crowds, the glory, the adulation. Spanning a thirty-year stretch of time in Rabbit's life, the four-book narrative begins with a game (Rabbit at twenty-six inserting himself into a group of high school kids playing basketball around a makeshift hoop in an alley), and it draws to a close with another (Rabbit at fifty-six playing one-on-one with a kid in the black ghetto near his Florida condo, dropping his shots through a netless hoop, playing against a terrible pain in his torso until he falls, unconscious, to the ground).

It's a long time between games, with too little to fill it, since for Rabbit it is an emptiness that cannot be filled by wife or child.

What keeps Rabbit going, propelling himself through that emptiness, is his sense of himself as special. Adored by a mother who saw him as *her* hero, who thought that no woman would ever be good enough for him, who despised her own husband by comparison, then worshiped by cheering, screaming crowds who must have seemed only to be confirming his mother's valuation of him, Rabbit will spend the rest of his life looking to women for more of the same. To his high school girlfriend, who was there to witness his athletic exploits, he was "a winner" and she, of all the women to come, was "the best of them all," because it was with her that he shared his finest, most triumphant hours. To Ruth, the woman he briefly abandons his pregnant wife for, he's someone special, beautiful, who can (and does) make her do anything he wants. To Thelma, the woman he has a ten-year affair with after what was meant to be a one-time-only mate swap on a drunken Caribbean holiday, he is the culmination of many years of dreams, "lovely Harry Angstrom," so wonderful that he need only "shed [his] light" to warrant her love. Women are "checks" to be "cashed," "treasure" to be "bartered," his defense against feeling the poverty of self. Even his daughter-in-law, Pru, will one night become part of his "wealth," shoring up his fading sense of self at terrible cost to her husband, Nelson, Rabbit's own son.

But it is Janice, Rabbit's wife—"poor dumb mutt" Janice, as he always calls her—Janice whom he abuses so terribly over the years, leaving her when she is pregnant with their second child, leaving her again shortly after she gives birth because she will not (being but a few days postpartum, cannot) make love, leaving her yet again at the grave of that child after hurling the most hideous accusations at her, Janice whom he never ceases to undermine and put down, who is in some ways the most enduring of his fans. For her Rabbit is everything. Despite all that he's done and all that he becomes, despite her own slowly growing competence over the years, her knowledge that even as she was first getting to know him he was "drifting downhill," he always somehow remains that beautiful creature, "like a boy made of marble," whom she first saw on a basketball court when he was "a famous senior, tall and blond, and she a lowly ninth-grader, dark and plain." She loves him. Part of her knows that "her flying athlete" has been "grounded," but because of her love, part of her will always see him aloft, golden.

As it turns out, Rabbit needs Janice's love terribly and cannot exist without it. Years before the events of the last book in the quartet, at a moment of crisis in the life of his son, he asked Nelson, who takes after Rabbit far more than either man is willing to admit, "What are you going to do when you run out of women to tell you what to do?" Nelson's answer—"Same thing you'll do. Drop dead"—proves only too prophetic.

But Rabbit cannot admit to his need. He would feel himself unmanned by it. Like many men, he lives by the fiction that he yearns to be free, and the books chronicling his years are filled with words like "trap" and "claustrophobia" and "crowded" and "tied down" to express his sense that Janice has robbed him, that "the entire squeezed and cut-down shape of his life is her fault." When she begins to expand her own life, becoming "annoyingly full of new information, new presumption" (as he thinks of her), he cannot bear it. To a man shaped by the rules of sport, molded by the conventions of capitalism, now fallen from the ranks of heroes, all of life is a matter of who's up, who's down. If Janice is up, then he must be down. Her enhancement is his diminution. Indeed, he articulates this quite explicitly: "Growth is betrayal," he thinks, in his first awareness of the woman Janice is on her way to becoming.

So it happens that as Janice comes into her own, Rabbit experiences it as a taking away from him. She didn't mean for it to, didn't see it that way herself. She gives up the lover who first gave her "not only her body but her voice" in order to return to Harry, though she has first to humble herself by practically begging him to get into bed with her—a price she willingly pays. In the years to come she tries to keep herself attractive to him, is hurt by his repeated infidelities but lives with them, fails to understand that he cannot bear her new proficiency. "Aren't you proud of me?" she asks him once, after she begins taking the real estate courses she needs to get a license. Alas, "He preferred her incompetent." He takes to calling her Wonder Woman but misses his old superiority to her.

Perhaps if Janice had understood that, she would have disguised her powers better, for it's only on behalf of Nelson, their son, that she uses them to defy Rabbit, and then only when absolutely necessary for Nelson's well-being (which Rabbit never fails to construe as his own potential downfall. To Rabbit his children and grandchildren are not, as for many, his immortality, but the reverse—"nails in his coffin"). Janice didn't develop those new strengths to use them at her husband's expense and is cheerily convinced, right up to the terrible end, that he had been "beginning to respect her" for them.

At moments when she has some glimmerings of how he feels, she tries to give him back what he had. Far from enjoying his weakness, she is uncomfortable with it: "It feels wrong," and what feels right is "his sense of being generally cherished, his casual ability to hurt her, his unspoken threat to leave her at any moment." Their marriage depends so much on that imbalance that she even takes steps to restore it, to help them both maintain the fiction that it is she who has been the needier of the two. Thus she says to him, at a moment when she knows he's feeling threatened, knows he fears she may once again have slept with her old lover, Charlie, "You know I've always loved you, or wanted to, if you'd let me. Ever since high school. . . . That's one of the things Charlie was telling me last night, how crazy about you I've always been."

The unspoken secret at the core of their marriage, the one that glues them together perhaps even more securely than their shared guilt over the havoc they wrought in their early married life, is the knowledge they both have of Harry's need for her. Harry's mother and sister think Janice trapped Harry into marriage by getting pregnant. Harry likes to think that himself. And so, for the most part, does Janice. That's not quite the way it was, however. One night, with the crazed lucidity of the utterly miserable, Janice remembers how it really was, how in fact, far from having meant to trap him into wedlock, "she felt awful about being pregnant before but Harry had been talking about marriage for a year and anyway laughed when she told him and said Great she was terribly frightened and he said Great and lifted her put his arms around her bottom and lifted her like you would a child."

Being able to come to Janice's rescue must have been Harry's salvation, lost as he was in that early post–high school period of feeling forgotten, snubbed by the very community that had worshiped him so short a time before, foresaken by his first girlfriend, who upped and married someone else while he did his two years of military service. But they never discuss this, and except for Janice's one night of remembering, and a day some two decades later when Harry's sister is repeating the standard Angstrom accusation against Janice, and he corrects her, saying, "Maybe I trapped myself," neither ever seems willing to acknowledge it. Not to themselves and not to each other.

Maintaining the fiction ultimately proves impossible. And this will be Harry's undoing. We sense this at the beginning of the last book. When Janice starts talking about getting a job, Harry is threatened. "Wouldn't you like me better," she asks him, "if I was a working girl?" He doesn't like the idea at all but can't say so. "After all these years of his grudgingly sticking with her, he can't imagine him begging her to stick with him, though this is his impulse." More and more he will have to face up to his need of her, which goes far beyond the financial dependence he's willing to admit to. "Much as Janice irritates him when she's with him, when she isn't . . . he grows uneasy." When once again he runs out on her, he learns that "there is a whole host of goblins, it turns out, that Janice's warm little tightly knit body . . . protected him from."

To the very end of his life Harry remains trapped, not by Janice, nor by the love of any of the other women who have given themselves to him, sometimes with astonishing generosity, but within the terrible egoism of his "own pretty skin" (as Ruth puts it), where always what matters is that he be the "master," he be the one "on top." To his great loss, he will remain perpetually puzzled by "that strange way women have, of really caring about somebody beyond themselves."

Ruth, his old lover whom he deserted when she was pregnant, who seems in some way to continue to love him always, for all that she is bitter over what he did to her, is the one who understands it all best. As she explains to her daughter, Annabelle, who may or may not be Rabbit's daughter too: "Women get more out of life. With men, it's if you don't win every time, you're nothing." Her knowing this must be what makes it possible for her to have "mercy" on him in their last meeting, to let him off easy—declining his extremely belated offer of money, withdrawing even her minor jab at his appearance—despite her completely clear-sighted vision of his failings.

In a novel where the protagonist measures who's up, who's down, by body weight, who consoles himself at each new demonstration of his wife's growing competence by imagining that her girth is expanding as well, it's oddly fitting that the woman who paid so dearly for her wisdom should come to a remarkably good (and comely) end. Having been described on that earlier occasion, when Rabbit went out to visit her for what would prove to be the last time, as "fat and gray," "a shaggy monster, lonely," Ruth transforms herself, re-creates her life. "She's lost a lot of weight and dresses real snappy. I kid her, she has more boyfriends than I do," her daughter tells Rabbit as he lies in his hospital bed. Thus, when Annabelle later offers to bring Ruth to him, he must decline, on just those grounds: "You say she's lost weight and looks snappy. I'm fat and a medical mess."

For Rabbit, the experience of love can never take him beyond what he recalls so happily of his affair with Ruth—"that cloudy inflation of self which makes us infants again." Indeed, he seems to be returning to that infant ego state as he meets his end, for in his dying moments he is oblivious, once more and as ever, to the great gift his wife is offering him. This, finally, is Rabbit's trap, Rabbit's tragedy. And it is the same trap in which many of our manly heroes are caught. Because of the way they are raised, and the emotional shutdown that is required of them, it becomes all but impossible for them to reach out or be reached. Their distance puts them beyond the giving and receiving of many kinds of gifts.

MEN IN LOVE

Even as I remained puzzled by the amicable but pronounced distance that continued for many years to characterize relations between myself and my own son, I slowly began to understand more about the distance I observed between other mothers and their sons—and between husbands and wives. This new understanding came about as the consequence of professional training and experience.

After Michael went off to college I went back to school and eventually earned a graduate degree in social work. Over the years my clinical work at the Ackerman Institute of Family Therapy, along with my growing individual practice, resulted in my seeing more and more men, either alone or as parts of families. Many were of a type very familiar to me—intelligent, successful, verbally adept, but emotionally mute and tense. The more people I saw in treatment, the more surely the consistency of certain patterns emerged, and the more clearly I understood why. (Admittedly, this was not a scientific study, but since I have by now seen more than two thousand men in therapy, and many more women, some impressionistic conclusions about the factors that shape those patterns seem forgivable.)

As every therapist will agree, the loneliness of women in marriage is epidemic. Couples therapy is almost always initiated by women. The emotional inaccessibility of men is the primary complaint, accompanied, paradoxically (or so it seems), by resentment of their emotional dependency, which is generally covert. Conversely, men complain of feeling pressured, nagged, invaded, pursued. Hence the classic "pursuer/distancer" dilemma, so familiar in the consulting room, so identical to the fiction that Janice and Harry Angstrom maintained about their marriage.

A great many of the men I saw were angry at their mothers, and had frequently generalized this anger to women as a class and to their wives in particular. The odd thing was that there was no pattern to this anger, other than the fact of it. If a man had an authoritarian or even abusive father, he was angry that his mother had not protected him. If she had protected him, he was angry that she had been overprotective, smothering. She was almost never there or she was always and overwhelmingly there, she was cold and distant or she was smothering and overclose—and so forth. What was really bothering these men, I wondered?

As a family therapist, I often asked to see the families of both husband and wife. The women almost universally agreed, generally with enthusiasm. The men agreed reluctantly, if at all. When either the father or both parents were alive, however, it was sometimes possible to persuade the man on the grounds that he needed to get closer to his father. I believed that myself. If there was only a wid-owed mother, then sometimes a man could be coaxed if I could make the case that the therapy process might help his mother be-come more "independent"—which often turned out to mean less of a psychological burden on him, less guilt-inducing, for many of these so-called dependent women enjoyed full, rich, active lives, even while continuing to long for more of a connection with their sons.

Predictably, the mothers complained that their sons didn't write, didn't call, gave only the most perfunctory signs of caring about them. Though that seemed true enough, generally these complaints were silenced by their husbands or their sons or, to my shame (in retrospect), by me.

At a certain point, however, perhaps about ten years into my prac-tice, I began to be aware of the very real pain these women were ex-pressing. Once I refused to buy into the standard notion that their complaints meant they wanted to take over their sons' lives, I was able to explore and eventually to validate their sense of loss and grief. I then began to question the cutoff from the sons' point of view, and was astonished by the response: I had tapped into a deep, secret well of pain. That was what lay beneath the anger. There were tears from men whose wives had never seen them cry, accusations of abandonment, a sense of loss at least as profound as what their mothers were expressing.

Eli, for example, a sophisticated, urbane thirty-eight-year-old man, twice divorced, came to see me because he was still mourning the end of his last marriage and trying to understand his inability to sustain a relationship. He wasn't too thrilled when I asked him to bring his mother with him to our next session. "My mother's not the problem," he told me. "She's not a central part of my life. I haven't even bothered to stay in close touch with her. Why should I? I'm almost forty, for heaven's sake!" Nonetheless, still protesting, he brought her. At first both were quiet. Then Eli's mother, a woman in her early sixties, described the pain she felt over her son's distance from her, becoming tearful as she talked.

Eli was unresponsive until I asked a simple question: "What's your earliest memory of a distance coming between you two?"

"I was six when she told me I was too old to sit in her lap." With that he started to cry.

The sadness of both mothers and sons—old mothers, grown-up, successful sons—seemed universal. Story after story unfolded with the same theme. Son: Where were you when I needed you? Mother: Trying to help you become a man. In the process, men had lost touch not just with their mothers, but with parts of themselves as well.

A Systems Approach to the Dynamics of Family Life

Though family therapy has been slow to come to grips with the changing realities of contemporary family life, its "systems thinking" analytic approach is in fact uniquely well equipped to do so, if we interpret "the system" to mean not just the enclosed world of the family itself, but also the society of which that family is a part. The rules and regulations of this larger system tell us what life is supposed to be: what a man is, what a woman is; what a man's role is, what a woman's role is; what constitutes a marriage; what intimacy means. Each of us is enmeshed in this system, our behavior subject to the socialization processes that structure relations between the sexes, our thinking about marriage, childrearing, and family colored by its basic assumptions. We may conform, we may rebel, but we can never escape the social system and its rules.

Within the larger system is the family system, in which all the general cultural rules and regulations are acted out idiosyncratically, family by family, depending on the interpersonal dynamics of the people involved. Within the family system are the individuals, each of whom has enacted, intrapsychically, his or her own unique integration of the other two systems. In short, contrary to Tolstoy's magisterial dictum, each family (as well as each individual within each family) is happy *or* unhappy in its own way.

The "Different Dynamics of Mother Withdrawal" listing in Chapter Four is a multipart description of the diverse ways in which women have responded to one of our culture's most powerful social injunctions: Turn the boy into a man. How that is achieved has been the subject of the first five chapters. The cost of that achievement is the subject of this one, which can best be demonstrated by looking at the lives of a few of the men whose mothers obeyed the injunction to pull back. Each woman did so for reasons general to the culture and particular to her own circumstances—as per the various headings under the "Mother Withdrawal" listing, a number of which are illustrated below.

Because the focus here is on the problems—what they look like, how they developed—I have not elaborated on the therapeutic journey toward resolution. Nor have I gone into much detail in these multigeneration stories about which family member came in first, with what initial presenting problem. The sheer recognizability of the men whose stories are told is all the message I want to convey. They are men whose personalities are familiar to all of us, for the culture that shaped them is the culture we live in. Perhaps an understanding of some of the factors that helped them become who they are, and a glimpse into what they have lost along the way, will help us to change some of our ideas about what manhood should be.

AVOIDING THE GRIEF OF PROJECTED LOSS

Angie and Her Sons, Noah and Ivan

NOAH: Older son Noah and his wife, Debra, the parents of daughters ages four and seven, met and married when they were both just out of their teens and have been together for about ten years. Though Noah never feels that he gets as much as he wants of the warmth and caring that attracted him to Debra in the first place, he gets enough to keep him semisatisfied, and in their initial therapy sessions he offers relatively few complaints about the marriage. Debra, however, does complain, for she experiences Noah's constant demands on her attention as childish, and she resents them for being disruptive of her relationships with her mother, her daughters, and her women friends.

Almost all of their important fights are about their respective mothers. Noah thinks that Debra spends far too much time with her own mother, far too little with Angie, his mother, whose frequent attempts at intimacy she constantly rebuffs. Though he himself is not close to Angie, he wishes that Debra would be a sort of bridge between them, never imagining that he and his mother could establish this connection themselves.

What Noah feels when he finds Debra in the middle of one of her hour-long daily phone calls with her mother is abandonment, loneliness, and jealousy, reminiscent of feelings from childhood that he only dimly recalls. What he expresses, and what he himself is aware of experiencing, is anger. Their phone bills are obscene, he tells me; why isn't dinner on the table and why didn't he have any clean shirts that morning, he complains to her. He speaks to her of his "rights" as husband and wage earner, not his needs.

He makes similarly tangential objections to the time she spends in other close relationships, especially with their children. Debra often complies with his demands as stated: dinners get made, shirts cleaned and ironed. But the subtext, the longing for connection, remains underground and unassuaged. Indeed, his ceaseless demands on her annoy her to the point that she offers him even less of what he wants, while giving him more of what he asks for. Her refusal to befriend Angie is her biggest weapon against him.

Before therapy, Noah could never admit to feelings of neediness. Only multiple sessions brought him to the point of remembering that seeing Debra on the phone with her mother conjures up feelings similar to those he had as a boy when he eavesdropped on his mother's endless phone calls with *her* mother—feelings he didn't know he had then and is only beginning to recognize now. It will take Noah a long time to be able to admit to what he wants from Debra, and from Angie too.

IVAN: Noah's younger brother, Ivan, also married young, and also married a woman who is very attached to her family of origin. Unlike Noah, however, he has enthusiastically joined his wife's family, so much so that his wife, Bea, is sometimes jealous. After all, he can spend hours talking to her mother, she complains, while his idea of intimacy with *her* is sex, with very little talk before, during, or after.

They have one son, Donald, who is six years old. Though Ivan is pleased to have a son and tries to relate to him, he finds it hard. In fact, most of Ivan and Bea's fights are about the boy. Ivan wants Bea to help facilitate his relationship with Donald by arranging events they could enjoy together, and by being their interpreter and intermediary, as in: "Your father loves you very much, but he works very hard and is tired when he comes home from the office, so you can't expect him to spend much time with you during the week."

Like Noah, Ivan wishes that his wife would also play facilitator with his mother. Given the warmth and welcome he has extended to hers, he can't understand why Bea won't accept Angie as an even exchange. Bea thinks Angie is "cold," however, and since she blames Angie for what she sees as Ivan's emotional deficiencies, she, like Debra, is rejecting of her mother-in-law. Though it hurts and offends Ivan when Bea tells him what a lousy mother Angie must have been for him to have turned out such a cold fish, he lets it pass because he'd rather she blamed his mother than him. Meanwhile, Bea secretly hopes to establish the kind of closeness with her son that she can't get from her husband. Also, there's a bit of one-upmanship with her mother-in-law in this endeavor: *See?* she wants to tell Angie. *This is what a mother-son relationship* should *be.*

Having found a surrogate mother in his mother-in-law, Ivan gets some of his emotional yearnings met through her and therefore is less needy in his marriage than his brother is. In general he has a greater sense of well-being, but he is disturbed by the sudden and inexplicable surges of anger he sometimes feels in his mother's presence, and uncertain about what it is his wife seems to keep wanting from him and not getting.

The underlying message Ivan and Noah both gleaned from their childhood was: only women know about relationships, and only women are supposed to need them. A real man is his *own* man. Of course the two brothers would never talk about any of this with each other. When together, they spend their time vying for position, making macho boasts about their work, their incomes, their cars, their houses, and so forth.

THE STORY: When Angie was twelve and her two brothers were ten and eight, their father died, though she doesn't remember grieving much because she had never been particularly close to him. Her already close relationship with her mother was further deepened after the death, however. "She depended on me a lot emotionally," Angie explains, "because as she always told me, 'The boys will go their own way but a daughter is for life.' " The two boys did as their mother hoped and expected: each grew up and became very successful in business, and both ended up living far from home, one of them halfway around the globe. "We're very proud of them," Angie says. But she and her mother rarely hear from them, except for greeting cards on birthdays and holidays, with short notes that seem usually to have been penned by their wives.

Angie married a rather remote but kindly older man when she was twenty, and had two sons. Though she regretted not having a daughter, Mitch was against having another child, as he was by then in his mid-forties and felt he was getting too old. When she first came to see me, at a time in her life when she felt torn between the demands of her mother and her husband, both of them ailing at the time, I asked her how her teenage sons were holding up under the trying circumstances at home. "Well," she said, "the boys have to take care of themselves, don't they? They have their own lives."

Angie is a very lonely woman now. Her mother is in failing health, and her marriage to Mitch has always been more cordial than intimate. She never felt close to her sons, having gotten the message early in life that you shouldn't try for that kind of relationship with boys because they will leave you before you know it. Moreover, it's not good for them to have too many feelings about their mother, because then they'll find it too hard to go when they have to. Though she doesn't expect much from them, she *is* very hurt by the response of their wives, who seem to want nothing to do with her, and have made little effort to include her in the lives of her grandchildren. As for her brothers, "They're gone," as she puts it. "Gone?" "Gone."

Two things Angie learned early: (1) loss is tolerable if you're not too attached; (2) women need to depend on one another for emotional sustenance. Never having made any demands on her sons, whom she loved and took good care of by her lights, she is deeply puzzled by their present attitude toward her. But they can explain it readily. "She was always more involved with her mother and her girlfriends than with us," they say, still hurt. The distance they perceived as rejecting she meant to be protective—of both them (their manhood) and herself (her vulnerability to loss).

Ivan and Noah are left with the belief that women relate to women, and men are supposed to tough it out alone, but they're having a hard time coping with the results of that belief. Noah is very threatened by his wife's relationship to their daughters, out of his fear that as the girls grow, the women will get closer and closer to one another and shut him out entirely. With such a big stake in the myth of masculine independence, however, he finds this fear difficult to confront. Hence his preoccupation with his rights (to clean shirts, homemade dinners), not his needs. All he wants, he says, is for Debra to act like a proper wife. What he really wants is for her to act like a mother—the mother he feels he never had. But it's very difficult for men raised to conform to the masculine model to admit to needs, which are always construed as weakness. To insist on their rights, however, is seen as strength. Neither Noah nor Ivan is getting what he wants from his wife, and neither is likely to until he can admit to his longings without feeling unmanned by them. Then perhaps there will be a place for Angie in their lives, and fewer inappropriate demands on Debra and Bea.

BUYING INTO THE NOTION OF DIFFERENCE

Mary Ellen and Gilbert

GILBERT: It took Gilbert almost two years of fevered courtship to get Liza to marry him—this despite the fact that he was a gallant suitor as well as a stable, hardworking man who had done what he called his "fooling around" in his youth and at thirty-two was now more than ready to settle down. He earned good money at his job as an electrician, the trade he had learned in the army, and he spent that money happily on Liza, taking her to the big Broadway musicals she loved so much, bringing her extravagant bouquets, buying her sexy lingerie and romantic gifts of jewelry, like the heart-shaped gold locket in which he had enclosed a little picture of himself. He was also an expert and considerate lover. Though he thought of himself as a man's man, not one of the "new men" so in vogue, he'd read enough of those popular magazine quizzes about how to treat a woman of the nineties to feel that he was a pretty sensitive guy where women were concerned.

Nothing was too good for his Liza, who had stirred something deep in him from the moment he saw her. There was only one name for this feeling—love, love at first sight. Though others said she reminded them of his sainted mother, he didn't really see the resemblance. Nonetheless, like his mother, Liza seemed to him everything a woman should be: pretty, which meant that she would make pretty babies, and possessed of a kind heart, which meant she would be a good mother to them. Whenever he said that to her, as he often did, Liza just laughed at him and didn't take those statements too seriously.

She knew, however, that she felt something was lacking in the relationship. When he asked why she was uncertain about marrying him, why she wasn't completely happy, she could only say that she didn't feel he really "knew" her; that he scarcely talked to her when they were together, and when he did talk it was mainly about himself or about the army buddies he played poker with on Monday nights, and the guys from work he bowled with on Thursday nights. He would be happy to talk to her about anything she wanted, he always told her, and meant it, but as he said to his friends, while he loved women he would never understand them. His buddies would laugh and drink to that—everyone toasting, *"Vive la différence!"*

When Liza spoke to her mother about her reluctance to marry Gilbert, she was reminded that she was already twenty-nine years old, and that with only a job as a dental technician between her and the streets, she needed to be thinking about her future. Besides, her mother said, "Gilbert's a good man (as men go), and he makes a good living and he's very good to you. What more do you want?"

"Somebody I can feel close to," she protested.

"Men are different, dear. Don't expect the impossible. Look at your father."

"Different how?"

"Just different."

Liza wasn't convinced, but she did keep mulling over what her mother had said. Browsing through a bookstore one day for one of the romances she liked to pass the time with on Monday and Thursday nights, she came across a book called *Men Are from Mars, Women Are from Venus* and, intrigued by the title, took it home with her. Its notion that men and women are simply and irrevocably different from each other was oddly consoling to her. Since there was nothing to be done about this difference except to make some improvements in interplanetary communications, there was no use in pining for what could never be. She decided maybe she would marry Gilbert after all. When she showed the book to Gilbert, trying to explain how it had helped her to come to a decision, he too liked the title (not to mention the effect it had had on his beloved), but he said he didn't want to read it because he wanted to keep the mystery in their relationship. He thought that was such an intelligent and witty thing to say that he repeated it at Monday night's poker game, where it was met with a lot of laughter followed by the telling of a great many off-color stories, which Gilbert enjoyed but would never have repeated in a woman's presence. After all, he had been brought up to respect women.

They had a lavish wedding. Though Gilbert would have preferred City Hall, he felt he owed it to Liza to let her have her big day. Women love to dress up and be seen, he knew. Men of course hate that sort of thing, but if they're good sports they'll put up with it for the woman's sake. Liza looked like an angel in her white dress and veil, while Gilbert felt like a fool when his buddies made fun of him in his "monkey suit," but both of them had a wonderful time at their wedding, and both felt ready for domestic life.

Liza has continued to work since their marriage, as they are saving for a house and the family they want to start. Gilbert has continued to be as loving a husband as he was a suitor, taking very good care of his wife. He carries heavy bundles for her, makes sure the car gets its tune-ups, fixes broken appliances, and handles all their finances, while Liza cleans the apartment and does the shopping, cooking, and laundry. And if she's tired, as she often is because she works much longer hours than he does, no problem. He's glad to take her out to dinner or help out around the house. Gilbert is a very happy man.

No surprises here. So why is Liza unhappy? Why does she sometimes find herself daydreaming about undoing that lovely ceremony that bound them together so short a time ago? Why does she continue to feel that she's sharing her life with a stranger? When she confides these subversive thoughts to her mother, hoping at least for some sympathy, her mother tells her she was spoiled by her father because she was so pretty and it's about time she woke up and smelled the coffee. After a quick rereading of her *Men Are from Mars* book doesn't do the trick for her either, she decides something must be wrong with her and starts seeing a therapist—secretly. She wants her marriage to work and hopes that therapy can "fix" her. The problem, she thinks, is simply that she lacks good communication skills, for books like the one she's consulted tend to persuade women that it must be their fault if they feel unheard.

THE STORY: Gilbert's mother, Mary Ellen, came from farm people in Iowa. She was a very attractive girl, and in fact was the Corn Queen of her home county when she was seventeen. The last of six children and the only girl, she'd been fussed over since birth, particularly by her five brothers, to whom she seemed a little doll, so perfect and pretty. Her mother loved to dress her up, much to the admiration of all the males in the family, who would exclaim over her when they came in from the fields. Being such an exquisite little thing, Mary Ellen herself was exempt from any kind of work.

Mary Ellen married at twenty-one—a city man. Christian had grown up on a nearby farm but left after high school, when he went to Des Moines and got a job in the loan department of a large bank. This was where Mary Ellen met him, one day when she accompanied her daddy into town to see about a loan. They were married a year later and had just the one child, for it was a hard delivery and it was decided that she was too delicate to have to go through such an ordeal again. Mary Ellen doted on Gilbert, so much so that Christian worried she would make a sissy of the boy. Boys are different, he tried to explain to her. She listened. Since Christian had to devote long hours to his job, trying to help local farmers avoid the foreclosures that were threatening so many people in that region, the solution was for her and Gilbert to spend as much time as possible at her parents' farm, where her brothers and father would give the little boy some light chores to do while Mary Ellen occupied herself with her mother and the neighbor women.

Gilbert remembers that his father always told him, "Respect your mother. We have to take care of her." He loved his mother passionately, and thought she was the prettiest, sweetest woman he had ever seen. When she died in a car accident during his senior year of high school, he was heartbroken. She'd never even gotten to see him graduate. Shortly afterward, with his father's blessing, he signed up for a four-year hitch in the army.

Meeting Liza shortly after getting out of the service was like a dream come true for Gilbert. Since their marriage he has continued to feel the same way about her, but he is deeply puzzled by her unhappiness, which he senses even though she no longer talks to him about it. As she explains in therapy, whenever she used to try to discuss her feelings of dissatisfaction, Gilbert would get such a hurt puppy-dog look on his face that she couldn't bear to pursue the subject. Besides, Liza is as puzzled by her unhappiness in the marriage as he is and doesn't really know what to say. As she is the first to admit, he is a good husband. He encourages her to dress well, doesn't mind the money she spends at the beauty parlor, never forgets a birthday or anniversary (including the anniversaries of their first date, their first lovemaking, and so forth). But everything about him is beginning to get on her nerves, even and especially all his offers of help around the house.

Though she doesn't yet know it, Liza is lonely in her marriage. Having accepted that men and women are from different planets, she finds herself feeling very isolated on hers. Gilbert relates to her as though she is a foreign, albeit deeply cherished object, which is a kind of love that cannot warm her. The reason she bristles so when Gilbert tells her he'll "help" her (though again she doesn't understand it herself) is that this is a typical male way of defining what it is that women are meant to do—simply by not doing those tasks most of the time, thus allocating them to the opposite sex. When a man "helps" his wife with the laundry, half of which is his, or says he'll "babysit" for the children, also half his, he's telling her what her job is, what her capacities are. Like many a well-intentioned man, Gilbert considers himself a thoughtful, generous husband and is utterly baffled by his wife's apparent irrationality—as is Liza herself—whenever one of his kind offers is met with annoyance rather than gratitude.

If and when communication from Venus to Mars begins to improve, as Liza becomes better able to articulate the reasons for her unhappiness, she may find that Gilbert does not want to hear what she needs to say. Her voice cannot be heard, her needs met, by a man committed to staying on Mars. But as a self-defined "man's man," Gilbert may not be able to meet her halfway. Like the authors of books such as the one Liza was once so enthusiastic about, he is convinced that men are men and women are women, our differences so profound that we can bridge them only by seeing ourselves as foreigners who must learn to speak each other's "languages." His *"Vive la différence!"* philosophy is the culture's way of perpetuating the idea of half people, reinforcing our belief that women have access to one set of qualities and abilities, men to another. Better communication skills will not solve Liza and Gilbert's problem, however, for it takes two whole people, who acknowledge that they live on the same planet—Earth—to communicate intimately, as Liza longs to do.

BELIEF IN THE UNKNOWABILITY OF THE MALE

Bonnie and Barney

BARNEY: At twenty-three, Barney still lives at home, despite the fact that he makes a good income and that he and his mother have very little to say to each other. Though generally silent and withdrawn in Bonnie's presence, Barney sometimes gives way to the fits of rage that seem to overtake him from out of the blue, and then he may destroy furniture, hurl things at Bonnie, or launch a verbal assault against her. He has never hit her, or any other woman, but he has gotten into a couple of serious barroom brawls after a few too many drinks. Bonnie sees his behavior as a legacy of the bad temper he inherited from his grandfather, her father.

Because she is always fearful of setting him off, Bonnie tends to tiptoe around her son and cater to him endlessly. Barney is both puzzled and maddened by the way Bonnie dances in nervous attendance on him: "It's like a constant buzzing in my ear," he says, though he can't tell you what "it" is.

Barney has a good job in construction, where his volatile temper is seen as strength and his silent application to the tasks at hand serves him well.

Olive, Barney's girlfriend, has been hanging around his house since they were both in high school, when she was always made welcome by his mother. Like Bonnie, she is a little afraid of Barney, and she depends on Bonnie for advice on how to "handle" him, which is a constant topic between the two women. Though Olive would like to marry Barney, or at least live with him, and Barney agrees that's the logical next step in their relationship, he always puts off the decision because for reasons he cannot fathom he feels uneasy about leaving his mother. His secret fantasy is that Olive will marry him and they can both live with Bonnie, for the underlying source of his reluctance is his fear of totally losing control without Bonnie to keep the situation stable.

Barney is aware of feeling different from other people, though he doesn't know why. When he starts to get overwhelmed by the loneliness and isolation that are always lurking just beneath the surface, he sometimes goes to a nearby bar looking for companionship. Often, however, he drinks too much and ends up getting into arguments, which occasionally lead to fights. Afterward he somehow feels better about himself. *I'm a man*, he thinks. *Sometimes men lose control because we just can't help it. It's in our nature. That's what Olive and Mom are afraid of.* Then he feels powerful for a while, but the feeling never lasts.

THE STORY: Bonnie was always afraid of her father. A stern, silent man given to occasional outbursts of monumental but inexplicable anger, he existed largely as a scary shadow figure in her mind. Her mother tiptoed around him and constantly admonished Bonnie and her two sisters not to upset him. No one questioned why. The assumption was: that's the way men are. How? Mysterious. You never know what will set them off.

After a series of short-term affairs in her twenties, Bonnie had a relatively sustained but casual relationship that went on for about four years and ended when she told her lover she was pregnant. She has never married—"Somehow it just turned out that way"—and Barney never got to know his father, who drifted away during the pregnancy.

Bonnie has a small but fairly successful catering business, which provides both money and a sense of accomplishment and satisfaction. She's had opportunities to expand, but that would mean dealing with corporate accounts—and the men who are generally in charge of them. "I'm never sure what those men want," she says. But she feels quite comfortable doing party planning and ordering with the well-to-do matrons whose elegant at-home dinners constitute most of her business now. In leaner times, she has been able to look to her sisters for financial as well as emotional support, for the three women have been close since childhood.

Men in general, and her son in particular, remain mysterious to Bonnie. Having gotten the message from his mother that he is alien, perhaps even dangerous, Barney has been made to feel that she knows some secret truth about him that she won't tell him. Perhaps that's what Bonnie and Olive are talking about when he walks into the kitchen unexpectedly and catches them whispering. Sometimes he dreams that he's a caged animal, a lion or a black panther. One night he dreamed that he was both the panther and the keeper who was afraid of him. He woke up in a cold sweat.

In therapy Barney is helped to articulate the frustration and confusion he feels about being kept at such a distance from the two most important people in his life. All three of them begin to question their tacit assumptions about the unpredictability and unknowability of men.

ELEVATION OF THE BOY

Rebecca and Colin

COLIN: Twenty-four-year-old Colin has been living away from home since he finished high school. Despite his apparent independence, things aren't going well for him. He went out West with some vague idea of working on a ranch, or some other suitably masculine activity, but he soon drifted to Los Angeles, where he has lived a marginal life, on the fringes of the movie industry, ever since.

Hypersensitive to criticism and unable to take instruction, he never lasts at any of the jobs he charms his way into. "Thinks he knows it all," his bosses complain, before they lose patience altogether and fire him. He always manages to get by, however, because his mother, who believes that "a man is entitled to his adventure," can be counted on for occasional handouts, even though she has to send them secretly so that Colin's father doesn't find out about them.

When he first got to L.A. he met a woman ten years his senior and moved in with her. Given the youth obsession of the culture they live in, Colin was something of a score for her—cute, charming, presentable—and for several years she was happy to flatter and take care of him. Eventually, however, she got bored, and two years ago she found another, younger lover and ended the relationship. Since then he has had trouble finding a woman who truly appreciates him.

Colin is a deeply unhappy young man. He's always known he was special, so he can't quite believe how badly things are turning out. His steadily increasing dependence on drugs hasn't made him feel any better, but it has taken the edge off the panic he has started to feel lately. Though his mother reassures him that he's still trying to "find himself" and that a man of his rare qualities can't fail to do so eventually, he's beginning to wonder. (She's secretly worried too.) He'd like to talk to his father about some of his concerns, but he's afraid to, because he knows his father disapproves of him. "You need to tough it out, boy," his father is likely to say. "Can't always be depending on your mother to bail you out." Since nothing seems to pan out for him professionally, he's now spending most of his time looking for a woman who would really understand him. He thinks that's what he needs to get started. Started on what? He shrugs.

THE STORY: Rebecca, Colin's mother, grew up in a house full of women. As the last of four daughters she was well aware of her father's disappointment at not having a son and was determined to make it up to him. Little Becky would hear her mother sighing, "Poor man, he wanted a son, someone to go to ball games with, someone to laugh at his jokes," and she'd try to be that son—with mixed results, at best. She was the one he'd take fishing and horseback riding, it's true, but he never attended even one of her athletic competitions, although she excelled at virtually every sport. Indeed, if she tried too hard to please he'd get nervous and tell her to put on a skirt and start acting like a lady. So the message she got was a mixed one.

When she was eighteen she married Ian, a man's man who she hoped would be the son her father had always wanted. This worked out well, for the two men became fast friends, while Becky, no longer required to audition for the role of her father's son, turned herself into a model wife. The birth of their first child, Christina, was a disappointment to her, as she had so much wished to present her father and her husband with a boy. But before Christina was even out of diapers Becky was pregnant again, this time with Colin—her parents' first grandson.

Colin was a handsome, lively little boy and quickly became the center of the family. In the adoring eyes of his mother, father, and grandfather, he could do no wrong. If the two children fought over a toy, Christina was always encouraged to give way. Colin always got to choose the bedtime story, the television program, the dessert.

Becky reveled in Colin, her great accomplishment. Since his maleness was such a prize, she exaggerated all those qualities she defined as belonging to men. Christina she understood from the day she was born, she liked to say, but Colin—he was different. He was born loving trucks, trains, and guns. And the reason Christina always had to give in to him was that he was so much more aggressive than she that he wouldn't be able to bear defeat. "Boys are just like that," Becky explained to Christina, when the little girl objected to the unfairness of it all. The imperious manner he developed while still a toddler was only one more sign of his specialness.

Always pushed to the background, Christina kept trying for a place in the sun. She worked hard at making friends, was a second little mother to Colin, graduated from college, and then put herself through veterinary school. She's doing well now and occasionally supplements the money Becky sends Colin with gifts of her own.

Colin, however, faces a very uncertain future. When a boy is elevated on the basis of his maleness alone, he may be able, if he has the talent, to exploit that masculinity in one way or another. If gifted in sports he might become an athlete; if very bright he may compete and be successful in one of the venues where brains count; if he's great-looking he may be able to get by on looks and charm alone. But if, like Colin, he has no great intelligence, no special talents or attributes, only a great need to maintain the myth of his specialness, he's in trouble.

The most hopeful scenario for Colin would be that he find some woman who for reasons of her own wants someone to take care of (and perhaps to support). A sufficiently symbiotic choreography of matching needs might even result in an enduring relationship. Barring that, he may eventually get into trouble with drugs or petty crime. Though his mother would like him to come back home, since things don't seem to be working out for him in California, that would be hard for him to do without feeling his masculinity impaired. If he's lucky, maybe he'll get sick and have to be sent home, which would allow Becky, who's beginning to be seriously worried about him, to get him into therapy with someone who could address the underlying dynamics of this family.

FEMALE LACK OF SELF-ESTEEM, OR "NOT BURDENING THE BOYS"

Lily, Josh, and Mark

JOSH: Tess and Josh, both doctors and both recently divorced when they met, married each other three months after that first meeting. A year later Tess was begging Josh to see a therapist with her about their "communication problems," but he said he didn't have a problem, except for all the complaining *she* did, and she should go by herself if she wanted to. "You're beginning to sound like my first wife," he told her. "What do you women want anyway?" It was beyond him.

His mother hadn't prepared him for today's demanding women, he explained on one of the rare occasions when Tess was able to drag him to therapy. She had been a completely devoted wife and mother and he didn't understand why he couldn't find someone like her. What did his mother do? "Full-time housewife." Was she happy in that role? "I don't know, I never really thought about it. But I assume she was. Why wouldn't she have been?" If that was his ideal, why had he married a professional woman? "I wanted someone I could relate to as an equal. My first wife was a nurse and she couldn't understand what I was talking about half the time."

In therapy Tess spends most of her time complaining about Josh. "He's a wonderful man," she says, "but totally self-engrossed and wrapped up in his work. I know his work is important. I respect that. But mine is important too and he acts like it's just a hobby. If I complain that he never talks to me anymore, he'll tell me in great detail about the gallbladder he just removed. He really thinks that's what I want."

Whenever Tess describes one of these "conversations," she starts to cry. "He doesn't talk," she'll say, "he lectures. He doesn't see *me* at all. I could be tearing my hair out in frustration but he doesn't notice. And if he does, he just gets that look on his face—that *Uh-oh, she's got her period* look. *Better stay out of her way.*" Though they eat breakfast together every morning, and drive home together most nights after doing rounds at the hospital, they share very little. Mornings Josh hides behind his newspaper as he downs his coffee and croissant, and in the car at night he makes only perfunctory comments if Tess tries to engage him in a recap of their respective days. He needs to concentrate on his driving, he says.

Sex is a once-a-week thing, every Friday night. "If I want sex on Saturday morning, he'll say, 'Why? We had sex last night,' " Tess reports. Tess would like to have children, and at thirty-six is fearful of missing her chance to do so, but Josh has two from his first marriage and feels he's "done that deal already."

Within only one year of their wedding, Tess and Josh have moved from the excitement of their brief courtship to the tired, stale impasse of old marrieds.

MARK: Josh's younger brother Mark, also a medical school graduate, decided not to follow in his brother's footsteps as a surgeon but to become a psychiatrist. It was a difficult decision because he looked up to Josh, who told him psychiatry was a "phony" profession, but Mark persisted and is now both very happy and very successful in his work. Married for thirteen years to the same woman, an artist, Mark has a tempestuous but passionate, loving relationship with her. Mark is not like most men, Daphne says. "He loves the kind of intimate conversation that I think of as girl talk. He wants to know everything about me." So they spend hours talking, with Mark never tiring of Daphne's stories about her family and her childhood, and she never tiring of telling them. He's impressed by her depth of psychological insight, and gratified that she's willing to share so deeply with him. After these talks, they usually make love.

Almost forty now, Daphne would like to have a child, but Mark is reluctant, feeling that a child will turn Daphne into a "mother" and distance her from him.

THE STORY: Mark and Josh's mother, Lily, married late. A beautiful woman and a talented musician, she had hoped for a career as a singer. But she had been discouraged by her father from an all-out pursuit of that career. "Show business is no business for a woman," he used to tell her, "and anyway you ought to be thinking about finding a husband." So she never had the drive she needed to get it off the ground. By the time she met Howard she was thirty years old and had been reduced to performing at the occasional wedding or charity affair. When Howard launched an all-out attempt to get her to marry him, she gave in, out of a sense that she wasn't going anywhere in her life anyway. Maybe settling down in the suburbs with this nice middle-class orthodontist wouldn't be so bad. Within a year Josh was born, then two years later Mark, and four years after that Maggie.

The children became Lily's life—that's what everyone said. And she agreed. "If you're happy, I'm happy," she always used to tell them. She devoted her every waking hour to them, and they repaid her efforts by being children, and then adults, she could be proud of. The boys became doctors, Maggie an accomplished pianist, engaged to a historian of some renown. Each child now has a different relationship with Lily, and with his or her respective mates.

Josh adores Lily, indeed wishes he could find a wife like her, though he has little idea of who she is—or who his wife is, for that matter. Having taken his mother at her word, he can't understand how it is that Tess could fail to be happy when he is content. In fact, he can't see her as separate from himself at all (which was why his first marriage finally broke up), for women are invisible to him except as the means to his own happiness.

A man who does not know his mother as a separate person is at a great disadvantage with women generally. Like Josh, he may think he is treating a woman well, while expecting her to be as centered on him and his pleasures as his mother was. If his wife insists that she has needs of her own, as Tess has done, he will be perplexed and will tend to conclude that there is something wrong with her.

Mark has an intense but conflicted relationship with Lily, for he is ceaselessly longing for an intimacy from which she draws back. After a stormy adolescence, during which he threw himself into the antiwar and civil rights movements of the sixties, always challenging his parents' values, always questioning, he settled down. But he has never stopped wanting to understand his mother, to get to know her, despite the opaque mantle of happy motherhood in which she has wrapped herself. A similarly questing spirit marks his relationship with his wife and informs his work, but he can count on both his wife and his patients to respond. His mother, however, still eludes him, which makes him feel rejected. He is mystified by that feeling, since he can hardly think of Lily as rejecting him. After all, it was well known that she lived for her children.

"What's to tell?" Lily says when brought into the therapeutic process and confronted with her younger son's curiosity about her inner life, a curiosity that has continued unabated even though the questions, which she always responded to by shooing him away in irritation, have long since ceased. "What kind of mother would burden her sons with her own disappointments? I wanted them to do well in life. You make that possible by encouraging them, not by dragging them down with efforts to get their sympathy." Indeed she has so submerged her feelings by now that she believes her own story. "If my children are happy, I'm happy"—Lily's mantra.

Maggie knows better, for Lily shared more of herself with her daughter than she did with her sons. It's no secret to her that Lily is an intensely lonely, frustrated woman. She loves Lily, feels close to her, understands but does not admire the self-sacrificial spirit in which Lily raised her children. Indeed, she is determined not to emulate her mother, and has informed her fiancée that any decision about children will have to be deferred while she focuses on her career.

The myth that a woman ceases to be a person when she becomes a mother is still embedded in the psyche of women everywhere, which may help to explain why so many of the daughters of the self-effacing generation have postponed motherhood until their biological clocks approach zero hour. When a mother lives through her children, sharing nothing of her own hopes and dreams, disappointments, and dissatisfactions, her unknowability may not turn out to be such a great gift after all.

As John Updike said years ago, in an essay about his relationship with *his* mother, "The largeness of our mother-myth has a paradoxically dwindling effect upon the women concerned: they must be in all things motherly and become therefore natural processes rather than people." His subject is the great pleasure he has taken, in later life, in being able to get "behind the giant mask of motherhood" and coming to know his mother as a person. The idea that this might be a source of pleasure will come as a surprise to most men. But having watched the process in the consulting room, and having begun it with my own son, I can say that the pleasure is real, and mutual.

The alternative is the route Lily has chosen (though admittedly she took it to an extreme), which reminds me of that old comedy routine depicting a man making a phone call to his mother. "Hello," she answers, in a faint, remote little voice. "Mother, what's wrong, why do you sound so weak?" "You haven't called for a month." "Why should that make you weak?" "Well, I haven't eaten anything during that time." "Why on earth not?" "I didn't want you should call and my mouth would be full."

MEN AS FATHERS

Mother "disappears" herself from the life of her son so that he will become a man. The disappearing father, however, is a much more literal fact of life. It's estimated that 25 percent of the children in the United States have little or no contact with their fathers. But at the same time that fathers are disappearing at an unprecedented rate, books (and articles) celebrating the joys as well as the importance of fatherhood are appearing at an equally unprecedented rate, bearing such titles and subtitles as *Fathers and Daughters; Fathers of Daughters; Women and Their Fathers; Fathers and Their Families; Fathers, Sons and Daughters; Fathers, Sons and the Search for Masculinity; Finding Our Fathers; Men Coming to Terms with Their Fathers and Themselves; Becoming the Father You Wish Your Father Had Been; The Nurturing Father; Father Love; Fatherhood Today; The Role of the Father in Child Development; How Fathers Care for the New Generation; Between Father and Child; When Men Are Pregnant; Birth of a Father; Fatherhood in America; Fatherhood USA.* Last, and best selling of all, Bill Cosby's *Fatherhood.* That's quite a shelf-ful, though it by no means exhausts the list of such books—all of them published within the last decade or so.

Now that even some sociobiologists are saying that the nurturing behavior of mothers is not just a biologically programmed inevitability but the result of a complex interplay between hormonal and social factors, other researchers are suggesting that the nurturing behavior of fathers *does* have its source in nature. Thus developmental psychologist Michael Lamb did a study demonstrating that women appear to have no "biological superiority" to men in their caretaking abilities; while studies of nonhuman primate families by psychologist William Redican and others show that the males carry out a wide range of caretaking activities, feeding, grooming, carrying, and playing with their young. Indeed, "In some species of New World monkeys . . . the father assumes almost the entire burden of infant care." Fatherly caretaking is now being looked at as an instinctive behavior, a key factor in the perpetuation of the human race. And it's not just good for the kids; it's good for Dad too. He's happier, suffers less stress, lives longer, and so on. "Try it, you'll like it," is the gist of all the joys-of-childrearing propaganda targeted at the ambivalent males of our species. Even the paleontologist hero of one of the biggest box office hits of all time—*Jurassic Park*—gets converted (under extreme duress, admittedly) to dadhood.

Apparently, however, a lot of other men have tried it and didn't like it—so much so that they walked out. There's considerable speculation about why, much of it centered on the collapse of the old breadwinner ethos. In *The Hearts of Men* Barbara Ehrenreich describes the centuries-old expectation that boys would grow up, get married, and support their wives and children. "To do anything else was less than grown-up, and the man who willfully deviated was judged to be somehow 'less than a man.' " In other words, manhood was earned and defined by one's breadwinning capacity, and the fruits of this activity were conferred upon the nuclear family. A man supported his children, even if he wasn't intimately involved with their day-to-day care. That much most cultural analysts are agreed upon, as they are also in agreement about the fact that sometime in the last few decades, this arrangement began to break down.

Ehrenreich's provocative analysis departs from others, however, in not putting the blame for this collapse at the door of the feminist movement. It wasn't the fact that women could earn their own bread that caused men to decamp; it was a "male revolt" against the dreariness of their lives as breadwinners, she says. Beginning with the self-awareness of the "man in the grey flannel suit" whose dutiful pursuit of a career bought him a life in the suburbs that he found stultifyingly empty, aided and abetted by the playboys whose lubricious and marriage-free lifestyle was celebrated in the men's magazines, then echoed and extended by the beat heroes whose alternative but equally carefree "on the road" ethos was a rejection of both work and marriage, this mid-century revolt was the result of men deciding they'd had enough of the traditional role, according to Ehrenreich. The human potential movement, the male liberation movement, concern about the effects of type A behavior on male longevity, and the counterculture also played their part in consolidating the revolt and making it respectable. In short, men opted out of not just childrearing but of marriage and child support too.

Other cultural analysts, both liberal and right-wing, view the collapse of the breadwinner ethic as another kind of revolt—the result of men's anger with the feminist movement, which they see as having deprived them of their jobs, or at least of their dignity as patriarch of the family. "You don't need me anymore? Well, I'm outa here." Everyone agrees on the results of the revolt, whatever its source, and has reams of statistics illustrating its cost to women and children.

While I think there is much truth to be found in both these explanations—for men are not a unilateral group whose motivations are identical across boundaries of age, ethnicity, income, class, and color—there is yet another way of looking at what has happened. Though many men no doubt are in revolt against the breadwinner ethos in one fashion or another, many others, and not just from the middle class, are devout believers in it. It is their very inability to live up to it in an economy that is declining, as well as their confusion about how else they might play the male role in a culture that is changing, that is the problem.

The story told below describes a man who walks out on his children. I tell it not because I wish to move from mother blaming to father blaming, or because I am unaware of the millions of men who do no such thing, and the smaller but still substantial number who are now trying to forge new kinds of connections with their children, but because it sums up so much of what is wrong with the values of the society in which we live and by which we raise our sons. It is these values that help to make manhood—and fatherhood—such precarious enterprises in this day and age.

T.J.: *The Case of the Missing Father*

An ambitious and hardworking man, T.J. McDowell enjoyed great success as a real estate broker during the boom years of the eighties. His wife, Loretta, also sold real estate and also did well, though not nearly on the same scale. The first several years of their marriage flew by as both immersed themselves in work, which was their main topic of conversation with each other. Often work overlapped with private time, since Loretta's business required the occasional wining and dining of certain clients, and she liked to have T.J. with her on such occasions, especially if a large commission on a major commercial property was at stake. She knew that men tended to deal more comfortably with other men when big money was involved. For his part, T.J. loved coming in as consultant, for he was very good at what he did and enjoyed playing the expert.

This was exactly the life T.J. had been born and bred for. His father, a well-known, well-to-do trial attorney, had told him he could be anything he wanted. Though he had at first been disappointed that his son didn't finish college and chose not to go into one of the professions, he nonetheless bankrolled T.J.'s first real estate venture and rejoiced over his many successes during the years that followed. He was very proud of his entrepreneur son.

Eventually T.J. and Loretta used his substantial earnings to buy their dream house in the suburbs, with an eye to starting a family. Having waited until Loretta was thirty-eight, however, they found pregnancy an elusive goal. The fertility experts they consulted suggested that Loretta cut down on her workload, since stress was thought to be a factor in her inability to conceive, and soon she was spending more and more time at home. Both discovered that they enjoyed this new arrangement. T.J. thought it was great to have home-cooked meals, instead of going to restaurants every night as they had done before, while Loretta found satisfaction in the more creative aspects of homemaking—gourmet meals, orchid growing, decorating the house that had remained all but empty after they moved in. The more mundane aspects—cleaning, laundry, ironing—she continued to leave to the cleaning lady who had been seeing to their needs for years, but they cut her days from three to one a week.

On her thirty-ninth birthday Loretta found out she was pregnant—cause indeed for celebration. If anything, T.J. was even happier than Loretta. When the baby arrived, he surprised himself with the depth of his love for his little daughter.

Now Loretta quit work altogether and stayed home full-time, but T.J.'s life remained much the same. It was just that something wonderful had been added to it. They didn't go out very often anymore, but that was okay, since the forty-five-minute commute he had added to either end of his workday when they moved to the suburbs left him tired by the time he got home. Energy was also consumed by certain manly tasks Loretta had assigned to him—watering the lawn, insulating the attic, hanging wallpaper in the baby's room— out of her belief in the family myth (told to Loretta by T.J.'s mother) that he was a restless man who needed to be kept busy.

When Betsy was nine months old Loretta found herself pregnant again. Exhausted by her second pregnancy and overwhelmed by the job of taking care of a very active toddler, she asked the cleaning lady to return to her old three-day-a-week schedule—just as the bottom fell out of the real estate market. At first it seemed almost a lark, with T.J. spending more time at home with his family and being able to help out a bit when Thomas James, Jr., was born. He took pleasure and pride in playing with Betsy while Loretta nursed little Tommy, or in hoisting his infant son high above his head to the sound of delighted gurgles. He even hung a few of the prints Loretta had acquired when she took an art appreciation course in the months before the first baby arrived. But what had seemed a temporary aberration in the real estate market began to take on a more ominous cast as the months went by and business kept going progressively downhill.

Trouble set in on the homefront, too, with both Loretta and T.J.

feeling anxious about how to meet their expenses—a high mort-gage, what seemed like endless medical bills because of Tommy's multiple allergies, and all the many costs of the good life to which they had grown so accustomed. T.J. might have asked his parents for a loan to tide them over, but his father had died suddenly of a heart attack shortly after the new baby arrived, and his mother had then moved to Florida. He didn't want to burden her with his prob-lems. Though he was sorry his father was gone, he was almost glad the old man hadn't lived to see him in such dire straits.

One day T.J. suggested to Loretta that they let the cleaning woman go, thereby precipitating a tantrum the likes of which he would never have thought Loretta capable of. She catalogued all his faults, including, to his great surprise, his irresponsibility toward his own children, for whom he had never so much as changed a diaper even though he was happy to show up for playtime. She was sick and tired of waiting on him and his children, she shrieked. It was the worst fight they had ever had.

T.J. slept on the couch that night—or rather he didn't sleep, be-cause he was so upset. His whole world seemed to be falling apart. In the morning he got up while Loretta was still asleep, gave the children breakfast, and solemnly told them how much he loved them. As he was hugging and kissing them he heard Loretta coming downstairs—and fled.

Without really thinking what he was doing, he went straight to the apartment of a young secretary in his office whom he had long suspected of wanting to have an affair with him. There he related his sad tale, until Nesta took him in her arms and led him down the hall to her bedroom. What a dreadful woman Loretta must be, she agreed, wanting him to pay a cleaning woman three times a week when he could barely meet the mortgage, expecting him to spend so much time with the kids when he was trying his best to make a living for everybody.

T.J. missed his children terribly. He had only meant to stay with

Nesta for a day or two, until Loretta came to her senses and realized that she was driving him away, that she couldn't expect him to earn all the money *and* help with the kids. To hell with that!

But Loretta didn't call. She had been absolutely devastated by his departure. "I open my mouth once, and he's gone. I don't understand," she kept saying during her first therapy session, five days later. A week after that Loretta decided T.J. must not be coming home and took the steps she thought necessary to ensure her family's future. She refinanced their mortgage at a lower rate, put the cleaning woman on full-time, and went back to work. Since her end of the market had not been as hard hit as T.J.'s, she discovered that she could just about meet her monthly expenses, as long as she was willing to economize on all the extras.

After almost two months of silence T.J. swallowed his pride and showed up at their door. Betsy and Tommy were wildly excited, but Loretta was cool. She told him what she had done, then gave him a set of rules regarding his responsibility to the family. Unless he agreed to them, he couldn't come back, she said, although she very much hoped he would. T.J.'s pride was deeply wounded. Not that the rules were unreasonable, but who did she think she was, making rules for him? Even his parents hadn't been able to exert control over him, once he entered his teen years and began hanging with the cool crowd at school. Also, he felt humiliated by Loretta's newfound independence. As she continued talking, explaining that they would be able to make ends meet if she kept working full-time, which of course would mean his having to do more around the house, he brooded. Before she could even finish her speech, he walked out. He knew he wasn't going back.

Within six months he had filed for divorce, at Nesta's urging. Loretta agreed, and they arrived at a fairly amicable division of their joint property. Loretta would keep the kids, but T.J. was free to visit them as often as he liked during the week. Every other weekend he could take them for an overnight.

T.J. was deeply depressed. For months he couldn't muster the energy to see his children. It was just too painful for him. Having been through a divorce herself, Nesta understood that he needed time to recover. She demanded little and took good care of him whenever he would let her.

When the final decree came through a year later, T.J. worked up his nerve to go see the children. It was only his third visit since leaving. Not surprisingly, they were shy with him. Betsy told him, "I'm mad at you. You made my mommy cry." Tommy barely seemed to remember him. Loretta reproached him with his neglect. "I wasn't up to it while everything was still pending," he explained. "But now that the divorce is final, things will change. You'll see." And by the way, he had decided he wanted joint custody. No problem, Loretta said. His lawyer should call hers, and they could do the necessary paperwork. Next weekend, just as he'd promised, he came for the kids. Nesta had left to spend the weekend with a friend, so he and his children could have some "catching-up time," but he didn't know how to fill the hours. When they got fussy, he took them back to Loretta early. She suspected she'd heard the last about joint custody.

That very evening T.J.'s mother called from Florida. The market was picking up down there, she said. Why didn't he come check it out? After talking it over with Nesta, he decided it would be worth a try. He rationalized his absence from the children by telling himself that he would be able to send money, which was more important, given that Loretta gave them such good care. Though he was too late to get rich on the Miami boom, he did find he could make a decent living, and Nesta followed him within a few months of his arrival. As promised, he sent support money for the kids, as well as lavish birthday and Christmas presents, which Nesta picked out.

Two years later, however, he married Nesta, and first the presents stopped, then the money. It's been almost ten months since Loretta has had any communication from him.

T.J. never meant to abandon his children. Everything just got out of control. First there was that fight with Loretta, which took them both by surprise. Since they weren't in the habit of talking about how they felt, he didn't know how overburdened she was feeling with two small children to take care of; similarly, she had no idea how shaken T.J. was over his inability to provide for his family in the manner to which they'd all grown accustomed. He had begun to wonder if he would ever return to his previous income level, but he would never have wanted her to know this. It was too humiliating, too frightening. The issue of the cleaning lady hit them both where they were most vulnerable.

When T.J. went to Nesta's, he wasn't looking for sex, only sympathy, but things spun out of control there too. Though he'd planned to go home that night with his tail between his legs, Nesta made such a fuss over him that he began to feel like a man again. He'd almost forgotten what that feeling was like. After all, Loretta had been so tired ever since Tommy, Jr., was born that they rarely ever made love anymore. So he let a few days pass, telling himself that he needed this little respite for his sanity. He deserved it. His home life would be the better for it. One day led to another. Loretta, for her part, was too hurt to go after him. As the days turned into weeks, her grief turned to anger.

When T.J. finally went home, with every intention of kissing and making up, he couldn't believe how Loretta pulled the rug out from under him. She seemed to think she was now the man of the house. It was more than his pride could bear, and he saw he could no longer make a life with Loretta. Still, he had every intention of staying connected to his children, whom he really did love dearly. In fact, he thought of his move to Florida as something he was doing for them. Though he knew he'd miss them, he also knew that his first obligation as a man was to be a good provider, so he decided to be a stoic about it. He would go to Florida, make a lot of money, then return triumphant in the eyes of his children.

Unfortunately, he didn't make it big in Florida. Ashamed of being what he thought of as a failure, he never visited or sent for Betsy and Tommy. They were better off not seeing him in his present state, he told himself. An expert at cutting off his feelings, he soon ceased to miss his children. At certain movies—father-son things, particularly—he got a bit teary-eyed, but he never made the connection. After he and Nesta got married, he found it easier just not to think about the children, which was a relief, because remembering them caused him such pain. The child-support money was a casualty of that amnesia.

Male stoicism, emotional shutdown, the breadwinner ethic as a way of defining manhood, a subtle but pervasive belief in the inequality of the sexes, anxiety over his place in the pecking order, of both his family and his career—these are all factors in T.J.'s story. As long as we continue to raise our sons to serve a system that equates manhood with success, femininity with emotion and nurturance, we must continue to teach men to shut off their feelings, as T.J. has done. And like Loretta and her two children, their families will continue to suffer the consequences of their feeling "unmanned" if they are unable to succeed, even when it's because of circumstances far beyond their control. The result may very well be more and more fathers absenting themselves from their families—a phenomenon previously thought common only among the lower classes but spreading rapidly into middle- and upper-middle-class life.

BEING YOUR OWN MAN

T.J. liked to think he was a "self-made man"—a phrase we use to denote those who have made their own money. This was his bulwark against the precariousness of masculinity, as we've defined it in our culture. The values implicit in that phrase do not apply just to money, however; they are everywhere in our culture, or in that part of it relating to males. Mother pulls back from her son in order that he be able to "make something of himself" or "be his own man." The utter strangeness of the phrase "be her own woman" suggests how different are our expectations for sons and for daughters. That such expectations are no favor to men is the premise of this book.

In the last couple of decades more and more men themselves have begun to question these assumptions, and to suggest the possibility of changing them—hence books with titles and subtitles like *In Search of the Deep Masculine, Transformations in Masculinity, Dilemmas of Masculinity, The Limits of Masculinity, Beyond Masculinity, The Making of Masculinities, The Making of New Masculinities, Changing Masculinities, Changing Men, The Changing Face of American Manhood, The Male Ordeal, The Hazards of Being Male, The Male Ego, The Male Dilemma, The Wounded Male, The New Male.*

Like Robert Bly and Sam Keen, the authors of all of these books, some of which date back two decades or so, know that modern men are in trouble—indeed, in considerable pain. There is genuine and sometimes excruciating uncertainty in contemporary culture about what it means to be a man. The answers to that dilemma are various. Avatars of the mythopoetic men's movement counsel the beating of the drum and the showing of the sword to exorcise the "soft man" within, thus enabling the more authentic "hairy man" to prevail and to reconnect with his fierce, passionate nature. Other writers and preachers suggest that certain heretofore female-linked traits, a dash of sensitivity here, a dollop of tenderness there, the ability to shed a manly tear or two, the capacity to nurture one's own offspring, should be added to the overall recipe for making a man—the "new man." And whether they think men are too manly for their own good or not manly enough, just about everybody agrees that men should try to get in touch with their fathers by way of reclaiming, reconstituting, reshaping, or re-creating their masculinity.

"Father hunger" is the pop-psych trend of the moment, despite the fact that, like Laius and Oedipus, Rabbit and Nelson, many a father harbors competitive (if not murderous) instincts toward his son, instincts that will make the easing of that hunger all but impossible. That's one of the costs of living in what Rabbit describes to Nelson—at a moment when Nelson dares to question the value of competition—as our "dog eat dog" society.

Some of these attempts to wrestle with issues of masculinity are all to the good, some silly, some downright harmful. But none of them goes to the heart of the problem, and nothing beyond change of a first-order degree of magnitude can come of them.

The real pain in men's lives stems from their estrangement from women. They may be looking for their lost fathers in some ritual space, or bonding with their newfound brothers in the sweat lodge, but their feelings of loss are not going to be assuaged until that central fact of male experience is acknowledged. As anybody who works with the elderly will tell you, when octogenarians utter their dying words, it's "Mama" the men call for, never "Daddy." All this Bly-inspired howling in the wilderness for the father who was not there is wasted breath.

No adult male in our culture, however, can go off into the woods and cry for his mother. No way is that a permissible social construct. Yet that is whom many men long for. As a culture, we have to face up to that longing—its power, its persistence throughout a man's life, its potential for destruction when unacknowledged.

MICHAEL AND I

It would be presumptuous of me to say that Michael missed me when he went away to college. In the process of writing this book, however, and of asking him to review those portions of it that related to him, I certainly began to look at the past with new eyes, to face up to the fact that, with the best of intentions, I had caused my son pain. The moodiness, the remoteness from his family, the distance that I had seen at the time as normal adolescent behavior, the closed-off, cool silences I had accepted as inevitable and appropriate in a young college student living on his own, I now see as anger. And beneath the anger I see his pain. Since Michael was always too polite to express anger, and we don't allow our males to express pain—nor does any mother want to see that pain—it has taken me the better part of three decades to come to this understanding. In the consulting room I came to it much earlier; in my own life I would have to write a book on the subject before I could get there.

As the years went by, Michael graduated from college, went on to medical school in California, married, had a son, added a degree in public health to his résumé. He was a perfect fit within the parameters of what Joseph Pleck has described as the Male Sex Role Identity Paradigm. I was very proud of him. That he was also distant with the family (most particularly his mother), that he seemed often tense and anxious to leave when spending time with us, I rationalized as my problem—just another manifestation of my Jewish momism, to which I gave the usual negative spin. I was not happy about my relationship with my son, but when I occasionally tried to question him about it, in the most tentative fashion, I knew enough to back off when he indicated that he had no interest in such a discussion. That's what men are like, right? You can't talk about feelings with them. It was easier for me to talk to my daughter-in-law, and I often used her as my conduit to Michael.

Although I was dealing in my practice with mothers and sons whose issues might have reminded me of what I was going through with Michael, whenever vague awareness of the similarities began to surface I simply admonished myself against the therapist's danger of identifying with her patients.

At several times in those years I watched Michael go through crises that made me want to reach out to him, to talk to him about what was going on with him. But did I? Absolutely not. I suffered, and allowed Michael to suffer, in silence. After all (so my reasoning went): (1) Michael is a man. (2) Not only is he a man, but he's a married man. So who am I to involve myself in his life? He didn't ask for my advice, he'll be angry if I interfere, he knows what he's doing. Mothers can only exercise a regressive pull in times of crisis.

Did I have a secret pride—secret even from myself—in what I perceived of as his manly strength, which would surely prevail over all difficulties? I'm afraid so. I do know that I abandoned him again.

Abandoned him to the "masculine mystique" I had bought into at his birth.

The good news is that my decision to describe some of my own experiences in this book has helped us to talk—really talk. It's still not easy, but we're working on it. And that in itself—the acknowledgment of a problem, the joint commitment to working through it—is a huge difference. Writing this book and sharing it with Michael has been a process that illuminated much of the past for both of us.

Other mothers and their grown sons will surely find their own routes to rapprochement. I hope the book will help stimulate the desire for it, the understanding that it's possible, and the recognition that if a mother is unhappy about her relationship with her son, the chances are very good that he is, too, and that both will benefit from trying to do something about it.

Even stronger is my hope that the book may lead to a rethinking of how a new generation raises its sons—and daughters. The reparative work that Michael and I have begun is hard work indeed. Starting at the beginning, with infants and children, will be less difficult.

I say "less difficult" rather than "easy" because the courage it will take to turn so many cultural assumptions on their head is great. But if, as I believe, the mother-son relationship is the single most profound agent for the maintenance of the gender-divided and increasingly gender-antagonistic system we live in, then we cannot forfeit the opportunity to change that system.

In our willingness to re-examine the premises of our parenting lies our hope for all future generations of mothers and fathers, sons and daughters.

SEVEN

What Do Women Want?
What Do Men Need?

> No, I don't know what's to be done about war. It's
> manliness; and manliness breeds womanliness—
> both so hateful.
>
> —VIRGINIA WOOLF
> *Letters,* vol. 6

So far as I know, only one of the recent multitude of books on the masculinity crisis (most of them written by men) makes any acknowledgment of the painfulness of the early break between mother and son, or recognizes it as a problem that will reverberate throughout a man's life. *In a Time of Fallen Heroes: The Re-Creation of Masculinity,* by R. William Betcher and William S. Pollack, is the exception. Under the heading "The Trauma of Every Boy's Life," the authors speak of "what it must feel like for a little boy to no longer be able to hold onto his mother. Surely," they say, "this societally enforced separation from the most cherished, admired, and loved person in his life must be felt as a terrible loss. All the more so because it occurs in a family context in which sisters are encouraged to remain connected to her. . . . Men's traumatic experience of abandonment, though not consciously remembered, forever casts a shadow on their relationships. It is a sadness that cannot be named, a sense of yearning without a clear object."

Having described this loss so eloquently, Betcher and Pollack might be expected to decry it, to call for mothers to refuse to sanction it so as not to consign their boys to what the authors themselves describe as "a sad and lonely existence." It's an existence in which men do not necessarily "seek out aloneness" but rather "need to believe they are alone, or at least not dependent or needful . . . in . . . a relationship"; an existence requiring that the women in their lives be ceaselessly wary "of setting off the tripwire of men's anxiety about losing their self-sufficiency." For while "a man's independence may be only a face-saving illusion in his own mind . . . it is an illusion he will go to great lengths to preserve." A perfect portrait of Rabbit Angstrom, in all his pathos!

But nowhere, in this or any other of the books on the male dilemma, is there a call for putting an end to the "trauma" that sets this dynamic in motion. No: who boys "need to become" requires a trade-off between independence (to which men "cling") and intimacy (which men flee). Though they have just succeeded brilliantly in anatomizing the process by which men come to locate their "center of gravity . . . within themselves," while women—those sisters whom little boys enviously observe remaining connected to their mothers—learn to locate their "center of gravity . . . *between* themselves and other people," these authors still maintain that the relational differences between men and women are necessary and inevitable. This is typical of most of the writing on masculinity.

The "essentialist project," as Australian psychotherapist Michael White describes this prevailing school of thought, is "preoccupied with the question of men's nature, and with attempts to determine global and unitary truths about the essence of 'masculinity'—so that men might uncover it, reclaim it, perform it, and live a life that is true to it (e.g., Bly and Keen)." "Essentialists" generally look to biology as the root of all gender differences. But aside from those of anatomy, these differences seem to amount to little more than greater verbal ability in girls, and greater math ability, visual/spatial ability, upper body strength, and predisposition to "rough and tumble play" as well as other forms of aggression in boys—all of which (with the exception of upper body strength) are almost certainly the product of environmental as well as biochemical, hormonal influences, and all of which (again with the exception of upper body strength, and the *possible* exception of aggression) are extremely small in magnitude in any case.

Surely these modest, in some cases probably nonexistent biological differences cannot be held accountable for our differing capacities for intimacy. Only the developmental paths we obediently tread can explain that distinction. It's time to question those paths, to alter the socialization process that sends boys and girls down such different ones.

Of course that means questioning the destination to which those paths lead, as well. But few have the courage to suggest that we reevaluate our expectations of what men must "become," or that men might look to women to learn something of what *they* seem to know about relationships, even though it's something that men need to know. Why not? Because, "Rightly or wrongly men have an inherent resistance to being 'one down' and will not . . . accept women as their teachers."

WOMEN AND OTHER HALF PEOPLE

> A man's ambition with a woman's heart—'tis an acursed lot.
>
> —MARGARET FULLER—writer, scholar, and teacher—
> speaking of her own fate in early Victorian America

The world needs more sweeping changes than those proposed in most of the books that have come out recently—chief among such changes an end to the one-upmanship between (and within) genders. Despite the illusions that both men and women continue to maintain, men are not "self-sufficient" or "self-made"; no man is "his own man"; and men can't simply decide to "redefine," "remake," or "re-create" themselves. Mothers have a great deal to do with the making of men—and so do fathers, grandparents, siblings, teachers, mentors, and peers, as well as the man himself. All are part of the "system," be it the larger system of society, the more intimate one of the family, or the intrapsychic one of the individual. And because all such systems are interactive, while it is true that mothers do much to make men, they are also made by them.

A woman's feelings, values, reasoning processes, and performance as a mother are largely conditioned by the male power structure she serves. The gender split she must promote as part of her service to that power structure will deprive her of attributes that are rightfully hers, just as surely as it deprives her sons. But since our culture rewards instrumental rather than relational qualities, doing rather than feeling, success rather than caring, from a practical point of view it is she—and her daughters—who will be the more disadvantaged.

In short, the culturally acceptable mother-son relationship is a double-edged sword, denying men a crucial aspect of their humanity (which has been the focus of this book) and degrading women by stigmatizing those qualities considered "feminine" (which has been the subtext).

Even given the gender inequities that still exist, however, the average woman of today is considerably more advantaged than Margaret Fuller, that most brilliant and privileged of nineteenth-century women. Indeed, she's more advantaged than the young Adrienne Rich, dreaming about the child she was carrying in the mid-fifties, more than a century later, and but a moment ago in our collective memory: "When I first became pregnant I set my heart on a son. . . . I wanted to give birth, at twenty-five, to my unborn self, the self that our father-centered family had suppressed in me, someone independent, actively willing, original. . . . If I wanted to give birth to myself as a male, it was because males seemed to inherit those qualities by right of gender."

"Independent, actively willing, original": The woman who longed for those qualities had at the age of twenty-five written two books of poetry, one published the year she graduated from college, the second in press as she awaited the birth of her first child. But she still perceived herself as an inferior half-being, lacking in those very qualities that she in truth had in abundance, and determined (as she later describes the person she was at that stage of her life) to obliterate them in any case, so that she would be a proper wife and mother, doing *"what women have always done."*

Thanks in large part to writers and activists like Rich herself, women have now gotten a bit of what men have always had—the chance to participate in the marketplace, to take part in public life, to achieve new levels of independence, autonomy, and power, to reclaim those qualities that for so long seemed the exclusive possession of males. Now it's time males were given access to the emotional gratifications females have always known. Neither "ambition" nor "heart" should be the sole possession of either gender, and neither accrues more "naturally" to one or the other.

Unfortunately, we still believe in the complementarity—and symmetry—of opposites. Masculinity in our culture is defined as the opposite of femininity. Its foundation is the expectation that boys separate from their mothers, and in so doing deny and reject any quality within themselves that is associated with femininity. The genders are not opposites, however. Even those who come down solidly on the side of nature in the nature-nurture debate have to concede this reality—and more and more they do (though generally only in the fine print).

Just as they are not opposites, the genders are certainly not symmetrical, or equal, in the divvying up of the qualities that have been allotted to them. The typically female concern with and sensitivity to relationships, for example, which we understand to be a natural outcome of the fact that girls are not required to endure an emotional cutoff from their mothers at an early age, may also be a function of women's place in the social hierarchy. Instead of being a gender difference it may be "a way of negotiating from a position of low power," "a need to please others that arises from [that] lack of power."

Conversely, strength is considered a masculine quality. In the workshops I do with women, I often ask them to list the major characteristics they would like to see in a man, and invariably strength is at the top of the list. "How do you define strength?" is the next question, which is always met with some confusion. Not physical strength, they say. After much discussion, we generally reach the conclusion that "strength" in a man is a buzz word for "not dependent," meaning someone who takes responsibility for himself, and can take care of others when called upon to do so. There's no point in begrudging men the quality of strength. They need it. As do women. We live in tough times. Is there anyone who seriously thinks that women do not need to be strong? Or that, in the face of the changing realities of late-twentieth-century economic and family life, they have not become strong?

Because of our mental habit of thinking in opposites, however, of defining masculinity as the obverse of all that is associated with femininity, we fear that if women become strong, men will become weak. In times of change—and ours is a time of great change, thanks to feminism, the end of the cold war, and, less positively, the constriction of the global economy in general, the decline of the middle class in particular—those who have the most to lose are most vulnerable to such fears. Middle-class males are surely, as a group, those who have the most to lose. Like Rabbit, when feeling threatened they are apt to construe anyone else's gain as their loss. Thus, newspaper accounts of the Ms. Foundation's "Take Our Daughters to Work Day" quoted boys as young as thirteen and fourteen who feared that this single day of exposure to the workplace would put girls one-up in the job search some years hence. "They may take over my job. . . . They will take over every job that is in the whole world in the future" was a typical response.

Adolescent would-be breadwinners already anxious over the future appear poised to do battle in the gender wars, but they're just the youngest carriers of the zeitgeist. So it's not surprising that during the year this book was being written, newspaper headlines give evidence of a striking increase in gender antagonism, a frightening escalation of the hostility that is inevitable in a culture that expects boys to identify themselves as masculine by virtue of not being feminine, then further compounds the damage by viewing success and power as the very hallmarks of masculinity. In such a context, and at a time when men are fearful that many of their avenues for success are being cut off, it becomes very difficult for men to have any sense of empathic identity with women. Women-as-objects—of anger, lust, envy, contempt, rape, and even murder—are all too often the result.

The latest entries in the annals of gender hostility have names like Tailhook, Glen Ridge, whirlpooling, Spur Posse. Spur Posse may be the highest profile of all. This is because a number of the nine teenage boys who were arrested on charges of molesting and raping girls as young as ten years old, along with several other members of the loose-knit group that made a practice of vying for "points" in an ongoing competition for sexual supremacy, saw fit to hit the talk-show trail. Catapulted into the national spotlight by the media, the boys from Lakewood, California, appeared on one television show after another, where they seemed to be not just lacking in remorse but actually indignant that such fine specimens as themselves, most of them star athletes, could be accused of rape. "We're a bunch of guys that are—I mean, better than decent-looking. We don't have to go out raping girls." Attempts to understand their astonishing indifference, even arrogance, tended to focus on the usual culprits— the collapse of morality in society at large, the degrading influence of popular culture, the lenience, even indulgence and approval of many of the boys' parents, the promiscuity of the girls involved, and the catchall "Boys will be boys."

But what happened in Lakewood cannot fully be understood until we look beyond these platitudes to the kind of socioeconomic context provided by Joan Didion in *The New Yorker.* Lakewood is in aerospace country—McDonnell Douglas country, Rockwell country, Hughes Aircraft country—just a short drive away from the huge naval station at Long Beach. This sector of the United States economy is being devastated, Didion explains, and with it the hopes of all the young boys who until recent years had every reason to believe their future would be as comfortable and secure as that of their parents. Once out of high school, many of them seem lost, directionless. What had he been doing since graduation, one Spur Posse boy was asked by a *New York Times* reporter: " 'Partying,' he mumbled. 'Playing ball.' "

Perhaps no one expresses this sense of loss better than Dana Belman, the twenty-year-old credited with having founded the Spur Posse, who at the time of this writing is awaiting trial on unrelated charges of "stealing guns, credit cards and jewelry and trying to run over several girls with a pick-up truck." A 1991 graduate of Lakewood High, a champion wrestler named Performer of the Year by the Lakewood Youth Sports Hall of Fame, Dana is quoted by his mother as saying, "I want to be in the ninth grade again, and I want to do everything differently. I had it all. I was Mr. Lakewood. I was a star. I was popular. As soon as I graduated, I lost the recognition. I want to go back to the wonderful days. Now it's one disaster after another." This is the boy whose father proudly described him and his two brothers (one of whom was briefly in jail in the wake of the Spur Posse arrests) as "virile specimens."

Rabbit Angstrom was a lower-middle-class white boy, without much in the way of an education or any particular talent off the basketball court. But he had the good fortune to come of age in the fifties, when the economy was booming. Dana, a boy with a similar history of adulation in the sports arena, and presumably similar hopes and similar values, has no such luck.

In a culture that believes, as psychologist Joseph Pleck puts it, that "the fundamental problem of individual psychological development is establishing a sex role identity," a culture that views success and power as the touchstones for male identity, how is a boy like Dana to prove his masculinity? By sexual exploitation of women? By outlawry? Pleck, who has done some of the pioneering work in re-thinking sex roles and challenging the prevailing ideology, explains that our culture views "sex role identity [as] the extremely fragile outcome of a highly risky developmental process, especially for the male." And no wonder! As we have defined the male sex role, especially in its emphasis on winning and one-upmanship, it *is* an elusive outcome, to which many males in our society, through no fault of their own, will have little hope of access.

Until we are willing to question many of the specifics of the male sex role, including most of the seven norms and stereotypes that psychologist Ronald Levant names in a listing of its chief constituents—"avoiding femininity, restrictive emotionality, seeking achievement and status, self-reliance, aggression, homophobia, and non-relational attitudes toward sexuality"—we are going to continue to deny men their full humanity. Indeed, until we are willing to question the very idea of a male sex role, one that draws lines between appropriately male and appropriately female behaviors, we will be denying both men *and* women their full humanity.

BACK TO THE KITCHEN?

Women in their role as mothers are crucial to the necessary revisioning of society. So are men. Men can and should—and some of them do—change diapers, get up for middle-of-the-night feedings, prepare family meals, take the kids on weekend outings, help out with homework, coach Little League, lead Scout troops, and perform myriad other instrumental tasks that help to relieve women of the overwhelming burdens of childrearing in a society where the nuclear family is pretty much unsupported by the culture at large. There are some statistical indications (though they are far from clear cut) that more men, especially younger men, are becoming willing to pitch in, to do their share. In a society where women "worked roughly fifteen hours longer each week than men," for a total, over the year, of *"an extra month of twenty-four-hour days"* according to sociologist Arlie Hochschild, we can only hope that such men become the rule, not the exception.

It is, of course, ideal if fathers can go beyond those instrumental tasks and forge deep emotional bonds with their sons (as well as their daughters). But many of them can't, because in the process of becoming "masculine," they have been required to shut down emotionally, to deny the "feminine" qualities of empathy and connectedness that would make that possible. Men who have cut off their own feelings for decades are often incapable of doing the emotional work required.

The reality is that men were not raised for empathic parenting. If we tell women that they can't raise sons without a man, or that they must step aside at a certain point in their sons' development so that the boys' fathers become the dominant influence, then many of those boys will be, for all intents and purposes, parentless. Or worse: believing any man is better than none, women may stay with men who are abusive. As Michael White says, he has interviewed "many men whose fathers hadn't run out on their families who wished that their fathers had."

Of course, with so many men absent from their families, for complex reasons that have been only sketchily suggested here, some women don't have any choice about whether to turn their boys over to the man in the house. He's gone, and the avalanche of literature on the importance of a father to his sons, much of it written with the intention of luring men home, will not bring him back. It will, however, act to disempower women and thus to deprive their sons of the effective parenting they need.

So is the responsibility for nonsexist rearing of sons just one more burden for mothers to bear? I think women are and will continue to be burdened until they cease raising male children who in later life neglect, abuse, undermine, patronize, and look down on them. To raise sons who grow up to respect and love women—their mothers, their sisters, their wives, and their daughters—is not a burden.

Such boys will be genuinely equal partners in childrearing when the time comes; they will be the ones who make the terms "mothering" and "fathering" anachronistic, who will enable us to retire those words in favor of "parenting." "Parenting" is something that any caring person of either gender and any sexual persuasion can do. If there are two people—or more—doing it, whether it's a man and woman, two women, two men, or any conceivable combination of loving, competent adults who are passionately committed to the well-being of the child, so much the better for the child as well as for those who are taking care of him or her.

Perhaps this book will be interpreted as just another call for women to return to the old order, in which they were the arbiters of family life. But in fact women have never been the arbiters of family life, the creators of family values. They were and are agents of the system they live in, dedicated to creating the kind of men who it was thought would serve that system well. Now they must become agents of their own values, drawing up their own agenda. To do this does not mean trying to turn the clock backward to some imaginary idyllic time when men went out into the world and women stayed home with the children; it means committing oneself to the idea of a world in which gender does not separate people from one another, or from parts of themselves. It means honoring the potential for wholeness in each of us.

LOOKING TO THE FUTURE

What the world needs now is a different kind of man, what I've called in my title a "good" man, as opposed to the new man, who's not very new (or at least not very different), the soft man, the wild man, or any of the other masculine ideals currently being auditioned in our culture. The good man, like the good woman, will be empathic and strong, autonomous and connected, responsible to self, to family and friends, and to society, and capable of understanding how those responsibilities are, ultimately, inseparable.

However, we're afraid for our male children when they have too much tenderness or concern for others because we assume nobody but our kid has those qualities. "My wife . . . talks about raising our son or daughter in a nonviolent, nonsexist way," one man writes. "And who could argue that this wouldn't be the best of all possible worlds? But until I see it, I'm holding out the possibility that the world is going to continue in its dog-pack, Wild West show, high-sticking ways."

Similarly, when I do workshops, many women in the audience object: "But if I were to raise my son as you suggest, how would he survive?" The answer is: our men aren't surviving very well! We send them to war at eighteen to kill and be killed. They're lying down in the middle of highways to prove their manhood in imitation of a scene in a recent movie about college football. They're dying of heart attacks in early middle age, killing themselves with liver and lung disease via the manly pursuits of drinking and smoking, committing suicide at roughly four times the rate of women, becoming victims of homicide (generally at the hands of other men) three times as often as women, and therefore living about eight years less than women (though at the turn of the century the difference was only about two years, and in the nineteenth century men outlived women).

Will men pay a price if they cease to focus so exclusively on issues of success and dominance, if they learn the pleasures of empathy and connectedness, if they take their full share of responsibility for the physical as well as the emotional well-being of their children? Yes, they probably will. While they will almost certainly have fuller, healthier, happier, longer lives, there's no guarantee they won't lose something in the way of status, money, power, and privilege. It's just that what they stand to gain is worth so much more.

Of course it's not only the happiness and survival of individual men that are at stake. There's also the question of whether the world can survive a continuing struggle over the perks of masculinity. The world we now live in, embroiled in hideous nationalist and religious wars at best, teetering on the brink of nuclear annihilation at worst, is the product of cultures that believe that to be "masculine" is to dominate, to be a woman is to be less than fully human (beliefs that may help to explain the all but incomprehensible use of rape as a weapon of war). The world we now live in, where AIDS researchers from two countries spent their energies arguing about who discovered the virus instead of joining forces to defeat it, is a world that believes in competition, not cooperation. But the solitary hero who works alone in a little laboratory and makes great discoveries is not a hero for our time. Neither is the warrior or the junk bond king.

Our discoveries, our progress, and our survival demand that we make changes in our most fundamental beliefs about ourselves, including our ideas about the mother-son relationship. This is the relationship that Freud, speaking no doubt from the point of view of an adored and coddled son, described as "altogether the most perfect, the most free from ambivalence of all human relationships." I, on the other hand, would ask if it is possible to have a more ambivalent human relationship than that of a mother and son in our society.

As charged with ambivalence as that relationship is, it is also a relationship that offers us one of our greatest hopes for transforming ourselves and the world we live in—if we will but have the courage to make the necessary changes.

A Note from
the Author's Son

In 1990, at the age of forty-five, I found myself facing cardiac bypass surgery. I had just accepted a new job, which would involve a cross-country move, a substantial career change, and considerable high-pressure responsibility. On top of that, our son had recently departed for college in another city. Instead of acknowledging my limits in the face of such a combination of major life changes I decided to press ahead, making plans to move to the new city and job within weeks of surgery. It was a mistake. Not fully recuperated from surgery, I found the demands of my new surroundings and responsibilities overwhelming. Struggling with a sense of lost capacity, self-esteem, and confidence, I would not regain my equilibrium for many months.

Recently my mother explained to me that though she had believed I was heading for certain trouble by taking on so much at such a difficult time, she nonetheless kept silent. She had wanted to talk with me, to warn me, yet felt unable to approach me with her feelings and concerns. The emotional distance that had grown between us was too great to bridge even in a crisis. As a result, I lost out on opportunities for family support and closeness that would have helped sustain me in a time of trouble. My mother's rationale, that I needed to make my own decisions and that I would see her concern as unwanted interference, was based in the established patterns of our relationship. She was right in believing that I would almost certainly have stiffened at her approach, rather than expose any weakness or distress.

Over the past couple of years the roots of this distance between myself and my mother have been slowly coming into focus for me, along with an understanding that the consequent losses of family bonds and intimacy have taken a toll. It has been the shared experience of this book—my mother writing and me reading chapter by chapter, both of us remembering—which in large measure has unlocked a door to these lost connections. Our conversations about the book, at first formal and strained, have become increasingly comfortable and satisfying. We have some distance to travel, but we have begun to move closer.

This book captures so much of my own experience that it has jarred my understanding of important events in my life. This is true despite the fact that my perceptions and memories of certain situations are different from my mother's. She remembers withdrawing from me and characterizes the attic room of my teenage years as "exile," while I remember my own active distancing behavior and recall that room as sanctuary. On the other hand, when she draws from her bank of therapeutic memories the general conclusion that many boys "not only accepted but encouraged this distancing," I see clearly the shadows of our own relationship.

While this book has unique meanings for me, I believe it touches universal notes that will be useful to others. The notion that men who have lost touch with their mothers have lost touch with parts of themselves is a powerful one—powerful enough to provoke change. I am proud that my mother has had the courage to open these issues for me and herself, and for other mothers and their sons.

—Michael Silverstein
Olympia, Washington

Notes

vii "What do we fear?": Adrienne Rich, *Of Women Born* (New York: Bantam Books, 1977), p. 204.

ONE: CAUTIONARY TALES: FOR MOTHERS OF SONS
AGES ONE TO SIX

3 25 percent of our children: 1991 Census Bureau report, cited in *New York Times*, October 5, 1992. Women headed up 22 percent of those households, men 3 percent.

3 as it is in most people's: Frank Pittman, M.D., *New Woman*, September 1992, p. 47.

5 "Morel said": D. H. Lawrence, *Sons and Lovers* (New York: Penguin Books, 1948; originally published 1913), p. 24.

10 "he who mounts": Aeschylus, *Oresteia*, trans. Richmond Lattimore (Chicago: University of Chicago Press, 1953), p. 158.

12 to offer his sister: See Bruno Bettelheim's *The Uses of Enchantment* (New York: Random House, 1976) for interesting interpretations of fairy tales, and the psychological uses to which children put them.

14 two-thirds . . . in 1991: Tamar Lewin, "Rise in Single Parenthood Is Reshaping U.S.," *New York Times*, October 5, 1992.

16 by other males: David Cohen, ed., *The Circle of Life: Rituals from the Human Family Album* (San Francisco: Harper San Francisco,

1991). See p. 18 regarding Mormon ceremony; p. 38 regarding Jewish haircutting ceremony.

20 Despite his understanding: "A boy's mother is the first object of his love, and she remains so too during the formation of his Oedipus complex and, in essence, all through his life." Sigmund Freud, *New Introductory Lectures on Psychoanalysis,* in *Standard Edition of the Complete Psychological Works of Sigmund Freud,* ed. and trans. by James Strachey (New York: W. W. Norton, 1965), vol. 22, p. 104. Originally published 1933.

20 "man's relation to his father": Sigmund Freud, *Totem and Taboo,* 1913, in *Standard Edition of the Complete Psychological Works of Sigmund Freud,* ed. and trans. by James Strachey (New York: W. W. Norton, 1976), vol. 13, pp. 156–57. Originally published 1913.

20 the mother-centered home: During the colonial period of the United States, for example, "the father [was] the dominant figure in the family, yet by the 1830s he was secondary in the household." E. Anthony Rotundo, *American Manhood: Transformations in Masculinity from the Revolution to the Modern Era* (New York: Basic Books, 1993). Quite a change from the preceding century, when men were so central to the family that child-care manuals were commonly addressed to fathers. See also John Demos, "The Changing Faces of Fatherhood: A New Exploration in American Family History, in Stanley H. Cath, Alan R. Gurwitt, John Munder Ross, eds., *Father and Child: Developmental and Clinical Perspectives* (Boston: Little, Brown, 1982), pp. 425–45. Demos, too, remarks on the change that occurred in the early decades of the nineteenth century, when the advice books on childrearing began to be addressed to women, because "Mother was now the primary parent" (p. 431).

20 "to copulate with his mother": Paul Olsen, *Sons and Mothers: Why Men Behave as They Do* (New York: M. Evans, 1981), p. 59.

20 mother was not the prime actor: See George F. Mahl, "Father-Son Themes in Freud's Self-Analysis," in Stanley H. Cath, M.D., Alan R. Gurwitt, M.D., and John Munder Ross, Ph.D., eds., *Father and Child: Developmental and Clinical Perspectives* (Boston: Little, Brown, 1982), p. 62: "The developmental psychology that Freud elaborated . . . was predominantly a 'son psychology,' and to a large extent a father-son psychology. . . . Indications of Freud's great interest in the psychology of the father-son relationship are that (1) the major case histories he wrote after 1901 were all about sons (Little Hans, the Rat

Man, and Schreber . . . and (2) in those case histories the treatment of the father-son relationship greatly overshadowed that of the mother-son relationship."

21 Previously the goal: See Daniel Beekman, *The Mechanical Baby* (New York: Meridian, 1978) for a review of 500 years of ever-changing advice to parents on child care.

22 into Mother's lap: See Miriam M. Johnson, *Strong Mothers, Weak Wives: The Search for Gender Equality* (Berkeley: University of California Press, 1988), pp. 73ff, for a discussion of the shift from Freud's emphasis on the father and the Oedipal period to the new emphasis—by Jones, Klein, and Horney—on mother and the pre-Oedipal period.

22 a 1943 book: *Maternal Overprotection* is cited in the chapter on "Motherhood as Pathology" in Barbara Ehrenreich and Deirdre English's book *For Her Own Good: 150 Years of the Experts' Advice to Women*, which is an excellent description of the assault on mothers and motherhood (New York: Anchor Books, 1979, 1989). See also *The Feminine Mystique*, by Betty Friedan (New York: Laurel, 1984, originally published 1963) which discusses the phenomenon of mother blaming in "The Mistaken Choice," chapter 8.

23 not being too "permissive and affectionate": Benjamin Spock, M.D., and Michael B. Rothenberg, M.D., *Dr. Spock's Baby and Child Care* (New York: Pocket Books, 1985), p. 437. Beginning with the 1976 edition, fathers were urged to take on "half or more of the management of the children" during their weekend and after work hours, although the assumption still seemed to be that women were home full-time, p. 54.

23 a review of the relevant journals: P. J. Caplan and I. Hall-McCorquodale, "Mother Blaming in Major Clinical Journals," *American Journal of Orthopsychiatry* 55 (3) (July 1985): 345–53.

24 one commentator: Carole Klein, *Mothers and Sons* (Boston: Houghton Mifflin Company, 1984), p. 78.

24 "potency" he felt his father did not have: Philip Roth, *Portnoy's Complaint* (New York: Random House, 1969). Passages quoted appear on pp. 11–12, 274, ix (epigraph), 51, respectively.

26 "risk the other person": D. H. Lawrence, *Sons and Lovers* (New York: Penguin Books, 1948; originally published 1913). Passages cited are from pp. 261–62, 428–29, 341.

27 "left to my nurse": Edmund White, *A Boy's Own Story* (New York: E. P. Dutton, 1982), pp. 172–73, 71, respectively.

29 "more delicate": Jeffrey Z. Rubin, Frank J. Provenzano, and Zella Luria, "The Eye of the Beholder: Parents' Views on Sex of Newborns," *American Journal of Orthopsychiatry* 44 (4) (July 1974). Interestingly enough, the fathers were more extreme in their ratings of the differences than the mothers were. A few of the many other studies demonstrating these gender-based distinctions in parents' behavior are H. A. Moss, "Early Sex Differences and Mother-Infant Interaction," in R. C. Friedman, R. M. Richart, and R. L. Vande Wiele, eds., *Sex Differences in Behavior* (New York: John Wiley, 1974); Jean Berko Gleason, Rivka Y. Perlman, Richard Ely, and David W. Evans, "The Babytalk Register: Parents' Use of Diminutives," in J. L. Sokolov, C. E. Snow, eds., *The Handbook of Research in Language Development Using CHILDES* (Hillsdale, N.J.: Lawrence Erlbaum Assoc., 1993); Caroline Smith and Barbara Lloyd, "Maternal Behavior and Perceived Sex of Infant: Revisited," *Child Development* 46 (1978): 849–56, reporting a study in which mothers of infants were asked to play with a six-month-old baby they did not know. Some were told the baby was a boy, others a girl, and the manner of play followed accordingly. See also Jeanne Brooks Gunn and Wendy Schempp Matthews, *He & She: How Children Develop Their Sex-Role Identity* (Englewood Cliffs, N.J.: Prentice Hall, 1979), for a more complete review of the literature on this subject.

29 "reality-defining": John Condry and Sandra Condry, "Sex Differences: A Study of the Eye of the Beholder," *Child Development* 47 (1976): 812–19.

30 It was Talcott Parsons: The instrumental/expressive division between father and mother was described in *The Social System* (and other writings by Talcott Parsons) (Glencoe, Ill.: Free Press of Glencoe, 1951). We are still very much under the sway of these ideas, which long predated Parsons.

30 asked for a doll: Benjamin Spock, M.D., *Dr. Spock's Baby and Child Care*, rev. and updated ed. (New York: Pocket Books, 1985), p. 47.

31 Soon he responds in kind: When I first wrote this description of the breaking of the gaze between mother and infant son, I had not read *In a Time of Fallen Heroes*, by William Betcher, M.D., Ph.D., and William Pollack, Ph.D. (New York: Atheneum, 1993). They allude on pp. 35–36 to an article by Doris K. Silverman, "What Are Little Girls Made Of?," *Psychoanalytic Psychology* 4 (1987): 315–34, in which she reviews research on infants that she (and they) believes supports the idea that girl babies, being for various neurophysiological reasons calmer and more alert than boy babies, and in particular better able to sustain and return the gaze of their mothers, are thus better able to bond with their mothers and develop social skills. Perhaps we will never be able to say for sure who withdraws first, but this kind of research finding seems to me to display the bias our culture invariably has toward seeing males (even tiny infants) as active agents (usually of withdrawal) and females (especially mothers of sons) as passive objects—the "doing" versus the "done-to." Whenever possible, we like to put science—anatomy, biology, biochemistry, neurophysiology, and so forth—at the service of this view.

Two: Hero Tales: For Boys Ages Six to Twelve

38 highest-grossing comedy: *Variety*, January 11, 1993, p. 84.

40 "the work-home dichotomy": John Demos, "The Changing Faces of Fatherhood: A New Exploration in American Family History," in Stanley H. Cath, M.D., Alan R. Gurwitt, M.D., and John Munder Ross, Ph.D., eds. *Father and Child: Developmental and Clinical Perspectives* (Boston: Little, Brown and Company, 1982), p. 442.

41 Males over the age of five or six: See Daniel Beekman, *The Mechanical Baby: A Popular History of Writings on the Theory and Practice of Child Care* (New York: New American Library, 1977). See also Joseph F. Kett, *Rites of Passage: Adolescence in America 1790 to the Present*, especially pp. 11–29, for a discussion of how concepts of infancy and adolescence have changed over the ages.

45 one of the most extraordinary things: Deborah Tannen, Ph.D., *You Just Don't Understand: Women and Men in Conversation* (New York: Ballantine Books, 1991), pp. 245–54.

46 "Hey Myrna!": Stephen J. Bergman, M.D., Ph.D., "Men's Psychological Development: A Relational Perspective," presented at a Stone Center Colloquium on November 7, 1990.

46 "Don't need her": Eric E. McCollum, "You Never Forget How to Ride a Bicycle: Men Finding Their Mothers," in Michele Bograd, ed., *Feminist Approaches for Men in Therapy* (Binghamton, N.Y.: The Haworth Press, Inc., 1991).

46 "We were the boys": Tommy Hilfiger ad, *The New York Times Magazine*, Part 2, *Men's Fashions of the Times*, September 13, 1992.

47 our bad boys: Talcott Parsons, in *Essays in Sociological Theory: Patterns of Aggression in the Western World*, rev. ed. (New York: The Free Press, 1954). See pp. 303–22 especially. Parsons sees the "bad boy" pattern as being caused by males having to achieve their masculinity not so much by identifying with Father, who is generally absent, but by disidentifying with or differentiating from Mother, who represents femininity and "goodness" (p. 305). Parsons calls this a "defense against a feminine identification," a "reaction formation" (p. 305). As a product of her culture, the mother often colludes in this behavioral pattern: she "admires such behavior and, particularly when it is combined with winning qualities in other respects, rewards it with her love" (p. 306).

51 "Ancient Maternal Betrayal": the phrase is taken from Jane Lazarre, *On Loving Men* (New York: Dial Press, 1978, 1980), p. 157.

51 "every day of their lives": Adrienne Rich, *Of Woman Born* (New York: Bantam Books, 1977), pp. 204ff.

52 "I know how to compromise": Judith Arcana, *Every Mother's Son: The Role of Mothers in the Making of Men* (New York: Anchor Press, 1983), pp. 288–89.

52 "feminize her son": Lazarre, *On Loving Men*, pp. 156–57.

53 A salutary tale: Munro Leaf, *Ferdinand the Bull* (New York: Viking Books, 1936).

54 "dominate or be dominated": Audre Lorde, "Manchild: A Black Lesbian Feminist's Response," in *Sister Outsider* (Freedom, Calif.: The Crossing Press, 1984), pp. 75, 76.

55 "nature" is winning . . . over "nurture": See Christine Gorman, "Sizing Up the Sexes," *Time*, January 20, 1992, for the typical presentation of the nature-versus-nurture evidence; for an alternative summation of the research, with considerably more emphasis on environmental influences, and on the ability of human beings (as opposed to lower life forms) to alter their behavior, see Laura Shapiro, "Guns and Dolls: Scientists Explore the Differences Between Girls and Boys, *Newsweek*, May 28, 1990.

58 $1.1 million for the script: Bernard Weinraub, *New York Times*, March 9, 1992, p. C11.

Three: The Myth of the Male Role Model,
and Other Tales for Changing Times

75 "the courage of women": Adrienne Rich, *Of Woman Born* (New York: Bantam Books, 1977), p. 215.

76 Does he take after: Same Howe Verhovek, "Hold a Baby or Hold That Line?," *New York Times*, October 20, 1993, p. 1. Michael de Courcy Hinds, "Not Like the Movies: A Dare Leads to Death," *New York Times*, October 19, 1993, p. 1.

78 hero tales become extremely important: See Ronald F. Levant, "Toward the Reconstruction of Masculinity," Special Issue of *Journal of Family Psychology* 5 (3, 4) (1992), for a discussion of the relationship between the mythopoetic men's movement and current confusions about gender role. "The mythopoetic approach is an attempt to deal with the complexities of the post-modern world by returning to the pre-modern, pre-industrial age," he says. See also E. Anthony Rotundo's *American Manhood: Transformations in Masculinity from the Revolution to the Modern Era* (New York: Basic Books, 1993) for a discussion of the parallels between Bly's mythopoetic movement, with its embrace of rites and rituals from tribal cultures, and the turn-of-the-century "masculinist" movement, in which the use of such rituals was evident in the Boy Scouts, in the practices of men's fraternal organizations, and so forth. That both movements took place at a time of fundamental uncertainty about men's role in society, when men were feeling insecure and threatened, is probably not coincidental.

79 fourth-highest-grossing . . . number one: *Time*, June 28, 1993, p. 64.

80 "In the post–cold war world": Frank Rich, "Term Limit for the Man of Steel," *New York Times*, Arts and Leisure section, November 15, 1992.

81 return to life: Bill McTernan, "Another Superhero Goes Down," *Newsday*, June 5, 1993, part 2, p. 26. There were actually four would-be successors who made their debuts in April 1993, one of whom would be revealed as the resurrected Superman later in 1993.

81 "Men today consume": Mark Gerzon, *A Choice of Heroes: The Changing Face of American Manhood* (Boston: Houghton Mifflin Company, 1982), p. 5.

81 "To be honest": Quoted in Holly Brubach, "Musclebound," *The New Yorker*, January 11, 1993, p. 32.

81 Pop culture has responded: See Myriam Miedzian, *Boys Will Be Boys: Breaking the Link Between Masculinity and Violence* (New York: Doubleday, 1991), especially chapters 12, 13, 14, and 15, for a description of the escalating violence in male-consumed media.

81 in 1991 it was 28.9 percent: Susan Chira, "New Realities Fight Old Images of Mother," *New York Times*, October 4, 1992; figures based on Bureau of Labor and Census Bureau statistics.

82 recent newspaper headlines: Paul Taylor, "Missing Dads," *Atlanta Journal/Atlanta Constitution*, June 21, 1992; Nina J. Easton, "Life Without Father," *Los Angeles Times Magazine*, June 14, 1992; Marcia Slacum Greene, "Mothers, Sons Going It Alone," *Washington Post*, July 19, 1992; Tamar Lewin, "Rise in Single Parenthood Is Reshaping U.S.," second in a series, "Going It Alone," *New York Times*, October 5, 1992.

82 "Almost half of all female-headed families": Lewin, "Rise in Single Parenthood Is Reshaping U.S."

82 children under age six: C. M. Johnson et al., *Child Poverty in America* (Washington, D.C.: Children's Defense Fund, 1991).

83 children . . . do better . . . when there are two parents: Hundreds of studies concerning the disastrous effect of father absence on the psychosocial development of children seem to indicate a national catastrophe. See, for example, the studies cited in Michael E. Lamb, "Fathers and Child Development: An Integrative Overview," Henry B. Biller, "The Father and Sex Role Development," Norma Radin, "The Role of the Father in Cognitive, Academic, and Intellectual Development," Henry B. Biller, "Father Absence, Divorce, and Personality Development," and—for a contrarian view, suggesting that "fathers are far less important than mothers as . . . agents of moral socialization" (p. 375)—Martin L. Hoffman, "The Role of the Father in Moral Internalization," in Michael E. Lamb, ed., *The Role of the Father in Child Development* (New York: John Wiley & Sons, 1981, 2nd ed.). All but the last of these articles suggest that father absence is detrimental, not just because two people are better than one in the raising of a family but because fathers contribute something that mothers cannot due to differences of gender; and all draw support for their conclusions from the evidence of dozens, even hundreds, of studies, which are amply cited in their footnotes. As even the editor of the book concedes, however, "Where research has been done on nontraditional families (e.g., on father absence and maternal employment), it is plagued by . . . poor measurement and methodological inadequacy" (p. 33).

We cannot accept these studies at face value, for they do not adequately distinguish the effects of poverty, and of single mothers who are lonely and overworked, from the effects of father absence. Before we can come to conclusions about father absence, we need a much fuller understanding of the complex interactions among the determinants of psychological development; we need studies of children raised by two same-sex givers; and we need studies of children raised by one competent, financially stable person. Though studies of children of single mothers show that these children have a higher incidence of academic and emotional problems, it is impossible to evaluate those studies because they do not separate out the factors of poverty and immaturity from fatherlessness. To date, according to Carol Lawson, in "Single But Mothers by Choice" (*New York Times*, August 5, 1993, p. C9), "there have been no long-term studies of children with single mothers who are mature and financially stable."

83 "Who was going to show my son," "Fathers protect," "politically correct," "must bond with a man": The first two quotes are from *The Washington Post* and *The Atlanta Journal*, respectively. The Frank Pittman quotes are from *The Washington Post* and from *New Woman*, September 1992, p. 47, respectively.

85 "The male child develops": Joseph H. Pleck, *The Myth of Masculinity* (Cambridge, Mass.: The MIT Press, 1981), p. 53. See also Gerald I. Fogel, Frederick M. Lane, and Robert S. Liebert, eds., *The Psychology of Men: New Psychoanalytic Perspectives* (New York: Basic Books, 1986), introduction by Gerald Fogel, pp. 6–7, whose abbreviated summary of Freud's scenario for male sexual identity formation is as follows: "[T]he phallic-oedipal phase . . . is characterized in the boy by a wish to obtain exclusive sexual possession of the mother by defeating and eliminating the father. Under the threat of castration by his powerful, forbidding rival, the little boy renounces his incestuous infantile claims and solves his dilemma by identifying with the father, who is internalized as the psychic agency of the superego."

85 Boys identify with the aggressor: Nancy Chodorow summarizes Freudian Oedipal theory in carrot/stick terms: With the threat of castration as the stick, the carrot is "identification with his father, and the superiority of masculine identification and prerogatives over feminine," in *The Reproduction of Mothering: Psychoanalysis and the Sociology of Gender* (Berkeley: University of California Press, 1978), p. 94.

86   There is very little in the . . . literature: For a review of the psychological literature on father-son similarities, see Pleck, *The Myth of
Masculinity*, chapter 4, "The Acquisition of Sex-Typing."

86   before the Oedipal stage: John Money and Anke A. Ehrhardt,
Man and Woman, Boy and Girl (Baltimore: Johns Hopkins University
Press, 1972). Cited in Miriam M. Johnson's *Strong Mothers, Weak
Wives: The Search for Gender Equality* (Berkeley: University of Califor-
nia Press, 1988): They "have concluded on the basis of their work with
children with ambiguous genitalia that gender identity, the gut level
conviction that one is a male or female, is formed early, before eighteen
months, and therefore probably prior to the Oedipal period when
Freud thought gender differentiation occurred" (p. 196). See also Joseph H. Pleck and Jack Sawyer, eds., *Men and Masculinity* (Englewood
Cliffs, N.J.: Prentice Hall, 1974), for "The Myth of the Masculine
Mystique," Gloria Steinem, p. 135. "According to the California Gender Identity center . . . it is easier to surgically change the sex of a
young male wrongly brought up as a female, than it is to change his
cultural conditioning."

86   many studies of homosexual and lesbian parents: Daniel
Goleman, "Studies Find No Disadvantage in Growing Up in a Gay
Home," *New York Times*, December 2, 1992. See also Charlotte J.
Patterson, "Children of Lesbian and Gay Parents," in *Child Development* 63 (5) (October 1992): 1025–39, for a review of three dozen
studies showing that when children raised by homosexuals were compared with those raised by heterosexuals, there was "no evidence to
suggest that psychosocial development" among the former was in any
way compromised, or that they were "disadvantaged in any significant
respect" (p. 1036). See J. M. Reinisch, *The Kinsey Institute New Report
on Sex* (New York: St. Martin's Press, 1990).

87   10 million households: Marcia Slacum Greene, "Mothers, Sons
Going It Alone," *Washington Post*, July 19, 1992, p. A20.

94   "BIG men": Jeffrey P. Hantover, "The Boy Scouts and the Validation of Masculinity," in Elizabeth H. and Joseph H. Pleck, eds., *The
American Man* (Englewood Cliffs, N.J.: Prentice Hall, 1980), p. 296.

94   a favorable ruling: Jay Mathews, "Boy Scouts Allow Women
Troop Leaders," *Washington Post*, February 14, 1988, A16.

94   Bryan Archimbaud: James Dao, "Master Is a Woman," *New
York Times*, October 31, 1992. The statistics on female scoutmasters
and Scout membership are also from that story.

95 being "the arbiters of the child's acceptability,": Sara Ruddick makes this point in *Maternal Thinking: Toward a Politics of Peace* (New York: Ballantine, 1989), p. 42.

101 Even if he is . . . remote": As Bly told Jill Johnston, "I stopped regarding him as a peculiarly rejecting father—it was just a father." Jill Johnston, "Why Iron John Is No Gift to Women," *New York Times Book Review*, February 23, 1992.

101 "bad example": James Hillman, "Fathers and Sons," in James Hillman, *Blue Fire: Selected Writings* (New York: Harper & Row, 1989), pp. 220–21.

102 perversely unrealistic two-thirds: Susan Faludi, *Backlash: The Undeclared War on American Women* (New York: Crown, 1991), p. 142, citing Sally Steenland, *Women Out of View: An Analysis of Female Characters on 1987–1988 TV Programs*, Washington, D.C., report by National Commission on Working Women, November 1987, p. 6.

103 "space for them all": J. M. Barrie, *Peter Pan* (New York: Bantam Books, 1985). Quotes are from pp. 59, 105, 106, and 158 respectively.

FOUR: THE ADOLESCENT YEARS: ESTABLISHING—AND ENFORCING—MASCULINITY

107 "If . . .": *Kipling's Complete Verse: Definitive Edition* (New York: Anchor Press, 1989), p. 578.

108 mother-son incest: Statistics regarding sexual abuse vary widely from study to study. A recent book summarizing and interpreting the various studies concludes: "Our review of both the evidence and the arguments suggests that there appear to be no sound reasons to believe that we have been wrong in presuming the amount of sexual abuse by adult female perpetrators to be small. There is every reason to believe that child sexual abuse is primarily perpetrated by males and that male perpetrators may be responsible for more serious and traumatic levels of sexual abuse than female perpetrators." David Finkelhor and Diana Russell, "Women as Perpetrators," in David Finkelhor, *Child Sexual Abuse: New Theory & Research* (New York: The Free Press, 1984). Apropos of the fear of awakening incestuous impulses (in either mother or son) when a boy reaches adolescence, see also "Boys as Victims" chapter, pp. 165, 170, regarding the age of boys who were victims of sexual abuse by mothers. The median age was about eight, versus thirteen and a half for girls in cases of father-daughter abuse.

119 "alexithymia": Ronald F. Levant, "Toward the Reconstruction of Masculinity," in special issue of *Journal of Family Psychology* 5 (3, 4) (1992): 379–402. In his discussion of alexithymia, Levant cites a paper by H. Krystal, "Alexithymia and the Effectiveness of Psychoanalytic Treatment," *International Journal of Psychoanalytic Psychotherapy* 9: 353–78.

120 "strewn with the wreckage of . . . morals": Granville Stanley Hall, *Adolescence: Its Psychology and Its Relations to Physiology, Anthropology, Sociology, Sex, Crime, Religion and Education* (New York: D. Appleton and Company, 1904), vol. 1, xiv–xv.

120 "To be normal": Anna Freud, "Adolescence," *Psychoanalytic Study of the Child* 13 (1958): 255–78. As summed up in one of the books written by the many researchers (like Daniel Offer, Anne C. Petersen, Elizabeth A. Douvan, and Joseph Adelson) who now challenge this view, turmoil theory sees the adolescent "as needing to go through . . . crisis in order to separate from his parents and develop his own identity. If he does not . . . he cannot, by definition, grow into a mentally healthy, mature adult." Daniel Offer, Eric Ostrov, and Kenneth I. Howard, *The Adolescent: A Psychological Self-Portrait* (New York: Basic Books, 1981), p. 84.

120 test their mettle: For a revisionist view of adolescence, which contests the idea that it must inevitably be a period of *Sturm und Drang,* see books by Daniel Offer and his various coauthors, among them Daniel Offer, Eric Ostrov, and Kenneth I. Howard, *The Adolescent: A Psychological Self-Portrait* (New York: Basic Books, 1981); see also David G. Oldham, "Adolescent Turmoil: A Myth Revisited," in *Adolescent Psychiatry*, vol. 6 (Chicago: University of Chicago Press, 1978), pp. 266–79.

121 "Boys of seventeen": Rosellen Brown, *Before and After* (New York: Farrar, Straus & Giroux, 1992), p. 31.

121 male sexuality is . . . aggressive: Sociobiologists like Richard Dawkins and Edward O. Wilson, in books like *The Selfish Gene* and *On Human Nature,* have done a lot to spread the gospel of male sexual aggression as biologically determined—as the male means of ensuring that his sperm will impregnate as many females as possible and thereby perpetuate the species. Whether for human beings biology need be destiny is another issue, little emphasized in the work of most sociobiologists. Wilson himself believes that the impact of culture on mitigating aggression, especially violent forms of aggression, can be considerable. Still, we will not be able to "eliminate the hard biological substructure" of our nature, he says, until such time as we learn to alter our very genes. See Edward O. Wilson, *On Human Nature* (Cambridge, Mass.: Harvard University Press), chapter 5, "Aggression," p. 96.

Freud, of course, was inclined to believe in the supremacy not just of anatomy but of biology, specifically of libido. "The task of mastering such a mighty impulse," he said, ". . . is one which may well absorb all the energies of a human being," in *Sexuality and the Psychology of Love* (New York: Collier Books, 1974), p. 30. Hence Ellen Willis's observation: "The idea that untrammeled male sexuality must inevitably be repressive is rooted in one of our most universal cultural assumptions: that the sexual drive itself . . . is inherently anti-social, separate from love, and connected with aggressive, destructive impulses. In providing a modern, secular rationale for this idea, Freud reinforced . . . traditional Judeo-Christian morality." See Ellen Willis, *No More Nice Girls* (Hanover, N.H.: Wesleyan University Press, 1992), pp. 33–34.

121 "Boys will be boys": Lawyer Michael Querques in the Glen Ridge, New Jersey, case that dragged on for four years and was finally decided in mid-March 1993. Cited in *The New York Times*, March 19, 1993, p. B16.

122 as one of the Lakewood "scorers" was described: Quotes concerning the Lakewood Spur Posse are taken from accounts in *The New York Times*, March 20, 1993, p. A6; March 24, 1993, p. A14; and March 29, 1993, p. A13, respectively.

123 "Not asking more questions . . .": Brown, *Before and After*, pp. 237–40, 118.

124 "Most current theories": Stephen J. Bergman, M.D., Ph.D., "Men's Psychological Development: A Relational Perspective." A Stone Center Work in Progress, No. 48, 1991.

124 "first individuation": See Louise J. Kaplan, Ph.D., *Oneness and Separation* (New York: Touchstone, 1978), for the most thoroughgoing account of the first individuation. Her work owes much to Margaret Mahler's. See also Margaret S. Mahler, F. Pine, and A. Bergman, *The Psychological Birth of the Human Infant* (New York: Basic Books, 1975).

124 "second individuation": See Peter Blos, *On Adolescence: A Psychoanalytic Interpretation* (New York: Free Press, 1962); and Peter Blos, "The Child Analyst Looks at the Young Adolescent," in Jerome Kagan and Robert Coles, eds., *12 to 16: Early Adolescence* (New York: W. W. Norton, 1971, 1972).

124 "Identity versus role confusion": Erik H. Erikson, *Childhood and Society* (New York: W. W. Norton, 1963), p. 261.

124 "the children to be brought up": Erik H. Erikson, "Womanhood and the Inner Space," chapter 7 in *Identity: Youth and Crisis* (New York: W. W. Norton, 1968), p. 283.

125 Those at the lower end of the scale: No longer willing to accept the moral and personality development scales that depict women as stalled on the lower rungs of the ladder, where relationships matter more than rules, subjectivity swamps the priorities defined by an abstract code of justice, and context muddies what should be a Platonically pure, neatly dualistic vision of right and wrong, women like psychologist Carol Gilligan, philosopher Sara Ruddick, sociologist Miriam Johnson, and others are challenging the work of the men (among them Lawrence Kohlberg, Murray Bowen, and Sigmund Freud himself) who devised those scales and hierarchies. See Sarah Ruddick, *Maternal Thinking: Toward a Politics of Peace* (New York: Ballantine Books, 1989); Carol Gilligan, *In a Different Voice: Psychological Theory and Women's Development* (Cambridge, Mass.: Harvard University Press, 1982, especially chapter 1); and Miriam M. Johnson, *Strong Mothers, Weak Wives: The Search for Gender Equality* (Berkeley: University of California Press, 1988).

125 "context of a . . . shared relationship with others": Murray Bowen, *Family Therapy in Clinical Practice* (New York: Jason Aronson, 1978), pp. 473, 472. See also Sigmund Freud, "Some Psychical Consequences of the Anatomical Distinctions Between the Sexes," volume 19, *Standard Edition*, pp. 257–58, in which he explains that since girls do not "smash" the Oedipus complex, perceiving themselves as *already* castrated, "for women the level of what is ethically normal is different from what it is in men." Hence the "character traits which critics of every era have brought up against women—that they show less sense of justice than men . . . [and] are more often influenced . . . by feelings . . ."

125 "sexual maldevelopment": Blos, "The Child Analyst Looks at the Young Adolescent," pp. 61, 59.

126 disidentifying with and becoming *unlike* Mom: Though he didn't use precisely the same language, Talcott Parsons made similar observations about the phenomenon of disidentification. Typical male behavior is characterized by what he calls "compulsive masculinity," which causes boys to "refuse to have anything to do with girls," to become interested in "athletics and physical prowess . . . in which men have the most primitive and obvious advantage over women," and to "become allergic to all expression of tender emotion"—these being their way of making "a defense against a feminine identi-fication." Parsons, *Essays in Sociological Theory: Patterns of Aggression in the Western World* (New York: The Free Press, 1954), p. 305. See also Ralph Greenson, "Dis-Identifying from Mother: Its Special Im-portance for the Boy," *International Journal of Psycho-Analysis* 49 (1968): 370–74. This was a very influential paper when it came out.

For more recent psychoanalytic views, see Gerald Fogel et al., *The Psychology of Men: New Perspectives in Psychoanalytic Psychology*, espe-cially Fogel's introduction, "Being a Man," p. 9: "Masculinity is often defined in relation to and in contrast to women; as boys and men we are dependent upon, threatened by, vulnerable to, and envious of women. . . . Not only must men struggle with the real and fantasy-distorted powers of women as objects, but also with those qualities and impulses within themselves that are perceived as womanly or woman-ish. Thus men's view of women becomes further twisted and confused. If women are not enough of a problem in their own right, they become so in their role as the bearers or symbolic representatives of various dis-avowed, warded off, unacceptable aspects of men." See also John Munder Ross's essay in the same volume: "Beyond the Phallic Illusion: Notes on Men's Heterosexuality."

126 in the name of autonomy: There was a brief period (mainly during the seventies), when it became fashionable in certain feminist psychological circles to argue that girls, like boys, needed to effect a cutoff from their mothers if they were to become fully realized selves. This was the period when, as Jean Baker Miller put it in her foreword to the second edition of her 1976 book (pp. x–xi), "the model of the new woman seemed to many people to be the model of the man . . . the only model of a full-fledged person." But the work of researchers and theoreticians like Miller, Carol Gilligan, and Nancy Chodorow has done much to redress this view. They argue that the "self-in-relation" that is the result of the female developmental experience is different from but not inferior to the "separate" self that is the culmination of male development. As Gilligan says, the latter "conception of adulthood is . . . out of balance, favoring the separateness of the individual self over connection to others, and leaning more toward an autonomous life of work than toward the interdependence of love and care."

See Jean Baker Miller, *Toward a New Psychology of Women* (Boston: Beacon Press, 1986). See also Gilligan, *In a Different Voice*, pp. 17, 156, and Judith V. Jordan, Alexandra G. Kaplan, Jean Baker Miller, Irene P. Stiver, and Janet L. Surrey, *Women's Growth in Connection* (New York: Guilford Press, 1991).

126 "Autonomy entails": Arno Gruen, *The Betrayal of the Self* (New York: Grove Press, 1988), pp. 2, 120.

127 depicts . . . girls as "mired in relationships": Gilligan, *In a Different Voice*, p. 156. Gilligan is critiquing the prevailing view.

127 "pawns of the ebb and flow": Bowen, *Family Therapy in Clinical Practice*, p. 475. Bowen is expressing the prevailing view.

132 "there is no context of assurance": Jean Baker Miller, "The Construction of Anger in Women and Men." A Stone Center Work in Progress, No. 4, 1985, pp. 6, 8.

132 "you strike out": *The Jane Whitney Show*, January 20, 1993.

143 the actual emotions "cannot be known": Miller, "The Construction of Anger in Women and Men."

148 to act authentically: See Ruddick, *Maternal Thinking: Toward a Politics of Peace*, p. 112. For Ruddick, the very definition of "inauthenticity" is the "repudiation of one's own perceptions and values," which she connects to mothers "who construct, before the eyes of their children, a world in which maternal values do not count," in which women accept the necessity , in Adrienne Rich's words, to *"travaillez pour l'armée"* (work for the army). Adrienne Rich, *Of Woman Born* (New York: Bantam Books, 1977), p. 190.

FIVE: LEAVING HOME: THE YOUNG MAN'S RITE OF PASSAGE

149 "Grown-up" . . . : Barbara Ehrenreich, *The Hearts of Men: American Dreams and the Flight from Commitment* (New York: Anchor Press, 1983), p. 181.

150 Journey from the "Motherland": "Motherland" is Sam

Keen's phrase. Sam Keen, *Fire in the Belly: On Being a Man* (New York: Bantam Books, 1991), p. 21.

151 "clean break": Robert Bly, *Iron John* (Reading, Mass.: Addison-Wesley, 1990), p. 19.

151 "To grow from man-child": Keen, *Fire in the Belly*, p. 16.

152 "an American thing": *People*, February 15, 1993, p. 54.

152 54 percent of eighteen- to twenty-four-year-olds: Statistics are from U.S. Census Bureau report, cited in *San Francisco Chronicle* article by Ramon G. McLeod, February 12, 1993.

152 more men than women: Jane Bryant Quinn, *Newsweek*, April 5, 1993, citing Census Bureau statistics showing that about 16 percent of twenty-five- to thirty-four-year-old males lived at home, versus about 9 percent of females, in 1992.

159 "Becoming One's Own Man": Daniel J. Levinson, with Charlotte N. Darrow, Edward B. Klein, Maria H. Levinson, Braxton McKee, *The Seasons of a Man's Life* (New York: Alfred A. Knopf, 1978), pp. 73, 60.

159 "Development itself . . .": Carol Gilligan, *In a Different Voice: Psychological Theory and Women's Development* (Cambridge, Mass.: Harvard University Press, 1982). Gilligan, Jean Baker Miller, Nancy Chodorow, and a number of other researchers and writers in the field are challenging developmental theories that undervalue relatedness. In earlier writings the goal was to re-evaluate women's experience, to show that it is different but not inferior; now there are somewhat tentative attempts to challenge traditional accounts of the male developmental model as well, to suggest that it's neither healthy nor inevitable. As authors Judith V. Jordan, Alexandra G. Kaplan, Jean Baker Miller, Irene P. Stiver, and Janet L. Surrey say in the introduction to *Women's Growth in Connection: Writings from the Stone Center* (New York: The Guilford Press, 1991), p. 7: "We are just beginning to think about the use of this perspective to better understand men; we know that the shift we are suggesting from a psychology of 'The Self' to one emphasizing relationships does not apply to women's psychology only." (See also chapter 4, "Empathy and Self Boundaries" by Judith V. Jordan, for an overview and challenge to the developmental theories emphasizing separation.)

A similar point is made in Terri Apter's book, *Altered Loves: Mothers and Daughters During Adolescence* (New York: Ballantine Books, 1991), which I think is representative of a growing number of books for a more general audience. Though it focuses mainly on challenging the conventional view that adolescent daughters must reject their mothers as part of their developmental process, it alludes often, if only parenthetically, to the possibility that the separation model need not necessarily apply to men either. Since I believe there is a potential for care and nurturing that is not only untapped in the male but actively squelched, I consider the reassessment promoted by such authors a great step forward.

160 "greater psychological distance": Levinson, "Becoming One's Own Man," p. 73.

165 "he was far too endangered": Robb Forman Dew, *Fortunate Lives* (New York: Harper Perennial, 1993), pp. 230, 55, 28.

166 high rate of . . . suicides among young men: Among 15- to 24-year-olds, the male suicide rate is 22.2 per 100,000, the female rate 4.2 per 100,000—or less than one-fifth that of the boys. Statistical abstract of the United States, 1990, from the National Center for Health Statistics.

173 "At the beginning of my life": Richard Rhodes, *A Hole in the World* (New York: Touchstone, 1991), p. 15.

173 that too is a loss: Though the men's movement has spawned a revival of the notion that what's wrong with men today is "too much mother," there is beginning to be a recognition on the part of at least a few male members of the mental health community that in fact there is very often too little, and that this is a loss. Stephen J. Bergman, whose paper entitled "Men's Psychological Development" was cited in chapter 4, is one of these men. William S. Pollack, president of the Massachusetts Psychological Association and staff member at both McLean Hospital and Harvard Medical School, is another. He is quoted in Anita Diamant's March 14, 1993, *Boston Globe Sunday Magazine* article, "What's the Matter With Men?" on the subject of the boy's early loss of closeness to the mother and the pain he must feel as a result. See also "No Man Is an Island: Reframing Masculinity," the paper Pollack presented to the August 1992 Centennial Meeting of the American Psychological Association in Washington, D.C.; and his book, *In a Time of Fallen Heroes: The Re-creation of Masculinity*, coauthored with R. William Betcher (New York: Atheneum, 1993).

180 "Only Connect!": E. M. Forster, *Howards End* (New York: Vintage, 1989; originally published in 1910), p. 195.

181 "When I left home": Peggy Reeves Sanday, *Fraternity Gang Rape* (New York: New York University Press, 1990), p. 138. See chapters "The Initiation Ritual: A Model for Life" and "The Law of the Brothers" for an analysis of the meaning of fraternities in the lives of young men. Quotes cited in the text appear on pp. 179 and 157, respectively.

182 " 'Mommy!'. . .": Caryn James, *New York Times*, April 18, 1993, Arts and Leisure section, p. 11.

Six: Men in Relationships

189 "which makes us infants again": This and preceding quotes are from John Updike's *Rabbit, Run* (New York: Fawcett, 1960); *Rabbit Redux* (New York: Fawcett, 1971); *Rabbit Is Rich* (New York: Fawcett, 1981); *Rabbit at Rest* (New York: Fawcett, 1990). Quotes are from the following pages: "et cetera," p. 137, *Rest;* "ready for dinner," from epigraph to *Rich*, attributed to "George Babbitt, of the Ideal Citizen"; "remembered him when," p. 238, *Rest;* "best of them all," p. 184, *Run;* "shed . . . light," p. 391, *Rich;* "checks . . . cashed," p. 270, *Redux;* "treasure . . . bartered," p. 381, *Rich;* "wealth," p. 268, *Rich;* "drifting downhill," p. 423, *Rest;* "made of marble," p. 422, *Rest;* "dark and plain," p. 128, *Rest;* "grounded," p. 39, *Redux;* "Drop dead," p. 194, *Rich;* "her fault," p. 38, *Rich;* "new presumption," p. 339, *Rest;* "Growth is betrayal," p. 74, *Redux;* "but her voice," p. 54, *Redux;* "preferred her incompetent," p. 251, *Rest;* "nails in his coffin," p. 437, *Rich;* "respect her," p. 424, *Rest;* "at any moment," pp. 265–66, *Rest;* "I've always been," p. 267, *Rest;* "like you would a child," p. 232, *Run;* "trapped myself," p. 240, *Rich;* "his impulse," pp. 87–88, *Rest;* "grows uneasy," p. 184, *Rest;* "protected him from," p. 392, *Rest;* "pretty skin," p. 278, *Run;* "on top," p. 280, *Run;* "beyond themselves," p. 252, *Rest;* "you're nothing," p. 306, *Rich;* "mercy," p. 421, *Rich;* "a shaggy monster, lonely," p. 421, *Rich;* "more boyfriends than I do," p. 230, *Rest;* "medical mess," p. 242, *Rest;* "infants again," p. 104, *Rich.*

213 "the giant mask of motherhood": John Updike, " 'The Most Unforgettable Character I've Met,' " *Vogue*, November 1984, p. 441.

214 25 percent . . . no contact with their fathers: Richard Louv, "The Crisis of the Absent Father," *Parents*, July 1993.

214 no "biological superiority": Michael Lamb, "Qualitative Aspects of Mother-and-Father-Infant Attachments," *Infant Behavior and Development* 1 (1978): 265–75.

214   studies of nonhuman primate families: William K. Redican and David M. Taub, "Male Parental Care in Monkeys and Apes," in Michael E. Lamb, ed., *The Role of the Father in Child Development* 2d ed. (New York: John Wiley & Sons, 1981). Joseph H. Pleck, in *The Myth of Masculinity*, cites a paper by William K. Redican and Gary Mitchell, "A Longitudinal Study of Paternal Behavior in Adult Male Rhesus Monkeys," *Developmental Psychology* 8 (1973): 135–36.

214   "In some species of New World monkeys": Gary Mitchell, William K. Redican, and Judy Gomber, "Lesson from a Primate: Males Can Raise Babies," *Psychology Today*, April 1974, p. 66.

215   good for Dad too: See Rosalind C. Barnett and Nancy Marshall, "Men, Family-Role Quality, Job-Role Quality, and Physical Health," 1991, a manuscript submitted for publication that was cited in Ronald F. Levant, "Toward the Reconstruction of Masculinity," special issue of *Journal of Family Psychology* 5 (3, 4) (1992): 379–402. Barnett and Marshall found that men's parental role was a significant predictor of their physical health.

215   "To do anything else": Barbara Ehrenreich, *The Hearts of Men: American Dreams and the Flight from Commitment* (New York: Anchor Books, 1983), pp. 11–12.

224   "dog eat dog": Updike, *Rabbit Redux*, p. 74.

226   perfect fit . . . Paradigm: See Joseph H. Pleck, *The Myth of Masculinity* (Cambridge, Mass.: The MIT Press, 1981) for a description of the propositions that make up the Male Sex Role Identity Paradigm (summarized on pp. 4–5). The MSRI Paradigm, according to Pleck, has "dominated the academic social sciences since the 1930s, and more generally has shaped our culture's view of the male role" (p. 1). Pleck's book dissects the MSRI Paradigm to give us an immensely useful analysis of the flaws in our ideas about sex roles.

SEVEN: WHAT DO WOMEN WANT? WHAT DO MEN NEED?

229   "both so hateful": Virginia Woolf, *Letters*, vol. 6, ed. Nigel Nicolson (London: Hogarth Press, 1980), p. 464.

229   a problem that will reverberate throughout . . . life: One other book does acknowledge the break between mother and son, and some of the damage it causes, but views the break as unilateral—sons breaking away from their mothers. See Michael Kaufman, *Cracking the Armor: Power, Pain and the Lives of Men* (Toronto: Penguin Books, 1993).

230 The "essentialist project": Michael White, "Men's Culture, The Men's Movement, and the Constitution of Men's Lives," *Dulwich Centre Newsletter: Some Thoughts on Men's Ways of Being*, nos. 3, 4 (1992): 36.

231 differences . . . amount to little more: According to the latest account by Eleanor Maccoby, over the years even "sex differences in verbal abilities have faded." See p. 513 of "Gender and Relationships: A Developmental Account," *American Psychologist* 45 (4) (April 1990): 513–20. Other researchers feel confident that the mathematical gap will also fade when girls are given the same kind of access to and encouragement in the sciences that boys are. See Jacquelynne S. Eccles and Janis E. Jacobs, "Social Forces Shape Math Attitudes and Performance," *Signs* 11 (2) (1986): 368–80. Differences in spatial skills are also being re-evaluated, and are in any case modest.

Psychologist Maccoby is coauthor with Carol Jacklin of a 1974 summary and evaluation of all the significant work done to date on sex differences. Twenty years later this book is still one of the most widely cited and highly respected in the field, and its conclusions hold up, according to Maccoby. Since publication of *The Psychology of Sex Differences* (Stanford, Calif.: Stanford University Press), she says, "work on sex differences has become more methodologically sophisticated, with greater use of meta analyses to reveal not only the direction of sex differences but quantitative estimates of their magnitude. In my judgment, the conclusions are still quite similar to those Jacklin and I arrived at in 1974" (p. 513, "Gender and Relationships"). In sum, with the exception of aggression—which Maccoby and Jacklin, like many if not most other researchers, identify much more strongly with males than females—the latest studies continue to show that the genders are far more alike than unlike in personality traits and cognitive abilities.

But the case for sex differences of *any* degree of magnitude, in *any* of these areas, including aggression, is by no means airtight. See Anne Fausto-Sterling, chapter 5, "Hormones and Aggression," in *Myths of Gender: Biological Theories About Women and Men* (New York: Basic Books, 1985). Contradicting Maccoby and Jacklin, Brown University biologist Fausto-Sterling does a persuasive, in-depth critique of the rather sketchy evidence for a biological basis to male aggression. Few studies have attempted to correlate aggressive behavior *in humans* with testosterone levels (and the ones that have are inconsistent in their results), she says, and in any case it is unclear whether elevated testosterone is an effect or a cause of aggression. Moreover, "aggression" is inconsistently defined from study to study. "Rough and tumble play" is different from ambition and drive, which are in turn different from the intent to inflict harm on another, but the boundaries between these behaviors are often unclear when scientists talk about what they are measuring.

In chapter 2, "A Question of Genius," Fausto-Sterling critiques the evidence on sex differences in verbal, visual-spatial, and mathematical abilities as well, and finds even less evidence of them and less reason to credit biological explanations for them than do Maccoby and Jacklin. Similar conclusions about cognitive skills are reached in the following meta-analyses: Janet S. Hyde and Marcia C. Linn, "Gender Differences in Verbal Ability," *Psychological Bulletin*, no. 104 (1988): 53–69; and Janet S. Hyde, Elizabeth Fennema, and Susan J. Lamon, "Gender Differences in Mathematics Performance," *Psychological Bulletin*, no. 107 (1990): 139–55.

See also Joseph H. Pleck, Appendix A: "The Biological Basis of Male Aggression: A Critique," in *The Myth of Masculinity* (Cambridge, Mass.: The MIT Press, 1983). Pleck analyzes both human and animal studies attempting to correlate aggression and testosterone levels, concluding, "At the present time, the evidence in animals for hormonal factors in male aggression is strong (albeit complex). But comparable evidence for human male aggression is much weaker and less consistent."

231 "women as their teachers": R. William Betcher, Ph.D., M.D., and William S. Pollack, Ph.D., *In a Time of Fallen Heroes: The Re-Creation of Masculinity* (New York: Atheneum, 1993). Passages cited can be found on the following pages: "clear object," pp. 38–39; "lonely existence," p. 41; "great lengths to preserve," p. 40; "need to become," p. 36; "other people," p. 45; "as their teachers," p. 44.

233 "When I first became pregnant": Adrienne Rich, *Of Woman Born* (New York: Bantam Books, 1977) p. 191.

233 doing "*what women have always done*": Rich, *Of Woman Born*, p. 6.

234 "a need to please others": Rachel T. Hare-Mustin and Jeanne Marecek, "Gender and the Meaning of Difference," in Rachel T. Hare-Mustin and Jeanne Marecek, eds., *Making a Difference: Psychology and the Construction of Gender* (New Haven: Yale University Press, 1990).

This book is a particularly useful contribution to the discussion of the sociopolitical meaning and uses of gender differentiation.

235 "may take over my job": Kimberly J. McLarin, "Left Behind, Some Boys Feel Left Out," *New York Times*, April 29, 1993, p. B8.

235 Tailhook, Glen Ridge, whirlpooling, Spur Posse: In 1993, a Pentagon report on the annual Tailhook convention of U.S. Navy aviators suggested that 175 officers were involved in sexually assaulting 83 women in the course of a three-day orgy of drinking and debauchery (Michael R. Gordon, "Pentagon Report Tells of Aviators' Debauchery," April 24, 1993, *New York Times*, p. 1); three boys in Glen Ridge, New Jersey, were found guilty of sexually assaulting a retarded girl whom the defense claimed was an eager, active participant in sex acts that involved not just fellatio, but penetration with a broomstick and attempted penetration with a baseball bat (Robert Hanley, "3 Are Sentenced to Youth Center Over Abuse of Retarded Girl," *New York Times*, April 24, 1993, p. 1); a nationwide survey of American junior high and high school students found that more than two-thirds of the girls reported being touched, grabbed, or pinched at school (Melinda Henneberger with Michel Marriott, "For Some, Rituals of Abuse Replace Youthful Courtship," *New York Times*, July 11, 1993, pp. 1, 33); and a phenomenon known as "whirlpooling," in which groups of teenage boys at public swimming pools in New York City converge on young girls for the express purpose of sexual fondling, entered the contemporary lexicon. Boys and girls alike identified whirlpools as a symptom of the "growing sexual hostility" between the genders. "All boys are dogs," as one girl summed it up (Michel Marriott, "A Menacing Ritual Is Called Common in New York Pools," *New York Times*, July 7, 1993, pp. A1, B2).

235 "don't have to go out raping girls": Joan Didion, "Trouble in Lakewood," *The New Yorker*, July 26, 1993, p. 49.

236 "Playing ball": Jane Gross, "Where 'Boys Will Be Boys,' and Adults Are Befuddled," *New York Times*, March 29, 1993, p. A13.

236 "with a pick-up truck": Ibid.

236 "I want to be in the ninth grade": Didion, "Trouble in Lakewood," p. 56.

236 "virile specimens": Gross, "Where 'Boys Will Be Boys.' "

237 "sex role identity": Pleck, *The Myth of Masculinity*, p. 3.

237 "avoiding femininity": Ronald F. Levant, "Toward the Re-construction of Masculinity," *Journal of Family Psychology* 5 (3, 4) (1992): 379–402.

238 "*an extra month of twenty-four-hour days*": Arlie Hochschild with Anne Machung, *The Second Shift* (New York: Avon Books, 1990), p. 3. Hochschild explains that she based her figures of fifteen hours a week and an extra month a year on time-use studies done in the 1960s and 1970s. See also her appendix: "Research on Who Does the House-work and Childcare," pp. 277–79, for a description of studies in the late 1970s and 1980s, most of them showing little change in the pro-portions of work done by men and women, others somewhat more op-timistic about improvements in the "leisure gap."

238 "wished that their fathers had": White, "Men's Culture, the Men's Movement, and the Constitution of Men's Lives," p. 51.

240 "My wife . . . talks": Bruce May, "In Fighting Trim" ("About Men" column), *New York Times Magazine*, September 2, 1984, p. 28.

240 nineteenth century men outlived women: National Center for Health Statistics, 1993 (from data to be published in the 1990 annual volume of *Vital Statistics of the United States*), regarding suicide rates; Myriam Miedzian, *Boys Will Be Boys* (New York: Doubleday, 1991), p. 318, regarding homicide rate, based on Statistical Abstract of the United States; Pleck, *The Myth of Masculinity,* pp. 150–51; and Barbara Ehrenreich, *The Hearts of Men: American Dreams and the Flight from Commitment* (New York: Anchor Books, 1983), pp. 69–70, regarding male and female life spans.

241 "altogether the most perfect": Sigmund Freud, "Femininity," in Sigmund Freud, *The Complete Introductory Lectures on Psychoanaly-sis*, trans. and ed. by James Strachey (New York: W. W. Norton, 1966), p. 597. Originally published as part of *New Introductory Lectures on Psycho-analysis*, in 1933.

Index

Abandonment, feelings of, 108, 131, 138, 162–63, 180, 190, 230
Abuse, physical, 51, 58, 238
Academic achievement, 111, 112–13
Achievement and status, seeking, 111–12, 237
Achilles, 10
Ackerman Institute of Family Therapy, 190
Adolescence, 87, 107–47
  aggression, 111, 120–21, 141, 143
  autonomy, myth of male, 124–27, 133
  case studies, 127–37, 139–47
  The Catcher in the Rye, 114–18
  competitiveness, 111–12
  devaluation of feminine qualities, 126
  developmental tasks, 107–8
  discipline during, 110, 146–47
  elevation of son, 110, 138
  emotional confusion of, 109, 131, 132
  fear of emasculating son, 110, 137, 138
  male role model, belief in, 110
  as pathology, 119–20
  peer group, 108, 138–47
  physical changes in, 109–10
  power and status in, 111–12
  pressure to achieve in, 111–13, 131
  proving masculinity in, 111–13, 146, 171–72, 237
  reluctance of mother to exercise authority over son, 110
  rituals of, 110
  sex drive in, 120–22
  sexual identification in, 107, 108, 145
  unknowability of the male, belief in, 122–24, 138
  violent behavior in, 111, 121–22, 129, 132, 133

withdrawal of mother, 107–8, 109, 110, 120, 123–24, 126, 127–28, 131, 132–33, 137–39, 147
  different dynamics of, 137–39
Adolescence: Its Psychology and Its Relations to Physiology, Anthropology, Sociology, Sex, Crime, Religion, and Education (Hall), 119
Adventurous behavior, 39
Aggressive behavior, 55, 231, 237
  in adolescence, 111, 120, 141, 143
  in one- to six-year-old boys, 32–35
  in six- to twelve-year-old boys, 39, 46
Alcohol abuse, 111
Ambitiousness, 39
American Graffiti, 160–62
Anatomical differences between the sexes, 231
Anger, 132, 157, 158, 159, 205, 225
  at mothers, 190, 203–4
  at women in general, 190
Apollo, 10–11
Arcana, Judith, 52
Archimbaud, Bryan, 95
Armed forces, 96, 181
Autonomy:
  achieving, 147–48
  defined, 137
  myth of male, 124–27, 133

Bar mitzvah, 110
Barrie, J. M., 102
Before and After (Brown), 120, 121–23
Behaviorists, 22
Belman, Dana, 236–37
Bergman, Stephen J., 46, 124
Betcher, R. William, 229–30
Blaming the mother, *see* Mother blaming

Blos, Peter, 119–20, 125
Blue Fire, A (Hillman), 101
Bly, Robert, 9, 10, 12, 78, 87, 101, 151,
   152, 160, 224, 225, 231
Bodies, Rest and Motion, 182
Bodybuilding, 81, 111
Bowen, Murray, 125
Boy Scouts, 94–95
Boy's Own Story, A (White), 26–27
Boyz N the Hood, 14, 101
Bravery, 39
Breadwinning role, 75, 223
   inability to live up to, 216
   revolt against, 215–16
Breastfeeding, 30, 31
Brown, Rosellen, 120, 121–22
Buddy, son as, 69–74

Campbell, Joseph, 9
Caretaking qualities, 44, 48–49, 75
   of fathers, 73, 214–15, 224
   son as mother's caretaker, 56–64
Case studies, 6–9, 16–19, 32–35, 59–74,
   89–94, 96–101, 127–37, 139–47,
   166–70, 172–80, 192–213,
   217–23
Catcher in the Rye, The (Salinger),
   114–18, 149–50
Childrearing by fathers, *see* Fathers
*Choice of Heroes: The Changing Face of
   American Manhood, A* (Gerzon),
   81
Circumcision, 15
Clinton, Bill, 56
Clinton, Hillary Rodham, 56
College, leaving home for, 160–70
Competitiveness, 39, 96
   in adolescence, 111–12
   case study, 96–101
   economic, 234–35
Cosby, Bill, 214
Couples therapy, 190
Crying, 84, 118, 147, 224
   anger as alternative to, 132
   by six- to twelve-year-old, 42, 43, 44,
      48, 54
   on starting kindergarten, 42, 43
   in therapy, 73, 142, 190, 191

Davis, Neil, 95
Decisiveness, 40
Delinquency, 111
Demos, John, 40
Developmental tasks in adolescence,
   107–8

Dew, Robb Forman, 164–65
Didion, Joan, 236
Die Hard, 13, 78–79
"Differentiation of self scale," 125
Discipline during adolescence, 110,
   146–47
Distancing, *see* Withdrawal of boys from
   mothers (and mothers from boys)
Dr. Spock's Baby and Child Care (Spock),
   23
Drug abuse, 111, 144, 145–46, 207, 209

Education, *see* Schooling
Ehrenreich, Barbara, 149, 215
Elevation of males, 35–36, 56–74
   in adolescence, 110, 138
   effect on adult relationships of, 206–9
Emotions and feelings:
   anger, *see* Anger
   crying, *see* Crying
   emotional confusion in adolescence,
      109, 131, 132
   emotional dependency of men, 190
   inaccessibility of men, 190
   not talking to sons about, 226
   repression of, 40, 43, 45, 55, 118, 148,
      223, 237, 238
      high cost of, 119
   see also Intimacy
Erikson, Erik, 119, 124–25, 159
Essentialists, 230–31
Estrangement from women, loss derived
   from, 225
Expressive mother, 30, 41, 44, 105

Fairy tales:
   elevation of men in, 57–58
   mother denial in, 12–13
Family system, 192–93, 232
Family values, 82, 83
Father figure, *see* Male role model
Fatherhood (Cosby), 214
Fathers, 214–23
   absentee, 82–83, 87, 105, 214, 217–23,
      238–39
   books about relationships with, 214
   boys as domain of, 3–9, 36, 138
   case of missing father, 217–23
   cult of father hunger, 101–5, 224
   differences in raising boys and girls, 3–5,
      21
   empathic, 238
   fatherhood as declining institution,
      81–82
   getting in touch with one's father, 224

inability of son to relate to women and, 26
instrumental, 30, 41, 44, 105
as nurturers, 73, 214–15, 224
as partners in childrearing, 237–39
physical abuse by, 51
single parent father as buddy to his son, 69–73
violent, 26
Feelings, *see* Emotions and feelings
Femininity, 41
defined as opposite of masculinity, 233, 234
"feminine" qualities of six- to twelve-year-old boys, 44–45, 47–49
stigmatizing of feminine qualities, 232
Feminist movement, 215, 234
men's anger at, 216
Feminizing influences, fear of, 4, 5–6, 9, 11, 16–19, 23, 52
in adolescence, 108, 138
Ferdinand the bull, story of, 53
Field of Dreams, 101
Fighting, 48, 54, 84, 96, 111, 141, 142, 143, 204
Film, *see* Movies
For the Boys, 148
Fortunate Lives (Dew), 164–65
Fraternal organizations, 181
Fraternity Gang Rape (Sanday), 181
Freud, Anna, 119, 120
Freud, Sigmund, 10, 20–21, 162, 241
Freudian psychology, 3, 11, 20–22
differences in raising boys and girls and, 21–22
Oedipus complex, 20, 21, 31, 60, 85, 86, 87
theory of identification, 85–87
Fuller, Margaret, 231, 232
Future, raising sons in the, 240–41

Gallant behavior, 40
Gang rape, 181
Gender antagonism, 235–37
misogyny, 126, 181
Gender roles, 40–41
changing, 76–81
mixed messages about, 76–78
movies and, 78–81
Gender split, 227
economic reasons for, 75–76
Gender-stereotyped expectations, 39–41, 67, 137–38, 146, 215, 223, 237
effect on adult relationships of buying into, 137, 198–203

first day of kindergarten, 42–43
as harmful to men, 223–24
of one- to six-year-old, 4–5, 29–30, 33
that sons will distance themselves as adults, 7, 138
leaving home, *see* Leaving home
Generation of Vipers (Wylie), 22
Gerzon, Mark, 81
Gilligan, Carol, 160
Glen Ridge, New Jersey, sexual assault case in, 121, 235
Godfather, The, 101
Great Britain, 150–51
Great Santini, The, 105
Greek mythology, 9–11
Gruen, Arno, 126
Guns, playing with, 51–52

Haley, Jay, 160
Hall, G. Stanley, 119, 120
Hamilton, Linda, 80
Hearts of Men, The (Ehrenreich), 149, 215
Hercules, 10
Heroic male, 81, 95–96
Hi Honey, I'm Home, 102
Hillman, James, 101
Hitchcock, Alfred, 27
Hochschild, Arlie, 238
Home Alone, 37–39, 40, 78, 79
Home Alone 2, 37
Homosexuality, 108, 133–37
as biologically influenced, 86
case study, 133–37
fear of, 86, 138, 237
mother blaming for, 23, 26–27, 135
Hook, 102, 103–5
Horney, Karen, 22
Hughes, John, 39
Human potential movement, 216
Husband substitute, son as, 64–68
Hysteria, 132

Identification, 85–87
with the aggressor, 85–86
sexual, 85–87, 107, 108, 145, 237
Identity crisis, 124, 159
Immigrant experience, 150–51
Impotence, mother blaming for, 23–25
In a Time of Fallen Heroes: The Re-Creation of Masculinity (Betcher and Pollack), 229–30
Incest, mother-son, 108
Independence, 2–3, 36, 39, 197, 230, 233, 237
as strength, 234

Indiana Jones trilogies, 101–2
Individuation, 124
Industrial Revolution, 40, 41, 75, 87
Inequality of the sexes, belief in, 223
Instrumental male, 30, 41, 44, 105, 232
Intimacy, 124, 231
  capacity for, 231
  trade-off between independence and,
    230
  see also Emotions and feelings

Jack and the Beanstalk, 57–58
James, Caryn, 182
Jason and the Golden Fleece, 10
Jones, Ernest, 22
Jurassic Park, 215

Karate Kid, The, 13–14
Kate and Allie, 102
Keen, Sam, 151, 152, 160, 224, 231
Kindergarten, 42–43
Kipling, Rudyard, 114, 125, 126
Klein, Melanie, 22

Lakewood, California, sexual assault case
  in, 121, 235–37
Lamb, Michael, 214
Latency years, 41, 60, 87
Lawrence, D. H., 5, 25–26
Lazarre, Jane, 52
Leaf, Munro, 53
Leaving home, 149–82
  abandonment, feelings of, 162–63, 180
  alternative rite of passage, 170–72
  arbitrary age for, 180–81
  case studies, 153–59, 166–70, 172–80
  for college, 160–70
  cultural expectations, 151–52
  early loss of mother and, 172–77
  expectations that sons will go out on
    their own, 151–52
  fear of impending separation, 158
  "getting a girl in trouble," 170–72
  immigrant experience, 150–51
  loneliness, 163–64, 182
  loss and, 150, 151
  in movies, 160–62
  opening discussion with your son about,
    163–66
  permission to stay home, 166–70
  reasons for our beliefs in necessity of,
    152–53
  reparation and reparenting, 177–80
  self-fulfilling prophecy, 153–59
  stigmatizing the stay-at-home, 159–60

*Leaving Home: The Therapy of Disturbed
  Young People* (Haley), 160
Lethal Weapon, 79
Letters (Woolf), 229
Levant, Ronald F., 118, 237
Levinson, Daniel, 159–60
Levy, David, 22
Lilith, 15–16
Little Man Tate, 15
Logical behavior, 39
Loneliness, 127, 132, 204
  leaving home, 163–64, 182
  in marriage:
    of men, 194–95
    of women, 190, 197–202
Lorde, Audre, 54
Loss, sense of, 229–30
  avoiding grief of projected loss of sons,
    7, 138
  leaving home, *see* Leaving
    home
  estrangement from women as cause of,
    225
  leavetaking and, 150, 151
  mother's, 190

McCollum, Eric, 46
Male liberation movement, 216
Male role models:
  in adolescence, 110
  case studies, 89–94, 96–101
  fear of failure, 96–101
  hero ethos and, 95–96
  identification, 85–87
  male therapist and, 88–89, 90–94
  modeling, 87–88
  myth of necessity of, 3, 9, 13, 14,
    17–18, 36, 81–101, 148
  women taking on role-model
    responsibilities, 94–95
Male Sex Role Identity Paradigm, 226
Male therapists and male role model, 88,
  89, 90–94
"Mama's boy" (sissy), 4, 8, 9, 11, 43,
  45–46, 89, 91, 137, 141
Marriage, 181
  basic assumptions about, 192
  loneliness of women in, 190
  pregnancy as reason for, 170–72
  unhappiness in, 127, 201, 202
  as way of finding Mother again, 182
Masculinity, 56
  in adolescence, 108, 146
    proving of, 111–13, 146, 171–72,
      237

beliefs about qualities of, 18, 19, 32, 39–41, 146
defined as opposite of femininity, 233, 234
infant behavior and, 30
the price paid for current beliefs in, 240, 241
reinstatement of traditional concepts of, 81
writings on, 229–31
see also Gender-stereotyped expectations
"Master Is a Woman," 95
Maternal Overprotection (Levy), 22
Melrose Place, 182
"Men and Their Mothers," 3
Men's movement, 224
"Men's Psychological Development: A Relational Perspective," 124
Midlife crisis, 127, 177
Migration, 150–51
Miller, Jean Baker, 132, 143
Milne, A. A., 26–27
Misogyny, 126, 181
Modeling theory, 87–88
Mormons, 15
Mother blaming, 19–27, 109, 226
for homosexuality, 23, 26–27, 135
for impotence, 23–25
for inability to relate to women other than mother in adulthood, 23, 25–26
for murderous behavior of sons, 23, 27
Mother denial, cultural manifestations of:
in fairy tales, 12–13
in movies, 13–15
in mythology, 9–12
religious rituals, 15–16
in tall tales, 13
Movies, 37–39, 40, 76, 106, 148, 182, 215
changing gender roles and, 78–81
cult of father hunger in, 101–2
elevation of males in, 58–59
independence of young boys, 37–39
on leaving home, 160–62
mother blaming in, 27
mother denial in, 13–15
Ms. Foundation, 234
Murder, 23, 27
Murphy Brown, 73–74
Mythology, mother denial in, 9–11

Nature/nurture argument, 231, 233
Nervous breakdown, 181
"New man," 72, 76, 77, 224

New York Times, The, 82, 236
1996, 182
Nurturing, 172
by father, 73, 214–15

Object relations, 125
Oedipus, 10, 11
Oedipus complex, 20, 21, 31, 60, 85, 86, 87
Of Woman Born (Rich), 75
Olsen, Paul, 20
One- to six-year-old, mother of, 1–36
aggressive behavior, 32–35
case studies, 6–9, 16–19, 32–35
differences in treatment of boys and girls, 4–5, 21–22, 23, 28–30
elevation of the boy over females in his life, 35–36
father's claim on boys, 3–9, 36
feminizing influences, fear of, 4, 5–6, 9, 11, 16–19, 23, 36
gender-stereotyped expectations, 29–30, 33
independence, 2–3, 36
male role model, belief in necessity of, 3, 9, 13, 14, 17–18, 36
mother blaming, *see* Mother blaming
mother denial, cultural manifestations of, *see* Mother denial, cultural manifestations of
overcloseness, 30–31
protectiveness, 2–3, 36
symbols that denote gender, 4
verbal and behavioral language of boys, 27–28
withdrawal of sons, 31–32, 42
Orestes, 10
Orthodox Judaism, 15–16
Othello, 37
Overcloseness, 30
Overfunctioners, 94

Parsons, Talcott, 30
Passive-aggressive behavior, 156, 157, 158–59
Passive-resistant behavior, 65–66
Peer group, 138–47
deviation from peer behavior, 108
peer pressures versus paternal authority, 144–47
relinquishing of the boy to the, 138–39
People, 152
Peter Pan, 102–3
Physical abuse, 51, 58, 238
Pittman, Dr. Frank, 3, 83

Pleck, Joseph, 226, 237
Pollack, William S., 229–30
Portnoy's Complaint (Roth), 24–25
Power and status sought in adolescence, 111–12
Pregnancy, 170–72
Program, The, 76
Projected loss of sons, 7, 138
  leaving home, *see* Leaving home
Protectiveness, 2–3, 36, 190
Psycho, 27
"Pursuer/distancer" dilemma, 190

Quayle, Dan, 82

Rabbit at Rest (Updike), 183, 184
Rabbit Is Rich (Updike), 183
Rabbit Redux (Updike), 183
Rabbit, Run (Updike), 183
Radio Flyer, 58–59
Rambo, 13, 79
Rape, 121–22, 235–37
Rationality, 39
Redican, William, 214
Relationship orientation of women, 233–34
Relationships, men in, 183–227
  avoiding the grief of projected loss, 193–98
  belief men don't need relationships, 196–97
  buying into the notion of difference, 198–203
  case studies, 191–92, 193–213
  cold mother, effect of having, 194–95
  distancing of sons and mothers, effect of, 191–92, 193
  elevation of the boy, 206–9
  expecting wives to be intermediaries in relationships with other family members, 194, 195
  as fathers, *see* Fathers
  female lack of self-esteem, effect of, 209–13
  insisting on rights instead of asking for needs, 194, 197–98
  jealousy of wife's relationship with her mother, 194
  in literature, 183–89
  marriage, *see* Marriage
  "not burdening the boys" syndrome, 209–13
  not recognizing women as separate persons, 212

"systems thinking" analytic approach, 192
  therapy including parents, 190–92
  unknowability of the male, belief in, 203–6
  with women, 189–213
Religious rituals:
  in adolescence, 110
  mother denials fostered by, 15–16
Rhodes, Richard, 173
Rich, Adrienne, 51, 75, 232–33
RoboCop, 79
Role models, male, *see* Male role models
Romantic relationship with a woman other than one's mother, inability to have, 23, 25–26
Roth, Philip, 24

Sabato, Antonio, 152
St. Elmo's Fire, 182
Salinger, J. D., 114–18, 149–50
Sanday, Peggy Reeves, 181
Schooling:
  excelling in school, 111, 112–13
  failure in school, 111
Schwarzenegger, Arnold, 80
Seductive mother, 108, 138
Self-esteem, female lack of, 136, 138, 209–13
  belief a woman ceases to be a person when she becomes a mother, 213
"Self-made man," 223
Self-reliance, *see* Independence
Sex drive, sanctification of, 120–22
Sexual assault, 121–22, 235–37
Sexual identity, 85–87, 107, 108, 145, 237
Sexual promiscuity, 111
Shakespeare, William, 37
Silverstein, Michael, 243–44
Single parents:
  African-American families, 14
  children raised in households headed by, 3, 81–82, 87
  father and son as buddies, 69–73
  fears of mothers raising sons alone, 9
  in television sitcoms, 102
Singles, 182
Sissy, *see* "Mama's boy" (sissy)
Six- to twelve-year-old boys, 37–74
  aggressiveness, 39, 46
  "ancient maternal betrayal," 51–56
  "bad boys," 46–47
  as buddy to his father, 69–73
  as caretaker of mother, 56–64

case studies, 59–74
differences in treatment of boys and girls, 42–43, 49, 51, 55
elevation of the son, 56–74
fear of alienating the male child from his culture, 51–56
"feminine" qualities, 44–45, 47–49
feminizing influences, fear of, 52
"good boys," 47
as husband substitute, 64–68
independence, 37–39
kindergarten, 42–43
as men-in-training, 39–51
qualities valued in, 39–41
repression of emotions, 40, 43, 45–46
withdrawal from mother, 42–44, 45, 49–50, 55
Socialization process, 28, 192, 231
Sons and Lovers (Lawrence), 5, 25–26
Spielberg, Steven, 103, 104
Spock, Dr. Benjamin, 22–23, 30
Sports, 111
Spur Posse, 121, 235–37
Star Wars, 101
"Stick-to-it-iveness," 95
Stoicism, 43, 223
Strecker, Edward, 22
Strength, 234
Suburban living, work-home dichotomy related to, 40
Suicide, 166, 174, 176, 177
attempted, 133, 134, 181
Superman, 80–81
Superman II, 40
"Systems thinking" analytic approach, 192, 193

Taboos, 108, 109
"Take Our Daughters to Work Day," 234–35
Tall tales, mother denial in American, 13
Tannen, Deborah, 28, 45
Television, 102, 182
Terminator 2, 79
Their Mothers' Sons (Strecker), 22
Type A behavior, 216

Under Siege, 13
Unknowability of the male, belief in, 122–24, 138

effect on adult relationships of, 203–6
Updike, John, 183–89, 213

Valerie, 102
Violent behavior, 111, 121–22, 129, 132, 133, 141, 143

Watson, John B., 22
When We Were Very Young (Milne), 27–28
White, Edmund, 26–27
White, Michael, 230, 238
Williams, David, 76
Williams, Robin, 103
Willis, Bruce, 78–79
Withdrawal of son from mothers (and mothers from sons):
in adolescence, 107–8, 109, 110, 120, 123–24, 126, 127–28, 131, 132–33, 137–39, 147
different dynamics of, 137–39, 193
dynamics of, 137–39, 193
dread of homosexuality, 86, 138
elevation of the boy, *see* Elevation of the boy
fear of exercising control over male child, 138
female lack of self-esteem, 136, 138, 209–13
gender-stereotyped expectations, *see* Gender-stereotyped expectations
male ownership of the boy, 3–9, 36, 138
projected loss of sons, 7, 138
seductive mother, fear of, 108, 138
unknowability of the male, *see* Unknowability of the male, belief in
effect on men's adult relationships, 191–92, 193
one- to six-year-old, 31–33
six- to twelve-year-old, 42–44, 45, 49–50, 55
as traumatic experience, 229–30
see also Leaving home
Woolf, Virginia, 229
Wylie, Philip, 22, 162

You Just Don't Understand (Tannen), 28, 45

FOR THE BEST IN PAPERBACKS, LOOK FOR THE

In every corner of the world, on every subject under the sun, Penguin represents quality and variety—the very best in publishing today.

For complete information about books available from Penguin—including Puffins, Penguin Classics, and Arkana—and how to order them, write to us at the appropriate address below. Please note that for copyright reasons the selection of books varies from country to country.

In the United Kingdom: Please write to *Dept. JC, Penguin Books Ltd, FREEPOST, West Drayton, Middlesex UB7 0BR.*

If you have any difficulty in obtaining a title, please send your order with the correct money, plus ten percent for postage and packaging, to *P.O. Box No. 11, West Drayton, Middlesex UB7 0BR*

In the United States: Please write to *Consumer Sales, Penguin USA, P.O. Box 999, Dept. 17109, Bergenfield, New Jersey 07621-0120.* VISA and MasterCard holders call 1-800-253-6476 to order all Penguin titles

In Canada: Please write to *Penguin Books Canada Ltd, 10 Alcorn Avenue, Suite 300, Toronto, Ontario M4V 3B2*

In Australia: Please write to *Penguin Books Australia Ltd, P.O. Box 257, Ringwood, Victoria 3134*

In New Zealand: Please write to *Penguin Books (NZ) Ltd, Private Bag 102902, North Shore Mail Centre, Auckland 10*

In India: Please write to *Penguin Books India Pvt Ltd, 706 Eros Apartments, 56 Nehru Place, New Delhi 110 019*

In the Netherlands: Please write to *Penguin Books Netherlands bv, Postbus 3507, NL-1001 AH Amsterdam*

In Germany: Please write to *Penguin Books Deutschland GmbH, Metzlerstrasse 26, 60594 Frankfurt am Main*

In Spain: Please write to *Penguin Books S.A., Bravo Murillo 19, 1° B, 28015 Madrid*

In Italy: Please write to *Penguin Italia s.r.l., Via Felice Casati 20, I-20124 Milano*

In France: Please write to *Penguin France S.A., 17 rue Lejeune, F–31000 Toulouse*

In Japan: Please write to *Penguin Books Japan, Ishikiribashi Building, 2–5–4, Suido, Bunkyo-ku, Tokyo 112*

In Greece: Please write to *Penguin Hellas Ltd, Dimocritou 3, GR–106 71 Athens*

In South Africa: Please write to *Longman Penguin Southern Africa (Pty) Ltd, Private Bag X08, Bertsham 2013*